Stay-At-Home Mothers:Dialogues and Debates

The publisher gratefully acknowledges the support of the Canada Council for the Arts for its publishing program.

Demeter Press logo based on the sculpture "Demeter" by Maria-Luise Bodirsky <www.keramik-atelier.bodirsky.de>

Printed and Bound in Canada.

Library and Archives Canada Cataloguing in Publication

Stay-at-home mothers / edited by Elizabeth Reid Boyd and Gayle Letherby.
Includes bibliographical references.

ISBN 978-1-927335-44-4 (pbk.)

1. Stay-at-home mothers. I. Letherby, Gayle, editor II. Reid Boyd, Elizabeth, 1968-, editor

HQ759.46.S73 2014 306.874'3 C2014-904585-9

Demeter Press
140 Holland Street West
P. O. Box 13022
Bradford, ON L3Z 2Y5
Tel: (905) 775-9089
Email: info@demeterpress.org
Website: www.demeterpress.org

Table of Contents

Dedications

To my beloved daughter Jessica Moncrieff-Boyd, my reason for 'being there'.

Elizabeth

Gayle would like to dedicate this book to the memory of her mother Dorothy Thornton (1931-2012). Loved always and forever.

Gayle

Acknowledgements

My thanks to the amazing Demeter Press who continue to make motherhood an important area of scholarship. Particular thanks to Andrea O'Reilly and Lyndsay Kirkham for their support. For editorial and research assistance, much appreciation to Ann-Claire Larsen, Wendy Reid, Bethwyn Rowe and Tracey Stephens, and for timely technological help, thanks to Catherine Marinceu. Above all, thanks to the chapter authors and stay-at-home mothers who contributed to this book.

Introduction

ELIZABETH REID BOYD AND GAYLE LETHERBY

INTRODUCTION

Stay-at-home mothers and the 'mommy wars' are a continuing phenomenon worldwide. This volume is the first international edited collection exploring debates and issues surrounding mothers returning to/staying at home from a variety of countries and perspectives.

Mothering at home remains a significant social and gender trend. Over the few last decades, there have been many books exploring questions, issues and policies surrounding working mothers. This volume explores the flip side – mothers staying at home. It provides a new, international perspective to enable a new discussion: Why are mothers still staying at home? Which mothers? In which countries? Under what conditions? What types of rhetoric are invoked - personal choice or political push? Which national policies benefit them? Which do not? What debates do such polices provoke?

In much media and public discourse, stay-at-home mothers remain separated in the private sphere, but they also remain in the media spotlight. This book uses feminist scholarship to reconsider this gendered location and women's place in it. Themes and issues are identified as relevant to the contemporary discourse and debates surrounding stay-at-home mothers and framing their experience from countries as diverse as Ireland and

Israel, and along socio-economic lines, from teenage mothers in the UK to highly-educated women in the US.

Many chapters draw on empirical data on mothers staying at home, including statistical trends, as well as conceptual discussion and analysis of the topic, to enable comparison and exploration and scope for contrasting views. Longer, traditionally presented chapters provide these national/theoretical perspectives. Diverse voices of stay-at-home mothers are also represented in shorter chapters that include auto/biographical reflections/short position pieces.

Chapters include discussion and debate about the 'mommy wars' between working moms/mums and stay-at-home moms/mums; the idealisation and persistence of mothering at home and what it means; maternity payments and childcare policy; state enabling of mothers staying at home; eco-mommas, radical parenthood, the return of the domestic goddess and the green angel in the house; the mother at home assisted by a nanny; stay-at-home mothers and the media; the history of mothers staying at home; debates about the 'worthiness' of different mothers staying at home; teenage and/or poor mothers versus wealthy older 'yummy mummies'; the mother wars online; maternal ambivalence; and mothering as gift.

In this introduction, we first provide an historical background to this current scholarship on stay-at-home mothers and more recent feminist analyses, before turning to how this book enriches, problematises and builds from this scholarship, and why this is important for all, whether stay-at-home mothers or those in paid work.

STAY-AT-HOME MOTHERS: HERSTORY

Stay-at-home mothering has an historical heritage. In ancient Greek thought, a clear separation existed between the public sphere (the polis) and the private sphere (the oikos). For centuries, men made 'his' story in public, while women made 'her' story in private. Men took part in the productive world as workers and citizens, while women remained in the reproductive world of care, as mothers and wives.

This (ideological) construction of care disguised that for centuries, all around the world; women have not only worked in the home, but also in fields, factories and workshops. At the turn of the 20th century, it was rare for married women to be employed: in 1900, only 5 percent of married women were employed, and by 1940, this had only risen to 15 percent. Two exceptions were African American households, of which as many as 20 percent were headed by women, and farm wives (almost half of all married women in 1900) who were an integral part of their family's work, although not counted as such in employment statistics (Reid Boyd and Letherby 2010, 2011, 2014).

Traditionally, what have been characterised as the male (public, productive, culture, work) and the female (private, reproductive, nature, care) spheres have also been differently valued. The world of work has historically dominated, and been valued over the world of care. Men have been associated with productive labour, and women have been associated with reproductive labour. This traditionally female labour has included tasks ranging from bearing children to those which have become associated with rearing children and having a family – the emotional support and nurturing of family members, the buying and preparation of food and clothing, planning and organising, and a wide variety of associated tasks. A woman's identity and her work in the home have long been bound together in a woman's eyes as well as those of her culture. Caring has evolved as a gendered concept (Poole and Isaacs 1997). It is within this context that stay-at-home mothering takes place.

TAKING SIDES: FEMINIST RESEARCH ON STAY-AT-HOME MOTHERS

Feminist analyses have long demonstrated that mothering in the private sphere has been less than perfect, no matter how idealised. Feminist critiques in the 1960s and 1970s highlighted inequitable power relations in the home and the sexual division of labour (Greer 1970, Oakley 1974) as well as the dissatisfaction and loneliness experienced by many women (Friedan 1963). Friedan argued that women had succumbed to a feminine mystique of a full-time housewife, forfeiting their whole selves. In the media, this was reflected in representations of women in television series as contented housewives. Part of this mystique was full-time motherhood, which had been pressed upon women in a post-World War Two spate of information (see, for example, Bowlby's Child Care and the Growth of Love (1953), which stressed the crucial importance of a maternal attachment figure, and warned against infant-mother separation). Bemoaned was women's lost femininity due to their war work, and women were urged to rush back home again and devote their lives to their children (Friedan 1963). This ideological construct, however, hid the paid work of women. Many mothers in previous generations suffered the same pressures as mothers today. Many women of childbearing age were well educated and/or equipped with skills relevant to the workplace, but they were also living in a culture where it was considered best for mothers to stay-at-home with their children. Mothers who worked outside of the home often cited financial necessity, as working mothers do today.

Child-rearing manuals became popular from the 1950s onwards and these emphasized the good mother/ideal mother as the mother who was responsible and devoted and who put her children before anything else including her own sexual and intellectual identity. Such publications were presented as scientific tracts, written by officials in various levels of government and members of the medical, nursing, and psychological professions – people whose knowledge of children was (and is) frequently based on a professional rather than a parental relationship. Paediatricians such as Benjamin Spock and social psychologists such as Penelope Leach, all argue/d that consistent nurture by a single primary care-giver is absolutely crucial. Day-care centres, pre-schools, spouses, and baby-sitters may help out but they are viewed as incidental to the bond the child really needs with an individual adult, usually the biological mother (Reid Boyd and Letherby 2014).

More radically, beyond a feminine mystique, it was argued that reproduction itself was the cause of female oppression, and that technology and artificial reproduction was the way forward for women; freeing women from the embodiment of bearing children would revolutionise caring for them (Firestone 1972). Liberation from motherhood, for Firestone at least, involved liberation from the female body. But not all feminist theorists, towards the end of the 1970s, shared Firestone's view. Adrienne Rich (1976) distinguished between the 'experience' of mothering and the 'institution' of motherhood. Further, for Rich, the experience of motherhood suggested new possibilities for mothering and her critiques of the institution of motherhood pointed to the way these possibilities were controlled and constrained, and all too often, damaging.

The strong differences between Adrienne Rich's writings on motherhood and the work of Firestone, centred on the potentiality of the female body. For Rich, women were presented with the possibility of converting physicality into both knowledge and power. Rich's (1976) work (also see Dinnerstein, 1977) is an example of a 'maternal revivalism' characteristic of late 1970s and 1980s feminism (Segal 1987). These theorists began to write of 'mothering in a different way, to grapple with the full psychological complexity of women's desire to mother, and the full political significance of the institution of mothering' (Segal 1987).

Within the psychoanalytic framework of object relations, mothering was understood to be developmentally, rather than biologically, destined. Nancy Chodorow's work represented a significant directional shift for feminist theory in her argument that mothering was not 'natural' but developmental. Two other works published in the 1980s, influential with regard to stay-at-home mothering, examined moral differences between women and men, developed in childhood and becoming apparent in adulthood. Carol Gilligan (1982) argued that female and male children's moral development differs, and that as a result women were more empathetic and compassionate than men. For Sara Ruddick the work of mothering was illuminated by 'women's ways of knowing' (1989: 41), which include protection, nurturance and training. Mothering engenders these ways of knowing, which then, in turn, re-engenders mothering (Ruddick 1989: 41).

While Ruddick's argument could be used to encourage men to mother, critics suggested her theory, and the work of Gilligan, ran the risk of essentialism, if not biological determinism, and at the very least, the idealisation of motherhood. Falling prey to essentialism was 'problematic, not because its insistence on articulating women's experience in terms of gender is universalising and normalising, but because this participates in the same logic that underwrites the solidification of identities on which oppressive deployments of these categories also depend' (Di Quinzo 1994) – stay-at-home mothering being a case in point. For Lynne Segal (1987) while maternalist revivalist theories both reflected and reinforced changes within the women's movement, they were (essentially) flawed. They ran the risk of solidifying the very aspects of femaleness, or femininity, of not biological destiny, which earlier feminists had sought to challenge and reject.

In the 1990s, it was argued that the 1970s call for equality formed part of what Anne Phillips (1999) termed assimilationist strategies, or those of 'sameness' which, crucially, requires a point of reference, and, in comparison between the sexes, the point of reference is always a man' (Bacchi, 1990: x). The 'maternal revivalism' cited by Segal (above) is also, like sameness, in reference to men, but emphasises difference, especially on the grounds of maternity. Such maternal revivalism can also be considered an aspect of cultural feminism. Phillips has suggested that there is both a strong version of this position, cultural feminism, which calls for a revaluation of traditionally female qualities and roles, and a weaker version, which accepts convergence as a condition of equality (1999). For stay-at-home mothers, these have proved powerful and divisive underlying constructs framing women's experience and although not the remit of this chapter similar arguments can be made for the identity and experience of women who do not mother children; either by choice or involuntarily (see Letherby 1994).

BACK TO THE TRENCHES: METAPHORS AND MOMMY WARS

Over the last two decades, the mommy wars have been an enduring metaphor to describe an assumed conflict between stay-at-home mothers and working mothers. This discourse surrounding predominant roles and expectations concerning femininity, womanhood and conceptions of 'women's place' has subsequently been rendered in various media / cultural representations. The 'at home mother' versus the 'out at work mother' debate has relegated mothers to a particular space for their parenting role. In the media worldwide, a discernible divide which separates mothers at home (and familialists) and mothers at work (and feminists) has persisted over the last decade, playing into beliefs about what constitutes good mothering.

The fires of the mommy wars continue to be fanned. However, there are increasing critiques regarding the split between women. As authors in this volume argue, it is time to move beyond the Mommy Wars that fans the flame of dissent among women, and that mothers are more supportive of each other than media portrayals pretend. Research in this book suggests that while the media generated conflict is compelling, it is largely untrue and that neither group judge each other harshly.

What the mommy wars disguise is the relationship between mothers at work and mothers at home. Mother-work may be described as physical, mental, emotional and spiritual relational work that crosses the boundaries of public and private, work and home. There are women and men at home and women and men at work in relation with each other. But the power of the childcare debate, as a discourse that defines childcare as a woman's interest, even though as a process, it crosses the boundaries of work and home, ensures that the responsibility for child caring ultimately remains with women and their individual choices. As Adrienne Rich argued: "the absence of choice remains the great unacknowledged reality, and in the absence of choice, women will remain dependent upon the chance or luck of their individual relationships" (1976: 659).

There are current signs that the stay-at-home mother is getting more than a nostalgic look of longing in her guise as domestic goddess or 'lady of leisure' (who lunches) from 'superwomen' for whom over-work, not under-work, is the new problem with no name, with associated adverse health and wellbeing outcomes. Such has been the difference between men and women's leisure time as women have returned to the paid work force (while most retain the primary responsibility for home and family care) that women's leisure has been conceptualized as a form of resistance). While the roles remain largely class and cost bound, there are some indications that the domestic goddess, rather than the superwoman of the second wave, is gaining a foothold as an aspirational ideal.

Many stay-at-home mothers would not necessarily identify with feeling like a Goddess – although some mothers in this book somewhat ironically claim the title. For some it is a struggle to maintain self-worth and a sense of identity. As chapters in this volume reveal, many stay-at-home mothers develop strategies to maintain their public social identity and private feelings of self-worth when they leave their jobs, resisting society's attempts to categorize them in a diminished or marginalised role. The work of stay-at-home mothers is emotionally, physically and mentally taxing – a long way from being a goddess of luck.

STAY-AT-HOME MOTHERS: RECLAIMING A CONFLICTED SITE

Stay-at-home mothering in the domestic sphere was once portrayed as a site of oppression for women. Today, it is also being reclaimed as a location of feminism activism. Stay-at-home mothering remains a complex site of women's work and care, with costs and benefits, losses and gains. It also remains a site of continued conflict. Such divisive conflicts distract from the continued public/private dichotomy and the dual burden of work and care with which many contemporary mothers continue to struggle. In such conflicting circumstances, women have been striking (sometimes poor) bargains to meet dual demands of work and home. Regardless of their so-called choices, mothers continue to be 'framed' as oppositional good or bad mothers, rather than mothers doing their best.

A fully human re-visioned ethics of care is beyond duality and opposing choices, it goes beyond personal, national or moral traditions. Such an ethics will re-frame care – moving beyond limited options of so-called gender appropriate childcare choices. New childcare choices will emerge when the caring needs of women, men and children are envisaged, beyond male and female, beyond public and private, beyond working and stay-at-home mothers. The mommy wars continue to disguise the continuity and commonality across the life course between women and the choices they make at different life stages. Recognising and understanding stay-at-home mothers is a vital step for the future. Only then can we appreciate the value of their gift.

VARYING MOTHER VIEWS: IN THIS VOLUME

Stay-at-Home Mothers: Dialogues and Debates is not for or against mothering at home, though it includes debates around the topic, and indeed, is likely to provoke them. In the 1960s and 1970s, stay-at-home mothering in the domestic sphere was portrayed as a site of oppression for women by second wave feminism. Today, in the 21st century, the tide has turned, and stay-at-home mothering is increasingly being reclaimed as a location of third wave feminism activism.

As this volume reveals, mothering at home is a complex site of women's work and care, with costs and benefits, losses and gains, pains and pleasures. It is been a site of continued conflict: between parents over the sexual division of labour; between paid and unpaid work; between mothers at home and mothers at work, between various kinds of feminists, and between partisan political agenda and policies. Such divisive conflicts distract from the continued public/private dichotomy and the dual burden of work and care with which many contemporary mothers continue to struggle. In such conflicting circumstances, women have been striking (sometimes poor) bargains to meet dual demands of work and home. Regardless of their so-called choices, mothers continue to be 'framed' as oppositional 'good' or 'bad' mothers, rather than mothers doing their best.

Yet it is not debates between women, or feminist debates, or opposite positions held by mothers, which remains problematic. It is the point of reference; the prior privileging and advantaging of hierarchical and gendered work/care norms. This volume looks closely at how the gendered parameters of the child care debate work and how they are sustained. It explores the discourses that continue to reinvent and reinforce old dualisms and divisions shaping women's lives. It is only by unravelling these discourses and perceiving the dualisms that lie beneath them, that we have any hope of such divisions being dissolved. We must look more closely at the divisions that constrain women's lives, and point out that they need not be permanent, they can be altered, and that they might only consist of a flimsy membrane - and membranes, as every mother knows, cannot permanently hold water.

Social transformations involve a relationship between positions. We argue for recognition of the relationship between mothers at work and mothers at home, for clearly, in the childcare debate, nothing is gained when they are set up as opposites. The 'mommy wars' continue to disguise the continuity and commonality across the life course between women and the choices they make at different life stages. Recognizing and understanding stay-at-home mothers, beyond current dichotomies and debates, is a vital step for the future.

In this volume, it has not been possible or even desirable for every viewpoint of stay-at-home mothers to be represented. Nor does it attempt to look at work-life balance from opposing sides of stay-at-home mothers versus mothers in paid work debate – resisting such division. New volumes such as Bernie Jones' *Women Who Opt Out: The Debate Over Working Mothers and Work-Family Balance* are also providing well-balanced accounts of such debates, and future research will hopefully follow in this important area. The aim of this volume is to keep its focus on stay-at-home mothers.

BOOK CONTENTS

It is time for the voices of Stay-at-Home Mothers to be heard. What they say may surprise you. The main body of this volume is divided into four sections: The Mommy Wars: Communications Across the Barricade; On the Home Front: National Perspectives; New Angels and Old Demons: Manifestations of Mothers at Home and When the War is Over: Re-Imagining Stay-at-Home Mothering. Each section contains five to eight chapters, and as a whole provide a rich analysis of the experience of stay-at-home mothers, the impact of the 'mommy wars' on mothering for this group, and more generally and offer a challenge to dominant perceptions and, often contradictory, expectations of mothers.

The first section - The Mommy Wars: Communications Across the Barricades – includes five chapters which all highlight the challenges that stay-at-home mothers face. This section begins with a chapter by Stacey E Rubin. "So, What Do You Do? An Exploration of the Experience of Highly Educated Stay-at-Home Mothers" focuses on the experience of highly educated stay-at-home mothers and in particular the benefits and drawbacks of staying at home. Here again internal and external expectations and drivers are significant and the acceptance of ambivalence is key here. Keren Epstein-Gilboa's discussion of "Maternal Ambivalence: Breastfeeding Mothers' Attempts to Resolve the Conflicting Desire to be Close to Children and to Fulfil Western Conceptualizations of Self Worth and Equality" reflects on the complexity of feelings women feel when wanting to stay close to their children whilst at the same time fulfilling themselves through work. External expectations and internal struggles are central to Epstein-Gilboa's analysis. Lisa Hotaling also focuses on autobiographical experience. In "Navigating the Narrow Pass of Motherhood" she, like Epstein-Gilboa, is concerned with balancing mothering and professional (and academic) identities. Hotaling offers her chapter as a suggestion on how women can avoid the pitfalls of depression and anxiety such balancing can lead to. Ending this section, in "Are 'Mommy Wars' Real?" Brianne Janacek Reeber and Paula J. Caplan argue that the 'Mommy Wars' is part of the fabric of misogyny and mother-blaming, casting mothers against each other. Yet, drawing on data from an online questionnaire Reeber and Caplan show that mothers often go to great length to give mothers in the other group the benefit of the doubt.

There are seven chapters in On the Home Front: National Perspectives, which, as the section title suggests, explore stay-at-home mothering experiences for women in different countries and cultures. Other differences such as age, religion, race and class are also relevant to the analyses here. The section begins with a chapter by Anne Allgood Berry, Yoshie Sano, Mary Jo Katras and Jaerim Lee. In "Staying At Home: Low-Income Mothers in Rural America" the authors report on a longitudinal study of rural, low-income mothers across the United States. They found that a significant number choose to stay-at-home to care for their children in spite of the financial hardship this decision may bring and argue that policy makers need to better understand this population if policy is to be effective. In "Stay-at-Home Jewish Mothers: A Jewish Israeli Perspective" Darya Maoz reflects on the decisions of and consequences for educated Jewish Israeli mothers who choose to stay-at-home. Maoz considers the perceived and objective conflicts for women in this situation. Geraldine Brown, Geraldine Brady and Gayle Letherby focus on the contradictory expectations of young mothers in their chapter "Young Mothers in the UK: Push and Pull Factors Relating to Choices to Stay-at-Home or Not". Mixed messages to access education and training whilst at the same time engaging in all-encompassing mothering, coupled with complex extended family relationships complicate the choices for young mothers. "Mothering from a Caribbean Perspective: Challenges, Determination, and Survival" written by Janet Haynes focuses on the period between 1977 and 2000. Haynes develops a race, class, and gender framework within which to understand a Caribbean perspective of balancing the role of motherhood, kinship care, and work. Valerie Heffernan in "Mediating the Mommy Wars in Contemporary Germany" considers the position of stay-at-home mothers in Germany, with a particular focus on how they are represented in contemporary 'mommy lit' and in German literature and media more generally. In her chapter "Integrating Choices: 'Being There for My Children' and 'Being a Citizen Worker': Irish Survey on Stay-at-Home Mothers" Noelia Molina explores and examines the trends, motivations and experiences of stay-at-home mothers in Ireland. Molina investigates the specific challenges faced by Irish mothers and the implications for them of choosing to stay home. The section concludes with a paper that deals with the Australian experience. In "The Mommy Curve: Stay-at-Home Mothers in Australia" Elizabeth Reid Boyd and Anne-Claire Larsen reflect on the changing attitudes towards stay-at-home mothers in Australia. Reid Boyd and Larsen suggests that relocating stay-at-home mothering as part of the child care cycle, rather than a 'pick a side' child care choice can lead to a positive future for mothers and children.

The eight chapters in New Angels and Old Demons: Manifestations of Mothers at Home highlight how stay-at-home mothers manage expectations of them whilst maintaining a sense of self within and beyond motherhood. The authors in this section also offer a challenge to some taken-for-granted assumptions regarding mothers to decide to remain at home to care for their children. In "Cyber-Mothers: Mothers at Home, Online" Pamela Weatherill argues that the virtual spaces inhabited by mothers provide a third space for women to gain and provide support, converse and share mothering experiences. Weatherill examines how the internet is used by mothers-at-home as a distinct cultural landscape and argues that cyberspace is a place where the divisions of mothers at home versus mothers at work break down. Beth Anne Shelton and Rebecca Deen's chapter "Are Stay-at-Home Mothers Really at Home?: U.S. Mothers' Volunteer Work in Schools" encourages us to challenge the assumption that stay-at-home mothers do not work outside of the home. Data from the authors' research highlights the role of volunteering in stay-at-home mothers' lives and this and other aspects of their data challenge popular conceptions of those who stay-at-home and those who do not. Pamela Redela's focus in "Eco-Momma: The Green Angel in the House" is on the new expectations of middle class American mothers. Redela draws on ecofeminism to explore the relationship between independence and attachment parenting with reference to this model. Dianna Shandy and Karine Moe's chapter also considers the US experience. In "Smart Women, Different Choices: College-Educated Women with Children Negotiating Work and Family" the authors draw on qualitative and quantitative analysis to discuss the benefits and drawbacks to using these macro-level data to understand trends that frame at-home motherhood in America. This mixed method approach allows an examination of the meanings of shifts in the demographics of stay-at-home motherhood. Rebecca Bromwich in "'But She Has A Nanny'... With Accompanying Eye Roll – Considering Mother work With a Live-In Caregiver" provides an autobiographical account of her experience as a mother of four young children with a full-time live-in caregiver. Bromwich begins a consideration of racial, gender and global differences and inequalities with reference to domestic employment, an issue that has been little considered previously In "'Quiet Desperation': The 'Retreat' and Recuperation of the Housewife and Stay-At-Home Mother on Popular Television" Anna Bautista reports on how the dominant discourses surrounding predominant roles and expectations concerning femininity, womanhood and conceptions of 'women's place' are perpetuated through the media, specifically television. Bautista suggests that popular television currently appears to be reverting female characters back to the domestic space as part of a renewed, and re-appropriated, focus on domesticity. In "Making it Work", Catherine Fournier suggests that working outside of the home can be a false economy for mothers and their families. Amongst other things she considers the significance of lower tax brackets, income splitting, trading work-related costs for time-related savings and also short and long-term savings to the physical, emotional and psychological health of the family when someone is in the home. Finally, Kathryn Clarke considers in her personal essay, "The day after, and The Day After That: Reflections on Keeping Your Options Open", that when the journey to parenthood has been arduous, life after birth may not be well-thought-through.

The final main section the book When the War is Over: Re-Imagining Stay-at-Home Mothering contains five chapters which, like some of those in the previous section, encourage us to rethink both the stay-at-home mother experience and the 'mommy wars' which inform, confine and judge women's choices. In "How Alternative Mothering is Transforming American Stay-at-Home Motherhood", Hallie Palladino argues that stay-at-home mothers are often early adopters of alternative parenting practices. She adds that the debate over the potential benefits and drawbacks of these choices tends to get conflated with the mommy wars precisely because these practices are associated with mothers at home and are commonly dismissed as little more than the misguided fallout of an intensive mothering mentality. Palladino challenges this. Solveig Brown's insists that "It's Time to Move Beyond the 'Mommy Wars'". In her chapter she draws on data focusing on the diverse thoughts, feelings, and experiences of middle-class and upper middle-class stay-at-home US mothers residing in the Minneapolis and St. Paul metropolitan area. Brown suggests that media discourses ignore the diversity of mother's lived experience and obscure the broader social, emotional, and structural factors that individual mothers routinely navigate. In "Seeing Themselves: Stay-at-Home Mothers Reject Stigma" Hester Vair considers the stay-at-home motherhood with reference to Canadian middle-class ideals. Women are either vilified for their attachment to oppressive roles for women, or valorised for their rejection of the selfish pursuit of individual success. A study of stay-at-home mothers on the East coast of Canada explored their view of mothering and their sense of themselves in the world. Drawing on stay-at-home mother's experience Vair asks whether their subordinate status enables these women to develop a liberatory critique of society. Tara Ulbrich, in her chapter, "Motherhood as an Act of Personal and Social Co-Creation", impresses upon us that the time has come to reclaim the beauty of mothering by unshackling the endeavour from consumption and reconnecting to its inherent creativity. She concludes that homemakers can design a personal and social future. Finally, in her chapter "The Free Gift: How U.S. Stay-at-Home Mothers Sustain Themselves in a Culture of Nonreciprocity" Ana Villalobos reflects on how women emotionally sustain themselves in the face of near constant giving, especially in work identified cultures that under values care giving.

The complexity of stay-at-home motherhood and mothering is evident from this collection. There are differences, even contradictions, in the chapters that follow, highlighting the need to move beyond stereotypes, the necessity of focusing on real mothers' experiences. We hope you enjoy reading the chapters as much as we have, they will certainly make you think.

REFERENCES

Bacchi, Carol 1990 *Same Difference: Feminism and Sexual Difference.* Sydney: Allen and Unwin.

Badinter, Elisabeth 1980 *The Myth of Motherhood: An Historical View of the Maternal Instinct.* London: Souvenir Press.

Jones, Bernie. D. 2012 *Women Who Opt Out: The Debate Over Working Mothers and Work-Family Balance.* New York: New York University Press.

Bowlby, John 1953 *Child Care and the Growth of Love.* London: Penguin.

Chodorow, Nancy 1978 *The Reproduction of Mothering: Psychoanalysis and the Sociology of Gender.* Berkeley: University of California Press.

Di Quinzo, Patricia 1994 "Exclusion and Essentialism in Feminist Theory: The Problem of Mothering." *Hypatia* 8(3): 1-20.

Dinnerstein, Dorothy 1997 *The Mermaid and the Minotaur.* New York: Harper Colophon Books.

Doucet, Anne 1995 "Gender Equality and Gender Differences in Household Work and Parenting." *Women's Studies International Forum* 18(3):271–284.

Eisenstein, Hester 1984 *Contemporary Feminist Thought.* Sydney: Allen and Unwin.

Firestone, Shulamith 1972 *The Dialectic of Sex.* London: Paladin.

Friedan, Betty 1963 *The Feminine Mystique.* London: Penguin.

Gilligan, Carol 1982 *In a Different Voice.* Cambridge: Harvard University Press.

Greer, Germaine 1970 *The Female Eunuch.* London: Harper Collins.

Henderson, Karla Hodges, and Beth Kivel 2002 "Context and Dialogue in Research on Women and Leisure." *Journal of Leisure Research* 34(3): 253-271.

Letherby, Gayle 1994 "Mother or Not, Mother or What?: Problems of Definition and Identity." *Women's Studies International Forum* 17(5): 525-532.

McDonald, Paula, Lisa Bradley, and Diane Guthrie 2005 April "Good Mothers, Bad Mothers: Exploring the Relationship Between Nonmaternal Childcare and Mother's Labour Force Participation." *Journal of Family Studies* 11(1): 62-82.

Oakley, Anne 1974 *The Sociology of Housework.* Bath: Marin Robinson.

Phillips, Anne 1999 *Which Equalities Matter?* Cambridge: Polity Press.

Poole, Marilyn, and D. Isaacs 1997 "Caring: A Gendered Concept." *Women's Studies International Forum* 21(4): 529-536.

Reid Boyd, Elizabeth, and Gayle Letherby 2010 "Stay-at-home Mothers." In *Encyclopaedia of Motherhood.* A. O'Reilly and J.G. Golson eds. London: Sage.

2011 "Stay-at-home Mothers." In *Encyclopedia of Women in Today's World.* M. Stange, C. Oyster, and J. G. Golson eds. London: Sage.

2014 "Stay-at-home Mothers." In *Mothering: A reader.* A. O'Reilly ed. Toronto: Demeter.

Rich, Adrienne 1976 *Of Woman Born: Motherhood as Experience and Institution.* London: Virago.

1986 *Blood, Bread and Poetry. Selected Prose 1979–1985.* London: Virago.

Ruddick, Sara 1989 *Maternal Thinking: Towards a Politics of Peace.* New York: Ballantine Books.

Segal, Lynne 1987 *Is the Future Female? Troubled Thoughts on Contemporary Feminism.* London: Virago Press.

Section I: The Mommy Wars: Communiques Across the Barricades

1.

So, What Do You Do?

An Exploration of the Experience of Highly Educated Stay-at-Home Mothers

STACEY E. RUBIN

INTRODUCTION

When pregnant with my first child, I remember reading *What to Expect When You're Expecting* by Heidi Murkoff and Sharon Mazel (1984) and feeling more prepared for what was before me throughout my pregnancy and the birth. But when I decided to stay home and put my counseling career on hold to be with my children, no such book existed, and I felt unprepared and alone in many of the complex feelings I experienced, including ambivalence about not pursuing my professional goals. I recognized that I was fortunate to be able to stay home, so my ambivalence was a struggle to accept. Unfortunately, women who decide to leave behind a career that they have worked hard to establish in order to stay home do not have the reassurance of what they might expect down the road. My goal in this chapter is to provide a kind of "what to expect" look at the decision to stay home for the highly educated mother.

I draw on both my past research (Rubin and Wooten 2007) and my clinical experience with the HE-SAH population. My research involved the transcription and thematic analysis of in-depth interviews with 10 HE-SAH mothers with at least a master's degree or higher to explore their individual experience and group themes. After discussing the purpose of the study, research participants were asked to consent to be included in the study and were also assured that all efforts would be made to protect their identities including the use of pseudonyms as well as the altering of any identifying information. In addition to my research data, I also include brief personal anecdotes from my patients that reflect important dimensions of the HE-SAH experience.

DECISION-MAKING PROCESS

Although some women decide before having children that they will stay home after the birth of their children, others go back to work only to discover the tension between the competing agendas of mothering and working. Regardless of how the decision unfolds, for most women the decision is emotional and made with much deliberation. When first researching and writing about this subject, myself and a colleague (Rubin and Wooten 2007:339) described the main components of the decision to stay home as beliefs and circumstances. However, over the past six years of working with HE–SAH mothers, I have come to see these factors more specifically, not just as beliefs, but personal ideals, and not just any circumstances, but more specifically emotional experiences that shape the decision to stay home. This is not to say that more concrete or practical circumstances do not impact the decision, but rather that, in their subjective experiences, these personal ideals and emotional experiences are what women speak about most.

I have found that long before actually having children, women have a fantasy of what motherhood will be like; these fantasies are imbued with ideals for both their child and themselves. I believe that the same kind of striving for excellence that these women have put forth in other areas of their lives, such as education and career, comes into play in forming personal ideals around mothering. Among the personal ideals that come into play, many center on being emotionally and physically available as mothers. Women talk about the long-term investment of raising happy children who grow up to contribute to society. Although acknowledging that staying home is not a guarantee of their child's happiness or success, they believe that staying home is best. In her research article "Being There," Elizabeth Reid Boyd (2002: 467) found that, when considering their choice to stay home, mothers talked about being there for their children: "The women I interviewed were not simply speaking of a number of domestic and child-care chores that needed to be done, when they spoke of their desire to 'be there' for their children. They were describing emotional shift work, which, in their view, would need to be done by them". I found that some women focus on what is best for their child, yet women also have their own needs and expectations. In this vein, women often mention the desire not to miss out on their children's childhood talking about the short period of time in which their children are young. They consider their career as something less bound by time. For example, one physician and HE–SAH mother in my study stated that "you only get one shot at it and they're only little once and I don't know, I think passing the torch in the cycle of life is really important in terms of raising your children".

In forming their personal ideals around mothering, women use their own mothers as signposts on how and how not to mother. Having had a stay-at-home mother themselves impacts many women's decisions. Looking back, women often remember the experience of their mothers being home and want the same for their own children. In my study one woman explained, "honestly, it is like a fairy tale the way my mom raised us... she was just the ideal mother". In contrast, some women who also had stay-at-home mothers want to do things differently in their own SAH mothering. For example, women who had SAH mothers who seemed selfless and without their own needs express the desire to not be "martyrs" and to have their own needs met. Women want to be available for their children, but they often express their concern that they not live through their children. Women describe the need to value themselves as individuals in their own right with needs, desires, and dreams of their own. In addition, whereas some women identify with their own stay-at-home mothers, others counter-identify with their own working mothers and want to be a different kind of mother than they experienced. When discussing her wish to stay home, one HE-SAH described how her mother "was always working and, even though I could go to my dad, it seemed like she was never there and even when she was home she was tired and distracted"

Emotional experiences also come into play in the decision to stay home. Although some women know they will be stay-at-home (SAH) mothers, many women have the intention of staying at work and finding a balance between work and family. However, they often underestimate the challenges that lie ahead. They look back on the stress of being spread too thin or the extreme sadness they felt on their morning drive to work. The decision to leave work seems to evolve through these emotional experiences that clarify their desire to stay home. As ambitious women, the experience of not meeting one's standards is often a new and unsettling feeling. Missed recitals or being passed over for a promotion are the types of stories that pepper their descriptions of a gradual realization that they wanted to quit working. One attorney and HE SAH mother, in my study, remembered, "There's guilt either way. I'm not giving my child enough or I'm not giving my client enough".

Many stories highlight painful experiences of stress, separation, and longing; other stories are of joyful emotional experiences that shape their decisions. Women describe quiet moments nursing their infants or witnessing a developmental milestone such as their babies' first steps. It is difficult if not impossible to estimate the changes that take place in the female psyche after having a child. Psychoanalyst Daniel Stern (1995) coined the term "Motherhood Constellation" as an overall shift in mindset that occurs in the new mother. He states, "that with the birth of a baby, especially the first, the mother passes into a new and unique psychic organization that I call the *motherhood constellation*. As a psychic organizer, this 'constellation' will determine a new set of action tendencies, sensibilities, fantasies, fears, and wishes" (Stern 1995:171). Personal ideals and emotional experiences together seem to capture the essence of the "Motherhood Constellation" and its impact on the experiences and decisions of HE–SAH mothers.

As I have previously argued (Rubin and Wooten 2007:340), one other important factor about the process of deciding to stay home is that the decision is often questioned, revisited, and reevaluated. Questioning the choice to stay home often occurs and reoccurs. Women also revisit the idea of returning to work during transitions in life, such as children moving to an all-day school schedule. Many women comment that, when they do return to work, it is to fulfill something within themselves. They describe a very different motivation than they had before, as if they have reached a place where they have nothing to prove. As women describe it, the decision to stay home—rather than being linear—is closer to a loop of decide, question, evaluate, and re-decide. When evaluating their options it seems the logistics of working again and the juggling they anticipate lead many women to hold off from returning to work. One of my respondents, considered her options, said "there's just no way to say sorry, you know, I can't meet that deadline because my child has a soccer game".

BENEFITS

When describing the benefits of staying home, women describe benefits for themselves, their children, their spouses, and the family as a whole. In other words, staying home—although it does have downsides—is not usually experienced as a selfless decision. On the contrary, women describe wanting this life for themselves, not just for the benefit of their children and spouses.

"Time" is the most common word women use when talking about the upsides of staying home (Rubin and Wooten 2007:340). The time that becomes available allows for what I consider the three "Fs" of stay-at-home mothering: freedom, flexibility, and focus. Women describe being free to volunteer at their children's schools, do projects with their children, or run errands that they struggled to take care of when working. Flexibility is often described as being able to take something to school at the last minute or stay home with a sick child. The ability to focus also enables them to take care of and respond to the needs of their children and influence their development on a daily basis. Not only do women talk about the benefits to their children and themselves, but they also speak about their spouses and how less stressed they are as well. As a result of their decision to stay home, their husbands were also not spread so thin. Thus, although some of the benefits women describe are practical on the surface, a closer look shows that they amount to deeper, more emotional benefits.

CHALLENGES

When given the opportunity to discuss the difficult aspects of leaving behind a career to stay home with their children, HE–SAH mothers appreciate the opportunity to express and articulate their complex range of emotions. They know that having the option to stay home is a privilege and are often made to feel as if they should not complain; consequently, their feelings go unspoken. One patient discussed the judgment she felt from her sister—a working mother—who told her "it must be nice" when discussing her experience of staying home with her children. This signaled to my patient that she was lucky to be staying home and should not complain. Such statements shut down the expression or exploration of what it means to stay home. "It must be nice" translates into "I do not want to hear about your trivial problems when you are lucky to stay-at-home," thereby belittling the struggles HE–SAH moms face. Choosing to stay home is a privilege, but exercising the option to do so comes with its own costs; similar to the benefits, these costs might be concrete at one level (i.e., loss of income), but give rise to less visible but more psychological costs that are far from trivial.

As a psychotherapist, my work involves helping people understand and recognize patterns of experiencing themselves and others and the limits these expectations impose. Many times the question for my patients is "can

I be myself and be in a relationship?" Trouble often stems from feeling limited in their experience of the self (perceived or actual) by the needs of the other. This dilemma is particularly evident in patients who are HE–SAH mothers. By deciding to stay home, women replace the conflict of being spread too thin with being "just a mom." By putting on hold important aspects of themselves to have more time with their child women experience various forms of loss; these losses can trigger a cascade of further losses.

After being introduced at a luncheon as a mother of three, my patient who is a HE–SAH mother and architect reflected on how rapid of a descent her self-esteem took upon leaving behind her profession, or "past life" as she calls it, to become a SAH mother. She lamented, "I love being a mother but that's not all I am and, after quitting, it doesn't take long to lose the self-esteem we had through our work." The loss of professional identity that leads to further loss of self-esteem is a common experience among HE–SAH mothers. If we think of a highly educated, ambitious woman, we can see how she might rely heavily on her achievements in education and then in her career to develop her sense of identity and self-esteem. Thus, it makes sense that, when replacing career with its concrete achievements and external validation with SAH mothering and its fuzzier, more internal and intermittent validation, that one can experience a loss of self-esteem. Women are often left with a void that was occupied by their profession and struggle to replace what was lost.

Another common theme described among HE–SAH moms is the loss of independence. In a society that values self-reliance, making the choice to stay home sets women up to feel dependent and even vulnerable financially. Many women describe the emotional shift from earning their own income to relying on their husband's income. This asymmetrical economic position can lead to feelings of powerlessness. In another cascade of losses, the loss of financial independence often leads to a loss of power and equality with their spouse. When describing her need to get permission about purchasing decisions, one HE-SAH mother in my study stated "…I don't like asking for money…I'd rather have my own money." Another loss that women mention is the loss of a dream. For ambitious women who have carved out space in the public sphere, staying home to raise children can feel isolating and frustrating. Women often feel as if they have left their own dreams behind and as though their development has been forfeited for the development of their children and spouses. There is a certain anxiety that comes not only from leaving a dream behind, but also from feeling left out of the game and slowly losing one's edge. One respondent, a journalist reflected that "... the longer you don't work, your tools aren't sharpened."

Guilt and shame are also common. Shame researcher Brené Brown (2007:13) differentiates shame and guilt: "Guilt and shame are both emotions of self-evaluation; however, that is where the similarities end. The majority of shame researchers agree that the difference between shame and guilt is best understood as the difference between 'I am bad' (shame) and 'I did something bad' (guilt)." Women talk about the time they have devoted to their education and training and the feelings of guilt about wasting their skills by not working and guilt around not contributing financially to the family. In other words, they often feel that they have done or are doing something wrong by not making use of their education by working and thus feel regret. Shame emerges for HE–SAH mothers who have placed much of their self-worth in their career. One respondent, an attorney, described going to her female physician and lying about still practicing because of feeling shame about staying home. She recalled her doctor saying, "you can't be a housewife, no, no, that is not acceptable. Tell me you're not a housewife" She went on to describe her shame saying, "I lied... I like her and I want her to like and respect me. I hate to lose that respect. And I think you do".

Many women have spoken to me about feeling dismissed because they are SAH mothers. When remembering being shamed or dismissed one woman said she wanted to "raise it up the flag pole" that she was an attorney. Another patient, an entrepreneur recalled being at a dinner party after shutting down her business to stay home: "It was like I didn't exist as a person. Every question was about my husband and not one aimed at me. I remember feeling like I was in the Twilight Zone and couldn't believe I'd gone from owning my own business to being invisible. I was so angry."

Other challenges seem to fit into the more day-to-day hazards of the job. For example, isolation is a common challenge. One respondent, an attorney who quit working after her first child, remembered "So I had the baby, and I had practiced and all I knew were working women and I moved to a new town and ... I didn't leave my house the first year ... I was very isolated, and so it was, it was really hard, it was very, very hard. In fact I remember thinking I shouldn't be this sad". Women also talk about the 24/7 nature of the job of not having lunch breaks or leaving at five o'clock to grab cocktails with their colleagues. Although women enjoy flexibility, the downside for them can be the lack of structure throughout the day that can feel never-ending.

SELF-CARE AND PERSONAL GROWTH

After touching on the challenges of HE–SAH mothers, I would like to note that personal growth need not be on hold and, in fact, must be claimed to avoid the stagnation and frustration that can come with the HE–SAH experience. Many HE–SAH mothers work with me to find the wholeness and meaning of being a mother while also claiming space for themselves. I have found the process of continuing to grow and finding fulfillment in being a HE–SAH mother to have three overlapping layers:

1. A Supportive Inner World: The HE–SAH mother must cultivate a positive relationship with herself that involves an inner dialogue of support, respect, and purpose. In other words, if she does not respect her decision to stay home and does not feel a sense of purpose, she will struggle to be fulfilled and happy.

2. Layers of Support: The HE–SAH needs to find support from her spouse, family, and other HE–SAH mothers and her overall community.

3. Aptitudes and Outlets: The HE–SAH must find new ways to reactivate the dormant talents and aptitudes that remain untapped since leaving work.

A Supportive Inner World

HE–SAH mothers must make a shift from having external feedback to having to rely much more on their internal sense of themselves. Women who have harsh and critical internal voices will struggle to feel good about themselves. It becomes imperative to be aware of this internal system. For example, if she validates her sense of purpose and affirms who she is, she will tend to honor herself and her decision. However, if she degrades her decision and condemns who she is, she will struggle to feel good about herself. Another important aspect of her internal system is fluidity. By keeping a fluid attitude that the choice to stay home is not set in stone, she can embrace her experience and avoid falling in to the rigid mindset of feeling "stuck" in her role as an HE–SAH mother. In general, living with a negative internal system makes for a difficult journey as an HE–SAH mother and can lead to her living vicariously through her children to shore up her lack of purpose and self-respect.

Layers of Support

Equally as important as staying connected to all aspects of themselves is being surrounded by concentric layers of support. As noted, the middle of the system (the foundation) is the self; moving outward, the environment might affirm or discourage the HE–SAH mother. First, the partnership between her and her spouse should be evaluated to ensure that both partners feel loved, respected, and on equal footing. If an HE–SAH mother finds herself feeling devalued by her spouse, it would be important to address these issues and seek professional help, if needed. Moving further outward would be the layer of extended family if they live in town and are, in fact, supportive. Women often talk about the role of their parents or in-laws in the lives of their children and the support they feel by having family around to pick up some of the slack. In addition, a network of other HE–SAH mothers who share and therefore affirm their experience of staying home can provide another layer of sustainment. Women talk about play groups, book clubs, and occasional girls' nights out as ways of connecting with other women who share their experience. Finally, the layer of community involvement is also a layer of support and affirmation. HE–SAH mothers often find support and connection through their roles in parent–teacher organizations (PTOs), nonprofit governing boards, and other community activities.

Aptitudes and Outlets

Although she may not be working, the HE–SAH mother continues to have all of her talents that—if cut off—will leave her feeling frustrated. Claiming these parts of herself is important for personal growth, and she must pay attention to what is getting lost after her shift to staying home. I recall when a patient who had given up her pursuits in the art world to stay home with her three kids told me with excitement, "I said it, I actually answered when another mom asked me what I did, I told her 'I'm an artist' and it felt great!" My patient discovered that she had not only given up having a creative outlet but, more importantly, she had also stopped thinking of herself as an artist. However, over the previous six months, she had begun to paint and reconnect with her creative self. Embracing these other parts of the self that can become split off over time is enlivening and life affirming. Other women speak about maintaining their connection to their "working self" by attending professional conferences or reading their fields' journals to stay current. Also, by taking classes, joining bible studies, or participating in book clubs, HE-SAH mothers find ways to continue to learn and grow. They also find much meaning from volunteering their time to causes that are important to them. Often they are able to use their aptitudes to serve in their volunteer positions and therefore feel satisfied that their talents are not left dormant. Although growing and using one's talents is important, I will add one cautionary observation. HE–SAH mothers must remember to mold their aptitudes to the environment rather than the environment to their aptitudes. We have all witnessed the former powerhouse executive who takes over the class holiday party as if it is her next big project. HE–SAH mothers are most often doers, so it is easy to fall into the trap of using a simple pleasure such as a class party to meet unmet needs for accomplishment and validation. In this case, nobody wins. The teacher and students are left with a stressful but "perfect" party and the HE-SAH mother is most likely left feeling let down and tired.

CONCLUSION

The decision to stay home is an emotional one that involves finding one's own "true north" amidst feelings of ambivalence. It is this internal compass, rather than external validation and concrete accomplishments, to which the HE–SAH mother must constantly return in order to sustain her sense of self-worth and purpose. Although the gains are clear for HE–SAH mothers, the psychological downsides are considerable and valid. However, I have found that, when women can hold on to their confidence and continue to experience staying home as a choice they can change, they are able to follow their "true north" with fewer conflicts and less regret and stay truly engaged and present in their lives and the lives of their children and family. After all, being fully present for their children—both physically and emotionally—is what first led them down this road.

REFERENCES

Boyd, Elizabeth Reid 2002 "Being There: Mothers Who Stay At Home, Gender and Time." *Women's Studies International Forum* 25(4):

463–470.

Brown, Brené 2007 *I Thought It Was Just Me (but it isn't): Telling the Truth About Perfectionism, Inadequacy, and Power.* New York: Penguin/Gotham.

Rubin, Stacey, and Ray Wooten 2007 "Highly Educated Stay-at-Home Mothers: A Study of Commitment and Conflict." *The Family Journal* 15: 336–345.

Stern, Daniel N. 1995 *The Motherhood Constellation: A Unified View of Parent-Infant Psychotherapy.* New York: Basic Books A Division of HarperCollins Publishers, Inc.

2.

Maternal Ambivalence

Breastfeeding Mothers' Attempts to Resolve the Conflicting Desire to be Close to Children and to Fulfill Western Conceptualizations of Self Worth and Equality

KEREN EPSTEIN-GILBOA

INTRODUCTION

In my work as a psychotherapist and researcher studying breastfeeding families, I frequently encounter mothers struggling with conflicting desires to be close to their child, while simultaneously trying to fulfill western conceptualizations of self-worth, equality, and distancing from children, typically exemplified by a return to the highly valued work-place and roles outside motherhood. Maternal efforts, encouraged by others, to suppress feelings, to set boundaries, and to separate intermittently from a child, only increase ambivalence. In this chapter, I will demonstrate the process of resolving ambivalence by referring to my research on mothers engaging in physiological breastfeeding patterns and applying findings to processes associated with stay-at-home mothering (Epstein-Gilboa 2006, 2009).

MATERNAL DEVELOPMENT AND AMBIVALENCE

Multiple factors affect women's transition to mothering including; personal, cognitive, social and cultural influences (Mercer 1995; Rubin, 1984).

Ecological theory suggests that development is influenced by systemic messages (Bronfenbrenner 1979) and explains maternal struggle with family, friends, culture and former views. Mothers in western culture might be influenced by feminist conceptualizations voiced in the 1970s that are historically rooted (Plant 2010) and actualized by mothers in the present context (Cooper 2007). These theories propose that while motherhood may be influenced by individual narrative, (Chodorow, 1999) and is an emotional experience, it is nevertheless socially constructed and devalued by patriarchy (Rick, 1976). Equality in socially constructed motherhood may be achieved through shared parenting (Chodorow, 1978). Ultimate self worth is dependent on liberation from housework and child rearing (Firestone 1970/2003; Friedan 1963/2001). An associated cultural theme is reverence for distancing and independence (Grill no date; McKenna 1996; Valsiner 2000). Mothers may identify with and attempt to fulfill their perceptions of the culturally informed role of mother (Raffle 1999).

Pre-existing views may be challenged when women become mothers and reorganize family alliances, roles and tasks (Carter & McGoldrick 2004), form a new identity and cope with feelings associated with earlier relationships and emotional interchanges with the new infant (Cohen and Slade 2005; Cooper 2007; Fraiberg, Adelson & Shapiro 1987, Mercer 1993; Stern, 1977, 1998; Weininger 1992; Winnicott 1958). A sense of being emotionally stirred up by the infant helps mothers engage in caregiving behaviours (Stern 1998; Weininger 1992; Winnicott 1958). Caregiving enhances the transformation to motherhood (Nelson, 2003) and facilitates adjustment with subsequent births (Gameiro, Moura-Ramos and Canavarro 2009). Diverse perspectives imply that optimal caregiving includes observing, interpreting and responding accurately to infant needs, including proximity to mother (Klein 1932/1997; Mahler, Pine, & Bergman 1975; Stern 1977; Weininger 1992; Winnicott 1958). This quality is coined as sensitive or attuned mothering in attachment theory (Ainsworth, Blehar, Waters, & Wall 1978; Bowlby 1987). Thus, ambivalence might be triggered during the transition to mothering when former culturally instilled scripts are disrupted by erupting emotions, including a desire to be close to the infant.

PHYSIOLOGICAL BREASTFEEDING PATTERNS

Maternal infant proximity is central to physiologically based breastfeeding patterns (Epstein-Gilboa 2006, 2009). Physiological breastfeeding patterns reflect infants' and children's developmental continuum that concurs with the recommendations set by the World Health Organization (1981, 2013) where infants nurse within the first two hours after birth, breastfeed exclusively for approximately six months, and continue nursing for at least the first two years of life. Physiological patterns are based on infant and child needs and cues that are displayed frequently. These contribute to ongoing maternal-infant contact during and in-between recurring nursing sessions, and include proximity behaviours such as holding, carrying and co-sleeping. Recurring opportunities to respond to infant cues regarding and during breastfeeding contribute to the development of sensitive mothering styles (Epstein 1993; Epstein-Gilboa 2000, 2006, 2009). Maternal capacity for sensitivity is likely also to be influenced by the hormones prolactin (Sobrinho 2003) and oxytocin (Carter & Porges 2013; Feldman, 2012; Matthiesen, Ransjo-Arvidson, Nissen, & Uvnas-Moberg 2001; Uvnas-Moberg 2003) that not only produce and eject milk, but also contribute to a sense of relaxation, well being and feelings of love towards the infant. Oxytocin, the love hormone, is also released during skin to skin interaction (Gordon, Zagorry-Sharon, Leckman, & Feldman 2010), another important component of proximity behaviours associated with physiological nursing.

Mothers engaging in physiological breastfeeding patterns are not only challenged by salient cultural themes contradicting mother-infant closeness but also by non-breastfeeding norms established through a patriarchal medical system in western culture in the last century that pressure mothers to wean early and avoid proximity (Baumslag and Michels 1995; Dettwyler 1995; Epstein-Gilboa 2006, 2009; Minchin 1998; Mulford 1995; Newman 1995; Palmer 2009; Scott & Mostyn 2003). Interference in women's physiological continuums is likely sustained by unresolved patriarchal envy of female physiology (Epstein-Gilboa 2010). It is interesting to note that despite cultural pressure experienced nursing mothers and those with older nursing children resolve ambivalence, breastfeed into early childhood and stay close to children (Epstein-Gilboa 2006, 2009). An analysis of the themes associated with maternal development and resolution of ambivalence through physiological breastfeeding points to facilitative components relevant for all mothers challenged by former scripts, cultural dissonance and a new found desire to remain close to and at home with children.

AMBIVALENCE AND RESOLUTION IN MOTHERS ENGAGING IN PHYSIOLOGICAL BREASTFEEDING

The descriptions in this section include observations from my research (Epstein, 1993; Epstein-Gilboa 2006, 2009) and clinical experience. I have noted that mothers of infants several weeks to months old seem interested in child development and attuned to infant cues for nursing and proximity, yet complain about infants' endless needs and voice concerns about an impending loss of self. They anxiously disclose that their family reprimands them for constantly breastfeeding or holding the baby, and for neglecting self-care and other relationships. Similar messages to set boundaries and take breaks from infant care are echoed everywhere, and initially, make sense to them. Mothers long for rest from ongoing parenting; they want to stop criticisms and please others.

However, when mothers seem to trust the researcher or therapist they gradually and shamefully disclose that despite their exhaustion and need for time alone, they are overcome by a strange and erupting desire to remain close to their infants at all times. Some mothers admit that they are unable to break away from their infants, disappointing themselves and others. Outings without their infant(s) are stressful and feel forced, thereby fortifying anxiety. They fear that they are obsessed with the infant and that this fixation is harmful; they worry that their desire to mother and be close to the infant will take over their former selves, never allowing a return to past roles or jobs. In some cases mothers feel unwanted anger towards partners or others whom they perceive are pressuring them. Anger may be disguised as disagreement over infant care or manifested in a cycle of depression or self-deprecation as mothers internalize their fury. In all cases mothers seem overwhelmed by feelings they did not expect and are not sure how to handle.

The longing for closeness to the baby seems to be accompanied by an increasing need to protect one's offspring and a sense that only the mother knows how to care for the infant properly. These feelings provide insight into the paradoxical situation where mothers crave time alone and help with the never-ending tasks of motherhood, while at the same time they mistrust others and perceive help with infant care as interference. Certain family members, namely fathers, are trusted more than others and allowed to take over some tasks, usually under mother's watchful eye or direction. The need to control and ensure an infant's safety bewilders mothers who had previously intended on sharing all tasks equally with partners.

The ambivalence expressed by first time mothers is absent in the narratives and behaviours of mothers with older nursing children as with those with previous nursing experience. For some mothers the functional, psychological and hormonal processes associated with breastfeeding, and in a culture that denigrates nursing and mother-infant oneness, may be too overwhelming, contributing to early weaning and disregard for proximity behaviours. Yet paradoxically, the narratives of mothers who continue nursing suggest that similar processes that initially cause anxiety also help mothers overcome their feelings.

Recurring breastfeeding interaction seems to act as a tangible tool facilitating the development of sensitive mothering, enhancing child development and providing mothers with positive reinforcement, a sense of competency, efficacy, and pride Earlier confusion about protecting the infant evolves into a sense of pride and confidence that is evident in mothers' descriptions of their unique ability to console infants through nursing. These feelings enable mothers to focus on infants' needs in a relaxed manner while simultaneously engaging in other tasks, including breastfeeding in all contexts. Nursing outside of the home enhances a sense of freedom, but also implies that mothers have changed their scripts allowing them to ignore dissonance.

Changes in internal meaning are also illustrated in experienced mothers' descriptions of actions originally intended to meet infant needs that evolve into fulfilling interchanges for them. The reluctance to admit longing in early mothering contrasts with later proclamations asserting sole ownership of interactions enthusiastically described as intense, intimate, and unique. Hormonal influences affecting mood and positive regard for the infant, which contribute possibly to the complexity of sensations at the onset of nursing, become increasingly pleasant as the experience becomes familiar. Intense feelings are celebrated and concur with increasingly meaningful themes.

Mothers imply that interaction associated with breastfeeding compensates for perceived damage to their psyche and increasingly revered physiological continuum. Past negative birthing or breastfeeding experiences, and the inability to conceive and experience pregnancy, such as in the case of adoptive breastfeeding mothers, exemplify experiences portrayed as physiologically and psychologically damaging. Maternal sense of compensation through breastfeeding, and a growing respect for female physiology in mothers' narrative over time suggest that mothers create new measures for self worth, facilitating the resolution of earlier ambivalence.

Novel conceptualizations of self-worth are also evident in mothers' changed views of shared parenting from sameness to a complementary stance. This altered perspective also points to increasing maternal ownership of their unique physiologically based position. Mothers are seen as valuable tutors teaching fathers about breastfeeding and childbirth. Sensitivity to child cues increasingly supersedes parenting dissonance. Reliance on paternal support is contingent on fluctuating needs. Support might also be provided by the company of likeminded women that is valued by most mothers but not required by all.

Thus, mothers go through a complex change process. In place of earlier confusion, mothers openly proclaim their feelings and views, engaging in breastfeeding and proximity behaviours beyond infancy, despite that this is defiled in most of their social circles. Responsiveness to cues for nursing and proximity behaviours evolve into a child-focused parenting style and worldview. Mothers who report initially fighting the sense of being stirred up, proclaiming that infants would not take over their lives, later proudly change. Some forego work outside of the home for periods much longer than expected whereas others change professions to include child-oriented work. Some make changes after the birth of the first child and for others this happens with subsequent children. The sense of self and changed scripts extends for many beyond weaning, childrearing, and the family. Many, myself included, remain active advocates long after their children have weaned from the breast and home. New found self worth and belief in one's actions override cultural pressures and negativity.

IMPLICATIONS AND SUPPORT FOR PROCESSES FACILITATING STAY-AT-HOME MOTHERING

The research on mothers engaging in physiological breastfeeding patterns suggest that specific processes enable them to let go of previous convictions and remain close to infants. These findings most certainly have relevance for all mothers who are pulled to stay at home with children while struggling with pressure to do otherwise. Acknowledging, validating and normalizing conflicting feelings help mothers get in touch with internal processes rather than using emotional energy to subdue underlying thoughts and feelings.

One important implication of the processes associated with physiological breastfeeding is that mothers seem to create new measures for self worth that reflect a new reality and rising themes. The new ideas seem to help them accept rather than deny feelings triggered by mothering. Thus, helping mothers reframe issues and worthiness may facilitate decisions to stay at home with children.

The significant role that breastfeeding plays in the development of sensitivity and associated positive self regard suggests one might support mothers' trajectories by helping them find tangible tools, enhancing maternal responsiveness, sense of competency and associated positive reinforcement. The pattern of breastfeeding in all contexts illustrates how maternal internalization of practical skills, confidence, and increasing focus on infant and self as a mother overrides previous interests, including cultural criticism. This finding also demonstrates the facilitative function of multi-tasking, especially for outings with child in hand. In my experience mothers' express relief when they realize that they can go out with infants. This acknowledgement validates and allows mothers to accept their sense of being stirred up by infants and justifies the desire for ongoing proximity.

Multitasking and mothering in different environments help mothers find ways to retain parts of their former identity and stay in touch with the world outside of mothering, improving maternal mood. Liedloff's (1985) study on populations where mothers simultaneously socialize and tend to children's needs concurs with research suggesting that this practice supports emotional health during maternal transformation (Stern, 1988; Weininger, 1992; Winnicott, 1958). Mixed feelings about staying-at home mothering may be resolved by the realization that this does not mean sitting at home all day alone. The acclaimed reparative qualities of breastfeeding that facilitate mothering demonstrate the value of compensating mothers for perceived loss.

One may support mothers by helping them note and embrace new competencies that may compensate for perceived lost capabilities associated with work outside of mothering. The experience of breastfeeding mothers suggests that helping a mother enjoy a sense of intimacy and acknowledge her unique relationship with her child may compensate for feelings formerly felt towards others in the outside world. The evolving expert stance, and tutor role reported by breastfeeding mothers and their partners may certainly be applicable to other stay-at-home mothers who may have become specialists in child development, for example. Maternal realization of one's knowledge of and impact on child development may replicate the sense of agency that one experienced in outside employment.

The celebrated role of mother tutor in the couple relationship in nursing families concurred with their reframed views of parental sharing. This stance may help all couples cease scapegoating attuned parenting and women's changing goals after motherhood, and instead focus on underlying issues that might prevent a partner from supporting a mother's desire to be a stay- at-home-mother. Changed couple focus may facilitate mutual support, contributing to the resolution of ambivalence and ability to accept a desire to remain close to one's child.

An analysis of the resolution of ambivalence for mothers engaging in physiological breastfeeding suggests that letting go of unsuitable scripts, accepting and responding to one's sense of being stirred up by the infant, and reframing meaning to fit the new context leads to new terms of reference for self worth. These functions may help interested mothers actualize proximity behaviours and alter views about stay- at- home mothering practices. The changes in maternal scripts, long term influences, pride and enthusiasm exhibited by mothers, even after children are grown, point to the strength of women's trajectory through mothering. One might suggest that with experience mothers resolve ambivalence, enabling them increasingly to listen to their own growing voice and ignore cultural dissent, and make life changing decisions to stay home with their children.

REFERENCES

Ainsworth, Mary Dinsmore Salter, Mary Curtis Blehar, Everett Waters, and Salley Wall 1978 *Patterns of Attachment.* Hillsdale, NJ: Lawrence Erlbaum Associates.

Baumslag, Noami, and Dia L. Michels 1995 *Milk, Money and Madness: The Culture and Politics of Breastfeeding.* Westport, CT: Bergin & Garvey.

Bowlby, John 1987 *Attachment and Loss.* Toronto, ON: Penguin Books.

Bronfenbrenner, Urie 1979 *The Ecology of Human Development.* Cambridge, MA: Harvard University Press.

Carter, Betty and Monica McGoldrick, eds. 2004 *Overview: The Expanded Family Life Cycle: Individual, Family, and Social Perspectives.* 3rd ed. Boston: Allyn and Bacon.

Carter, C. Sue, and Stephen W. Porges 2013 "The Biochemistry of Love: An Oxytocin hypothesis." *EMBO Reports* 14(1): 12-16.

Chodorow, Nancy 1978 *The Reproduction Of Mothering Psychoanalysis and the Sociology of Gender.* Berkeley: University of California Press.

1999 *The Reproduction of Mothering; Feminism and Psychoanalytic The-*

ory; Femininities, Masculinities and Sexualities; The Power of Feelings. New Haven: Yale University Press.

Cohen, Lisa J., and Arietta Slade 2005 "The Psychology and Psychopathology of Pregnancy: Reorganization and Transformation." In *Handbook of infant mental health.* C.H. Zeanah ed. Pp 2–36. New York: The Guilford Press.

Cooper, Hilary Weiss 2007 *The Transformation of a Woman's Sense of Self After the Birth of her First Child.* New York: University of New York.

Dettwyler, Katherine A. 1995 "Beauty and the Beast. The Cultural Context of Breastfeeding in the United States." In *Breastfeeding: Biocultural Perspectives.* P. Stuart-Macadam & K. Dettwyler, eds. Pp 167–216. New York: Walter de Gruyler Inc.

Epstein, Karen 1993 "The Interactions Between Breastfeeding Mothers and their Babies During the Breastfeeding Session." *Early Child Development and Care* 87: 93–104.

Epstein-Gilboa, Karen 2006 "Systemic Interactions in Breastfeeding Families." *Dissertation Abstracts International* 68-01(B): 669.

Epstein-Gilboa, Keren 2000 "Fall The Psychological Reality of Breastfeeding." *Infant Mental Health Project Print*28: 18–21.
2009 *Interaction and Relationships in Breastfeeding Families: Implications for Practice.* Amarillo, TX: Hale publishing.
2010 "Breastfeeding Envy: Unresolved Patriarchal Envy and the Obstruction of Physiologically-based Nursing Patterns." In *Giving milk.* A. Bartlett and R. Shaw, eds. Toronto: Demeter Press.

Feldman, R. 2012 "Oxytocin and Social Affiliation in Humans." *Hormones and Behavior* 61: 380-391.

Firestone, Shulamit 2003 *The Dialectic of Sex: The Case for Feminist Revolution.* New York: Farrar, Straus and Giroux.

Fraiberg, Selma, Edna Adelson, and Vivian Shapiro 1987 "Ghosts in the Nursery: A Psychoanalytic Approach to the Problems of Impaired Infant-mother Relationships." In *Selected writings of Selma Fraiberg.* L. Fraiberg, ed. Columbus, OH: Ohio State University Press.

Frieden, Betty 2001[1963] *The Feminine Mystique.* New York: Norton Books.

Gameiro, Sofia, Mariana Moura-Ramos, and Maria Cristina Canavarro 2009 "Maternal Adjustment to the Birth of a Child: Primiparity versus Multiparity." *Journal of Reproductive and Infant Psychology* 27(3):

269–286.

Gordon, Ilanit, Orna Zagorry-Sharon, James F. Leckman, and Ruth Feldman 2010 "Oxytocin and the Development of Parenting in Humans." *Biol Psychiatry* 68(4): 377–82.

Grill, Robin N.d. "Banished! Are Parents who Follow Their Hearts Left Out in the Cold?" http://www.naturalchild.org/robin_grille/banished.html

Klein, Melanie 1997[1932] *The Psycho-analysis of Children.* Rev. edition. London: Vintage Books.

Liedloff, Jean 1985 *The Continuum Concept: In Search of Happiness Lost.* Reading, MA: Addison-Wesley Publishing Company.

Mahler, Margaret S., Fred Pine and Anni Bergman 1975 *The Psychological Birth of the Human Infant: Symbiosis and Individuation.* New York: Basic Books.

Matthiesen, Ann-Sofi, Anna-Berit Ransjo-Arvidson, Eva Nissen, and Kerstin Uvnas- Moberg 2001 "Postpartum Maternal Oxytocin Release by Newborns: Effects of Infant Hand Massage and Sucking." *Birth* 28(1): 13–19.

McKenna, James J. 1996 "Sudden Infant Death Syndrome in Cross Cultured Perspective: Is Infant Parent Cosleeping Protective?" *Annual Review of Anthropology* 25: 201–216.

Mercer, Ramona 1995 *Becoming a Mother: Research on Maternal Identity from Rubin to the Present.* New York: Springer.

Minchin, Maureen 1998 *Breastfeeding Matters.* Australia: Alma Publications.

Mulford, Chris 1995 "Swimming Upstream: Breastfeeding Care in a Non-breastfeedtng Culture." *Journal of Obstetric, Gynecologic,* & Neonatal Nursing 24(5): 464–474.

Nelson, Antonia, M. 2003 "Transition to Motherhood." *Journal of Obstetric, Gynecologic, & Neonatal Nursing* 32(4): 465–477.

Newman, Jack 1999 "Breastfeeding Myths Perpetuated by Culture, Society and the Health Care System." *Leaven* 35(5): 107.

Palmer, Gabrielle 2009 *The Politics of Breastfeeding: When Breasts are Bad for Business.* 3rd edition. London: Printer and Martin Ltd.

Plant, Rebecca Jo 2010 *Mom the Transformation of Motherhood in Modern America.* Chicago: University of Chicago Press. Raffel, Stanley 1999

"Revisiting Role Theory: Roles and the Problem of the Self." *Sociological Research Online* 4(2).

Rich, Adrienne 1976 *Of Woman Born: Motherhood as Experience and Institution.* New York: Norton.

Rubin, Reva 1984 *The Maternal Identity and the Maternal Experience.* New York: Springer.

Scott, Jane, and Tricia Mostyn 2003 "Women's Experiences of Breastfeeding in a Bottle-feeding Culture." *Journal of Human Lactation* 19(3): 270–277.

Sobrinho, Luis Gonc alves 2003 "Prolactin, Psychological Stress and Environment in Humans: Adaption and Maladaptation." *Pituitary* 6: 35-39.

Stern, Daniel N. 1977 *The First Relationship: Mother and Child.* Cambridge Massachusetts: Harvard University Press.

1985 *The Interpersonal World of the Infant.* New York: Basic Books.

1998 *The Motherhood Constellation.* London UK: Karnac.

Uvnas-Moberg, Kerstin 2003 *The Oxytocin Factor: Tapping The Hormone Of Calm, Love, and Healing.* Cambridge, MA: DeCapo Press.

Valsiner, Jaan 2000 *Culture and Human Development.* Thousand Oaks, CA: Sage Publications.

Weininger, Otto 1992 *Melanie Klein: From Theory to Reality.* London: Karnac Books.

Winnicott, Donald Woods, ed. 1958 *Collected Papers, Through Pediatrics to Psycho-analysis.* London: Tavistock.

World Health Organization 1981 *International Code of Marketing of Breastmilk Susbstitutes.* Geneva, Switzerland: World Health Organization. http://www.who.int/nutrition/topics/infantfeeding_recommendation/en/index.html

2013 "The World Health Organization's Infant Feeding Recommendation".

3.

Navigating the Narrow Pass of Motherhood

LISA CARLEY HOTALING

BACKGROUND

Mothering in the United States has come to reflect an untenable paradox for many new mothers. While more mothers than ever are attempting to manage the fine balance of parenting and maintaining a professional identity, there is a concomitant surge in new mothers opting to abandon their professional life for the opportunity to stay home full-time with their children. For many women, this isn't an authentic choice; rather, they are often forced to leave their careers behind because the cost of day care is prohibitive relative to their earning potential. The focus of this paper is an exploration of mothers who choose (out of desire or necessity, often indistinguishable) to stay home full-time with their children and how those achievement strivings, so ingrained from late twentieth century egalitarian educational pedagogies, converge with attachment parenting, which exerts a powerful force on women commonly referred to as the new momism.

The theoretical framework for this chapter emerged from the ground of my personal experience becoming a new mother and enduring a profound anxiety as I struggled to navigate what I have termed the narrow pass of motherhood.

I was in graduate school when I became unexpectedly pregnant with my first child. Attending graduate school for psychology was a primary goal, having children was not. My new husband and I even moved from New York to San Francisco so I could attend a specialized training program. Three months into my new graduate program, I became pregnant, while on birth control, and was faced with the first of many difficult decisions to come. I gave birth to a healthy girl, but just a week into my next semester, my daughter contracted a paralyzing illness and soon caring for her swallowed graduate school until it was no longer possible for me to continue my studies. I took a leave of absence for a full year, registered for classes the following fall, and discovered three months into that subsequent semester that I was pregnant again. We made yet another difficult decision and felt forced to move back to New York to be closer to family. I finished my coursework but had the thesis looming over me like a vast black hole: every time I got close to it, it would consume me. Eventually, I dropped out altogether and abandoned any hope of completing my studies.

My first panic attack washed over me when I was only a few weeks pregnant. I ended up in the hospital for the first of a dozen times. Now living in New York, a two year old and a newborn in my sole care (family support ironically fell through because it was perceived as unnecessary now that I was a full-time mom), I continued to slowly fall apart, anxiety ripping me to shreds, one convulsion at a time.

Seeing my anxiety giving way to lethargy, apathy and ennui, my husband suggested that I begin to make and sell the baby slings I had used for my own children. Baby slings are a somewhat complicated accoutrement, and women asked me to help them fit their babies after they were born. So, I found myself in the unusual and privileged position of being one of the first non-family members to be with a mother and her newborn. Women, one after another, openly shared their discontent, emptiness, and groundlessness. Each of these threads pulled together to form a tapestry of postpartum loss. These women inspired me to find the courage I had been lacking, and I began to examine my own pain, loss, and disconnectedness. I wasn't alone. This was both reassuring to me and deeply disconcerting. I wasn't alone! So many women were feeling this unbearable pain as they entered into motherhood. What was going on?

I began to wrestle with this pain, abstractly at first, looking for patterns, trying to tease out meaning, searching for root causes, and then the full weight of my choice to stay home pressed in on me like a suffocating blanket. In order to make this shift into full-time mothering, I had to snuff out an entire identity. The gasping for breath, the heart-twisting palpitations of my panic attacks were the death throes of my previous self, begging to be given one more chance at life. In the midst of this terrifying odyssey, I had a dream one night, both horrifying and enlightening:

While a hostage on the back of a terrorist dragon, I was pulled into a body of water and thrown from its scaly back, abandoned and drowning. When I surfaced, I found myself between the cliffs of a mythical narrow strait. On one side, Scylla, the many-headed dog-beast, so fearful of being swallowed by a male dominated culture, that she herself becomes the aggressor casting fatal arrows at any perceived threat. To my right, I felt the sucking water pull me as Charybdis threatened to swallow me whole, empty and without boundaries.

From this powerful metaphor, I began to conceptualize motherhood in terms of Ulysses' journey. This myth became the map of my own journey and subsequently manifested into my (finally) completed master's thesis.

Both Scylla and Charybdis were punished for extreme behavior: They inhabit the opposite posts of the narrow pass, so to speak, in the modern mothering dilemma. Does a new mother resolve her achievement strivings by adopting a stance of caustic independence, believing she needs no one to be a successful mother (like Scylla), or does she, like Charybdis, give up her achievement needs by a total loss of boundaries?

When I took to the task of conceptualizing the path new mothers were taking in an effort to find a sense of self after entering motherhood, I conceived several stages, beginning with pregnancy, that seem to outline the trajectory I observed many woman, including myself, embarking on after we had our first child. These steps are by no means universal; however, they represent an amalgam of what I experienced and what I was privileged to observe and hear told by mothers courageous enough to share.

THE NARROW PASS: A MODEL OF MATERNAL CONSTRICTION PREGNANCY

From the moment I discovered I was pregnant, I looked to the experts for direction. It was made clear by one "expert" after another that I was ultimately, singularly responsible for this baby growing inside me. I was indoctrinated in the sacrosanct ways of attachment parenting, which include a general disavowal of technological intrusions into the domain of motherhood. Women who are being initiated into the alternative parenting movement have to juggle some powerful forces, and I suggest that the movement, designed to support women, may in fact, be a subtle form of coercion. The pressure to have a home birth, for example, without medical intervention, can exert a powerful force on an expectant mother. Your strength as a woman begins to be measured by the birth you choose.

BIRTH

Due to pre-existing health conditions, mine was a high-risk pregnancy and hence necessitated a hospital birth. Because I did, in fact experience some complications during delivery, I was given Pitocin and pain killers. I fought with the delivery nurses until I faltered with exhaustion. In my case, if I hadn't allowed them to administer those interventions, I may have lost my baby. Even though those interventions ultimately saved my daughter's life, I felt I had failed as a mother who should be strong enough to deliver her child naturally. This feeling of inadequacy became the permanent backdrop to my early mothering experiences.

ADJUSTMENT

Nursing, another mandate of the natural parenting movement, like attaching to baby in a moment of Nirvanic bliss, proved to be yet another area of profound failure for me. I ignored the pain each and every time my daughter latched on; I ignored the fact that she was losing weight and that when I pumped, I saw blood in my milk. It wasn't until my daughter entered the "failure to thrive" zone and I was told that there was a problem with my mammary glands that I stopped nursing. So concerned was I with doing the "right" thing as a mother, I ignored my body completely.

Many women I interviewed had made the decision to stay home when they realized that nursing was incompatible with their work schedules. This is a complicated issue because while I agree that the workplace needs to accommodate nursing mothers in myriad ways that are currently being ignored, mothers are needing to nurse their babies now, not in the future when policies change. We should work to change accessibility to nursing in the workplace; however, when we are faced with the reality that we cannot nurse our babies (or even pump discreetly) in the workplace, mothers must make a choice about continuing to nurse or alter their employment situation.

Leaving the workplace also leaves many women dependent on another (an economically stable partner, spouse, etc.) for the first time in their adult lives. This adjustment extends beyond an economic dependency on their partner but also includes a difficult transition into a role that has few markers for achievement. It's also an increasingly isolated role, often comprising of mother and baby for hours at a time.

CONFORMITY

There is an experience of sheer isolation when mothering in the United States. We are mothering basically alone, not connected to a community within which to parent. Additionally, we are parenting in such a way that our work comprises our childcare responsibility rather than our children being integrated into our work.

I reached out, practically in desperation, for other mothers. On the one hand, making these connections was very positive as I began to move out of the house and into the world again. On the other hand, connecting with other women who were also staying home with their children served to reinforce the parenting choices I made. There was such a strong desire to overcome the isolation that I often molded myself to fit another mother's model of parenting, reflecting her values and agreeing with her ideas which likely included, at least to some degree, the mandates of the "new momism." I would continually compare myself and wonder if I was adequate to the task of mothering at all, but I never shared those fears with anyone, least of all other mothers.

CAREERISM

In discussions with other mothers while preparing my thesis, I discovered that we all felt a similar pressure from the culture to do more, to centralize our child even more, to put our own needs in the background until the edges of own identity became increasingly watercolor washed into those of our children.

This represents a turning point in my model. All the stages up to this point felt very difficult for me. I had had to wrestle with choices and weigh my options against very powerful messages. When I committed myself to this role as a "stay-at-home mom", I felt a palpable release of tension. My feeling of anxiety diminished, belying an increasing need to repress my dissatisfaction, and I accepted my role with renewed vitality. Motherhood thus became a career, and I was bound and determined to do my very best at it.

In my Herculian striving for perfection, I could not give myself without feeling under-appreciated. Not feeling met with adequate praise, I couldn't help but begin to feel a deep resentment. I was completely defined by my role as mother. My need for external agency got foisted on my daughter as I attempted to demonstrate, through *her* achievements, ("*Why yes she started walking at just nine months, and she read her first word when she was just two...*") just what a great mother I was.

I am suggesting that there is an apparent but often overlooked irony that women have on the one hand rejected many aspects of the culture that are deemed masculine, technologies being a clear example, while unwittingly accepting all the messages of the Good Mother, which have also emanated from the predominantly patriarchal culture. I am suggesting that as a mother's achievement needs get further sublimated through co-opting the male model of achievement she rejected in the first place (competition, individual achievement, etc.), her acceptance of the Good Mother motif becomes even more entrenched, even as she more thoroughly rejects the masculine culture around her. The untenable position this puts her in increases her repressed anxiety and as a necessary palliative she becomes more dogmatic.

DOGMATISM

A mother's display of superiority in the realm of parenting may actually reveal her deep sense of subordination in a culture that values only male paradigms of achievement which largely happen "out there" in the world, rather than those that take place in the relative privacy of the family home. However, driven by the need to display supremacy, she often excludes her partner or spouse from participation in parenting.

Not only is the partner thus excluded from the domain of parenting, but other mothers who do not espouse the exact same parenting values are also excluded. The more dogmatic a mother becomes, the more isolated she becomes, and her circle of friends becomes exceedingly homogeneous and limited in scope. "I can't let my son play with Jack any more because his mother allows him to eat Cheetos/play with toy guns/stuff crayons up his nose/(fill in your own parenting faux pas d' jour)". My own special dogmatism revolved around fast food and "unnatural" peanut butter. The dogmatism we feel engenders an increasing exclusivity, which undermines the need for connection and affiliation; thus a palpable sense of loss is experienced. Once these connections become strained, mothers now often find that our achievement needs have led to a dogmatism that in fact undermines our affiliative needs.

What really emerged for me here was insecurity about my job as mother, without external signifiers for appraisal. My identity was inextricably linked with the idea that I was what I achieved, and yet this new role of motherhood had remarkably few atta-boys or year- end bonuses attached. *How was I to measure my success? And why does no one see what a great job I am doing*? I began to fuel a quiet anger, its embers ignited when my parenting was questioned or my efforts were unseen.

ANGER AND RAGE

I have tried to demonstrate how our "willing" subjugation to the cultural messages lead us to an ultimate subjugation of our own self, in the ostensible service of our children, but really in acquiescence to a cultural imperative suggested both by the patriarchal powers and by the other women who have co-opted the imperative of total mothering.

Only a few years into motherhood, I found myself often exhausted to the point of not being able to get out of bed. I would get migraines, violent stomach cramps, body aches, and panic attacks too numerous to count. These little illnesses emerged as a somatic expression of my buried anger. This anger after the birth of my daughter crept in as dust through a window screen, imperceptible in the moment yet cumulative over time.

The perpetual and mundane tasks of picking up toys, tuna cans and unread Tolstoy (launched from my dust-covered book case) day after day, while feeling that the stars were aligned if I could get a shower in, began to accumulate, suffocating me from within. One day, when my daughter was about two years old, the phone rang and I had to walk across the dining room, barefoot, to answer it. I stepped on a wooden alphabet block with sharp edges. In a fit of rage, I picked up the block and threw it across the room so hard that it temporarily lodged in the wall. I felt a volcanic explosion rise up in me, and I looked for anything else I could throw into a wall.

Even after the birth of my second child, this scenario played itself out innumerable times with Legos, Tinker Toys, and plastic dinosaurs. However, one night, in the aftermath of another fit of rage, I looked around me and saw the debris of be-headed dolls, busted crayons and bona fide terror on my daughter's face, and I knew that something had to change; I had to change. I was accustomed to walking away from these scenes and shutting myself up in my room to cool down, but this time, I went *into* the rage. I sat myself down in the middle of the mess I had made worse, and I rode the dragon to its depths.

As I looked at the internal terrain of my anger, I was seeing, for the first time, the emptiness of my internal landscape. When I reached beyond the anger, I felt an abject terror. My rage would be triggered when I had to pick up after the kids because deep inside I believed that it was fundamentally beneath me to be picking up their toys when I could be (*should* be) in graduate school finishing my degree. And yet that was just the beginning. When I rode the anger deeper, I experienced the emptiness of the pursuit of achievement, that if I couldn't be present in the moment to celebrate my children's creativity rather than see the mess, then this anger would not merely stay contained within me but would swallow me like a snake consuming its own tail.

The idea of a human being's inherent need to grow is central to humanistic psychology, and it cannot be understated that motherhood, as idealized in our culture today, demands nothing less than a kind of "otherhood" where the self of the mother is whittled away. When faced with our own anger, the resulting feeling is profound guilt. "Aren't I supposed to just *love* motherhood?"

GUILT

Real guilt arises from not being true to oneself, to one's own nature. Humans must grow, must become, and have a responsibility to make meaning toward a deeper way of being. It is not possible, I believe, to turn one's back on growth without consequences.

Feeling a growing resentment at my own increasing dependency, lost independence, and lack of achievement, my suppressed anger began to burst out, which resulted in deep guilt. This movement from anger to guilt is a critical one because the affect of anger (which ostensibly can be managed) transmogrifies into guilt, an ontological state of being, for which there is no more "management." This point needs to be underscored because now I began to see that, in fact, my achievement needs weren't being gratified through self-abnegation. I began to understand that I could not get those needs met through my child and this caused enormous guilt that I had attempted to do so in the first place. However, I felt a profound guilt for "stepping-out" of the Good Mother role, even as I began to see its diaphanous composition. This untenable "narrow pass" caused me to further submerge my anger. Guilt threatened to swallow me whole, and I began to despair.

DESPAIR AND LOSS OF SELF

I often heard from friends in rare moments of quiet and candidness, "How could this have happened? I have no idea who I am anymore." The explicit awareness of a loss of self first came to me when I was unpacking in our new apartment, seven months pregnant. We had just moved from California to New York, and I came across a box I had not seen for several years. I pulled up one of the folded-under cardboard lips and discovered all the journals I have written since I was eighteen years old, about forty books in all, silent all these years.

After I got married, I had placed each one in this very box. These journals were my life, under construction, and sitting on the floor with them at my side, I was looking at an abandoned structure. Not only had I not seen these journals in several years, it occurred to me that my last words were written in a new journal just after the initial ultrasound for my first child. I had written only on the first page. The remaining blank pages were like tombstones yet to be engraved, waiting.

I shifted my weight from one arm to the other, resting my free arm around the circumference of my belly in a half-hearted hug. Hot tears dripped from the end of my chin and fell, glistening, onto the top of my hand. I bowed my head and apologized to my son, still transforming within me, holding so much promise and soon needing so much from me. "I'm so sorry," I whispered, "I wish I could tell you who your mother is."

I did not lose myself in that moment. It was a gradual erosion, occurring through thousands of moments in time, such that the falling away was barely noticeable; pieces of self swept off the contours of my identity, scorching anger left trenches that filled with tears that overflowed into this moment when, sitting on the floor, ripe for birth, my journals beside me, I looked at the landscape I had become, and it was unrecognizable. I had become profoundly alienated from myself.

The self can be defined as the central perceiving, acting, and interfacing entity within the human being that guides and informs its meaning- making endeavors which are rooted in a fundamental, inherent need to grow. What does it mean then, to lose one's self? With my sense of self profoundly, radically slipping away, I had to somehow figure out how to let go of the false promises of actualization through the absolute care of others in order to save myself. Kierkegaard discusses two forms of despair: the despair of weakness and the despair of defiance. They are briefly characterized as follows: the despair of weakness is an effect of refusing to claim oneself.

This is the dread of autonomy as symbolized by Charybdis. In the end, she lost any sense of self and became one with the sea, sucking and heaving, without end or beginning. The despair of defiance on the other hand, or of "manliness" as Kierkegaard suggested, is understood as the awareness of one's despair of refusing to be oneself (autonomous agency). In the end, the individual loses herself in the awareness of her own weakness (dependency). In an effort to avoid a mature dependency, adhering instead to the dictates of autonomous male achievement models (even couched in "back-to-instinct" attachment parenting) as symbolized by Scylla, a mother unwittingly winds up utterly dependent and lost as symbolized by the voracious, sucking mouth of Charybdis.

CONCLUSION

It would be unkind of me to leave it at that, to outline a path to despair with no remedy offered. But, I have no words of wisdom. I only have my journey and my own twisted navigation. It has been several years since I completed my thesis and first conceived the narrow pass. I have found an uneasy peace. I completed one year into a clinical psychology doctoral program, but 1,200 miles from my children, who are now ten and seven years old.

After I was accepted to graduate school (for the second time), I explained to my daughter what it meant, that I would be moving away but that I would see her often and talk to her every day. I asked her to share with me her feelings about such a significant change. She shared this with me, "Mom, you have been there for me since I was a baby. You have supported me in everything I have done. It's time for me to support you now. I love you, and I *know* you love me. Now, go do your best!" Her maturity and confidence with such a difficult decision, (a confidence I lacked, frankly), brought tears to my eyes. Perhaps along the straddled path between achievement/abnegation, I found my way through the narrow pass after all: engendering in my daughter the belief that identity is not fixed in the past or situated in the future, not discovered in what I achieve or how much I give up; rather it is a unity, a whole, authentic self who celebrates the now, chooses in the present, knowing only this being in this moment is for certain.

POSTSCRIPT

After completing one year of my doctorate, I took another leave of absence as I attempted to carve a path between increased demands at school and another medical situation at home necessitating my return, full-time, to parenting. As the return to graduate school became untenable, I had to navigate, once again, the straits of the narrow pass. However, this journey is joyful. I have chosen to leave school behind at this time and follow a more balanced dream: I am developing a journal for mothers, aptly titled: *The Narrow Pass.*

4.

Are "Mommy Wars" Real?

BRIANNE JANACEK REEBER AND PAULA J. CAPLAN

> "With motherhood comes one of the toughest decisions of a woman's life: Stay at home or pursue a career? The dilemma not only divides mothers into hostile, defensive camps but pits individual mothers against themselves."
> —Leslie Morgan Steiner's *Mommy Wars*

HISTORY OF MOMMY WARS

Judging from newspapers, magazines, news reports, and television shows, in the United States stay-at-home mothers (SAHM) and mothers with paid work (MWPW) are at war against each other, and the story rages throughout the media, from *The New York Times* to "Dr. Phil." Recently, a number of media outlets (e.g., NPR, 2012; Fox News, 2012) treated as evidence of the "Mommy Wars" a woman journalist's statement that a political candidate's wife never worked a day in her life because she had been a stay-at-home mother; they might have treated it instead as one woman's comment about another woman. In this paper, we report the results of the first known study aimed to see whether Mommy Wars are real.

The media stories are based on small numbers of anecdotes, and there has been no empirical investigation of whether mothers really judge mothers of the other group negatively. What purpose is served by the spread of this notion? If these wars are real, that is consistent with the message of the forces of anti-feminist backlash (Faludi, 1991) that women are quick to attack each other.

From the first use of the term "Mommy Wars" in 1990 (Darnton), the assumptions made about mothers have been that they:

- are easily divided into two groups: SAHM and MWPW (Berg, 1985; Darnton, 1990; Gardner, 2002);
- have hostile feelings toward mothers of the other group (Berg, 1985; Darnton, 1990; Gardner, 2002; Oprah, 2007);
- feel the need to defend being SAHM or MWPW (Berg, 1985; Gardner, 2002);
- view their own group as a cohesive entity and do not willingly associate with the other group (Berg, 1985; Darnton, 1990; Gardner, 2002); and
- consider the other group inferior (Berg, 1985; Darnton, 1990; Gardner, 2002).

Factors and conditions relevant to the 1980s and 1990s, era of Mommy Wars' media debut, appear to have contributed to its birth. Pressure to do "intensive mothering" (Hays, 1996, 4) became prevalent in the 1980s, requiring more time and effort than ever before (trying to heed the advice of every childcare expert, even when they contradicted each other: Caplan, 2000), and "over-the-top levels of hypernatalism" involved a push for mothers' perfection in the conservative 1980s, when women were increasingly told their place was in the home (Douglas & Michaels, 2004, 205). Hypernatalism was seen in many movies and television shows that were either all about babies and children or featured births, especially the popular television show *thirtysomething* — premiering in 1987 and portraying "mothers [who] had chosen to return to the home and not work for pay," implying that women had a moral obligation to their children to do so (Douglas & Michaels, 2004, 209).

In an article about Mommy Wars on the *Washington Post's* "Style" page on January 3, 1985, called "Mothers Against Mothers," Barbara Berg did not use the term "Mommy Wars" but raised the primary issue, quoting catty comments about each other from both SAHM and MWPW. Berg alleged there was "growing animosity centering on a single question: Who makes the better mother, the one who stays home or the one who works?" (Berg,

1985) Nina Darnton coined the phrase, "Mommy Wars" in a 1990 *Newsweek* article beginning, "These are the Mommy Wars," followed by anecdotes about hostility that mothers in the two groups felt toward each other.

Women's magazines fueled the notion that Mommy Wars were raging. In a 1992 chocolate chip cookie bake-off in *Family Circle*, readers decided which Presidential candidate's wife made the better cookie—stay-at-home mom Barbara Bush or working mom Hillary Rodham Clinton. This followed Clinton's remark that as a working mother, she did not have time to stay home and bake cookies (Burros, 1992). (Clinton's cookies won.)

On November 10, 2003, Dr. Phil's "Mom vs. Mom" episode aired nationally. Onstage were Sonja, the representative mother with paid work, and Leah, a stay-at-home mother. The mostly female Dr. Phil audience was split into MWPWs and SAHMs purposely seated on opposite sides of the aisle. Immediately after the show's taping, the expert guests agreed that an "important conversation... attentive to all the complex issues of parenting" had taken place (Peskowitz, 2005, 33), but when the show aired, it was a "heavily edited show [that] featured an audience of mothers hurling insults at one another" (p. 33). The expert guests were angered and posted a statement of disapproval of the show on the Family Home Network's website, emphasizing that there is no war but rather a "common struggle to support our families financially and emotionally" (cited by Peskowitz, 2005, 35).

In an article called "Moms hating moms: The internalization of mother war rhetoric," Johnston and Swanson (2004) assert that "Mother War rhetoric does affect mothers" (506), based on interviews with 98 women, but they report no statistical analyses of data to support that claim, and their report is plagued by interpretive problems.

Recent books by academics (Douglas & Michaels, 2004; Peskowitz, 2005) lend themselves to popular consumption and are thought provoking but lack empirical data bearing on Mommy Wars' reality. Douglas and Michaels (2004) and Peskowitz (2005) claim that the existence of Mommy Wars is unsubstantiated and based only on media claims. In contrast, Steiner, in her book, *Mommy Wars* (2006), does not question whether Mommy Wars are real but rather assumes that they are and blames mothers for them.

Popular press and other media reports about Mommy Wars abound; a simple search for "Mommy Wars" in the online archives of *The New York Times* for all available dates brings up eight articles[1] (Allen, 2012; Clemetson, 2006; Brown, 2006; Bellafante, 2006; Wyatt, 2004; Stolberg, 2001; Spragins, 2001; and Richardson, 1992), but no author questions whether

Mommy Wars are real and pervasive except Allen (2012). Allen makes the important point that the conflict has been framed as involving SAHM and MWPW, whereas the focus needs to be on improving the cultural, social, and economic conditions that lead women into one group or the other. During the 2012 U.S. Presidential campaign, journalist Hilary Rosen's comment that Ann Romney was unqualified to advise her husband, candidate Mitt Romney, about economic matters related to women, because as a SAHM she had never worked a day in her life provoked reactions related to Mommy Wars. One of the most interesting was D'Arcy's (2012) *Washington Post* article, whose subtitle, "Mothers are not so easily divided," was an important echo of Allen's point and reflects progress toward dismantling the Mommy Wars myth.

CULTURAL CONTEXT OF THE DEVELOPMENT OF MOMMY WARS CONCEPT

The Second Wave of the women's movement, which began in the late 1960s and early 1970s, was continuing at the time of the initial media pronouncements about Mommy Wars in the 1980s and 1990s. Daughters of women who came of age at the beginning of the Second Wave found that, when they themselves came of age, the media were declaring that feminism was no longer needed, because equality between the sexes had been achieved. Many young women did not expect to be treated as second-class citizens (Gardner, 2002), so when they entered the workforce and became mothers around the time of Mommy Wars' media debut, many had thought to combine motherhood seamlessly and easily with paid work (Peskowitz, 2005). Even women who had started work in the 1970s and postponed having children until the 1980s believed they could "have it all" (Douglas & Michaels, 2004). But due to backlash against the women's movement (Faludi, 1991) and the failure to win many of its battles (pay was still far from equal, the glass ceiling in the workplace remained, and men still did far less than half of the childcare and housework: Pleck, 1997), being a mother with paid work was still extremely difficult. This rendered believable the claim in Mommy Wars stories that MWPW were jealous of SAHM. The Second Wave's emphasis on the importance of mothers' freedom to choose paid work rendered believable the claim that SAHM felt jealous of and were demeaned by those with paid jobs.

The backlash included major media figures' and political conservatives' claims that feminists considered mothers worthless (Caplan, 2000). This was untrue; nearly all feminists have always argued that becoming a mother should be a woman's choice "made as freely as possible, as should whether or not to stay at home with her children" (p. 126). Alix Kates Shulman, a prominent Second Wave voice, said, "I never felt any conflict between the [feminist] movement and motherhood. Feminism healed my conflicts. . . . In fact, it was as a mother that I most deeply engaged with feminists" (cited by Caplan, 2000, p. 126). Unfortunately, claims that feminists considered SAHM worthless have made the latter worry that perhaps they cannot be feminists and that feminists will judge them negatively for their choice (p. 127). Mommy Wars stories are part of this backlash, including false claims about feminism to set women up against each other.

METHODOLOGY

Participants

Participants were a convenience sample of 151 mothers located via an email sent to about 30 personal contacts including relatives, former teachers, and family friends, which included mothers and other people who may have had e-mail contacts for mothers. The e-mail[2] indicated that this was research about mothers, with no mention made of Mommy Wars. A link to the online survey was included, and recipients were asked either to take the survey if they were a mother of at least one child who was 18 or under and still living in her home, or to forward it to any mother they knew who was eligible. Recipients were assured of anonymity.

Questionnaire and Procedure

The purpose of the study was to find out if the media's claims about the dynamics of the Mommy Wars are true and whether SAHM and MWPW are at war with one another. There was no existing questionnaire to explore this, so one with both a structured, quantitative component and an unstructured, more qualitative one was designed based on media stories about Mommy Wars. The questions[3] were designed to gather demographic information, gauge awareness of the supposed Mommy Wars, and learn whether mothers are actually involved in them. Participants were encouraged to comment freely throughout the survey, with space for comments provided after each substantive question.

For items whose response choices were SAHM and MWPW, the order of the choices was counterbalanced. When a series of paired questions, one about SAHM and one about MWPW, was presented, the order within pairs was also randomized.

Demographics and Other Information

Participants were asked to state whether they are currently a MWPW or SAHM. Each was asked her age, number of children and their ages; whether other adults live in her household and help with childcare, and if so, her relationships to them; how many hours per week she takes care of children and does housework; who is the children's primary caretaker; her highest level of education; her race/ethnicity; her household income and whether or not her household depends on her income; and whether she reads mainstream popular women's magazines and/or less traditional magazines aimed at women. Those identifying themselves as SAHM were asked how they respond to people who ask their occupation. Those identifying themselves as MWPW were asked their occupation, whether they do the paid work inside or outside of their home, and the number of hours they work each week.

Hypotheses: Do Mothers Experience Mommy Wars?

The first set of hypotheses was designed to understand if mothers engage in Mommy Wars. On a scale of 0-10 (0 for "disagree strongly" to 10 for "agree strongly"), all participants were asked to rate the degree to which they agreed with statements about SAHM and MWPW, probing whether participants have negative feelings about mothers from the group to which they do not belong or about their own group.[4] The hypotheses were that mothers would agree with the following statements (rated 6-10) about the group to which they did not belong, which would be consistent with the reality of the Mommy Wars.

1. "I think that [MWPW/SAHM] are probably not realizing their full potential as individual women."
2. "I think that [MWPW/SAHM] are probably not contributing adequately to society."
3. "I think that [MWPW/SAHM] are probably denying their children a positive role model."
4. "I think that [MWPW/SAHM] are probably denying their

children adequate affection and opportunities for bonding."

5. "I think that [MWPW/SAHM] are unlikely to be very good mothers."

The second set of hypotheses and their converses was tested to understand if media claims about Mommy Wars dynamics were true. Then those who were aware of the notion of Mommy Wars were asked to explain their understanding of what Mommy Wars are, to see if it matched media descriptions.

6. SAHM and MWPW will prefer friends mostly from the same category as themselves.
7. SAHM and MWPW will say they feel judged negatively by the other group.
8. SAHM and MWPW will mostly say that they have to defend why they are a SAHM or a MWPW.
9. Respondents will have heard of the Mommy Wars.

RESULTS

One hundred fifty-one people took the online survey. Twenty of these dropped out before finishing, but four of the 20 were included in the analysis because they answered more than half of the substantive questions (beyond demographics). Thus, the total number of respondents for each question varies slightly. In the qualitative portion, respondents extensively responded to open-ended questions, and that material is used in the Discussion section to interpret some of the quantitative data.

Average age of respondents was 38.77 (n=135, SD=7.14, range 24-55), and the average number of their children was 2.1 (n=135, SD=1.01). Ninety-two percent of participants reported their race/ethnicity[5] as white, 4% Hispanic, 2% Black, 1% Asian-American, and 1% Native American. Seventy-six percent identified themselves as mothers with paid work and 24% as stay-at-home mothers. Highest levels of education obtained by respondents were: high school diploma (16%), 2-year degree (10%), B.A. or B.S. degree (47%), master's degree (19%), Ph.D. (2%), and professional degree (6%). Household incomes were: less than $40,000 (5%), $40,000-$60,000 (10%), $60,000-$80,000 (13%), $80,000-$100,000 (27%), $100,000-$200,000 (35%), and $200,000 or more (10%). Forty-six percent said that their households are not dependent on income from them and that therefore they could choose whether to work for pay or stay at home with their children (27% of MWPW, 97% of SAHM). Fifty-four percent of all respondents said they do not have the option of staying home, because their household depends on an income from them (73% of MWPW and 3% of SAHM). Chi-square tests showed no significant relationship between mother's status (MWPW or a SAHM) and household income, nor was there a significant relationship between mother's status and education. A significant relationship was found between mother's status and whether or not the household was dependent upon an income from the respondent ($p<.001$, $n=135$), with households of 73% of MWPW depending upon their income and the remaining 27% of MWPW choosing to work for other reasons. Three percent of SAHM stay home because they have no choice due to expense of daycare.

Occupations of MWPW mothers were 35% in education, training, and library; 16%, business and financial operation; 10%, management; 9%, sales; 8%, office and administrative support; 6%, healthcare practitioners and technicians; 4%, community and social services; 4%, healthcare support; 2%, personal care and service; 1%, legal work; 1%, transportation and material moving; and 4% did not provide enough information to be classifiable (Bureau of Labor Statistics, 2005). Of MWPW, 84% work outside their home, 9% from home, and 7% both inside and outside. Number of hours worked per week by mothers with paid work ranged from 5-60 (mean=35.6), and the sizable standard deviation of 11.5 reflects the great range and variability of time spent doing paid work. Ninety-six percent of respondents live with another adult in their home ($n=135$). All but three of these live with their spouse, five with their spouse and another relative, and one with her fiancé. Of respondents who live with another adult, 98% said that adult helped them with childcare. Ninety-three percent are their children's primary caretakers. Three respondents listed their spouse as the primary caretaker, two listed daycare, one listed a relative other than a spouse, and three shared responsibility with their spouse. Fifty-seven percent of participants said they read mainstream popular women's magazines, 10% said they read less traditional magazines aimed at women, and 4% said they read both kinds.

ARE MOTHERS ENGAGED IN MOMMY WARS?

For every hypothesis, the data failed to support claims about the dynamics of the Mommy Wars and were inconsistent with claims that the Mommy Wars exist.

The first set of hypotheses was tested to understand if mothers engage in Mommy Wars. The following hypotheses—that SAHM and MWPW would agree (6-10 on average) with the following statements about mothers of the other group—were not supported by the data.[6]

1. "*I think that stay-at-home mothers/mothers with paid work are probably not realizing their full potential as individual women.*" Hypothesis 1, that MWPW and SAHM will answer on average between 6 and 10 about the other group was not supported, meaning neither group believes that members of the other group fail to realize their full potential as women. (Of note, neither group believes their own group fails to realize their full potential as women, either.)

2. *"I think that stay-at-home mothers/mothers with paid work are probably not contributing adequately to society."* Hypothesis 2, that MWPW and SAHM will answer on average between 6 and 10 about the other group was not supported, meaning neither group believes that the members of the other group fail to contribute adequately to society. (Of note, neither group believes their own group fails to contribute adequately to society, either.)

3. *"I think that stay-at-home mothers/mothers with paid work are probably denying their children a positive role model."* Hypothesis 3, that MWPW and SAHM will answer on average between 6 and 10 about the other group was not supported, meaning neither group believes that members of the other group deny their children a positive role model. (Of note, neither group believes their own group denies their children a positive role model, either.)

4. *"I think that stay-at-home mothers/mothers with paid work are probably denying their children adequate affection and opportunities for bonding."* Hypothesis 4, that MWPW and SAHM will answer on average between 6 and 10 about the other group was not supported, meaning neither group believes members of the other group deny their children adequate affection and opportunities for bonding. (Of note, neither group believes their own group denies their children adequate affection and opportunities for bonding, either.)

5. *"I think that stay-at-home mothers /mothers with paid work are unlikely to be very good mothers."* Hypothesis 5, that MWPW and SAHM will answer on average between 6 and 10 about the other group was not supported, meaning neither group considers members of the other group unlikely to be good mothers. (Of note, neither group believes their own group is unlikely to be good mothers, either.)

The second set of hypotheses was designed to test if media claims about dynamics of the Mommy Wars were true. The original hypotheses and their negative converses were tested. The negative converses were all supported, indicating that none of the media claims about the dynamics of the Mommy Wars was true.

6. The negative form of Hypothesis 6 – "Neither SAHM nor MWPW will prefer friends in the same category as themselves"–was supported. A chi-square test was performed to see if there was a relationship between the mother's status (being a MWPW or a SAHM) and having friends in a category that would be consistent with the Mommy Wars. The results were not significant ($p>.05$, $n=135$), thus SAHM and MWPW are not significantly more likely to have friends in mostly the same category as themselves than in the other.

7. The negative form of Hypothesis 7 – "SAHM and MWPW will NOT say they feel judged negatively by the other group" – was supported. Chi-square goodness of fit test was performed on responses of each group with the

expected values of 50% saying that they feel judged negatively by the other group and 50% saying that they do not feel judged negatively by the other group. For SAHM, the test did not reach statistical significance; thus, the null hypothesis that there is a random distribution of responses cannot be rejected, but the negative form of the original hypothesis (as stated above) is supported because the responses of SAHM did not differ from chance. For MWPW, the test reached statistical significance ($p<.05$, $n=95$), because more MWPW do not than do feel judged negatively by SAHM (61%). A chi-square test yielded no significant relationship between mother's status and feeling judged by the other group.

8. The negative form of Hypothesis 8 – "Neither SAHM nor MWPW will mostly say that they have to defend why they are a SAHM or a MWPW" – was supported, and a chi-square test of the relationship between mother's status and whether or not one had to defend oneself did not reach statistical significance.

9. The negative form of Hypothesis 9 – "Respondents will not have heard of Mommy Wars" – was supported. A chi-square goodness of fit test, with expected values of a 50% response rate in both the "yes" and "no" answer choices for all respondents (the null hypothesis), reached statistical significance ($p<.05$, $n=131$), because more respondents had not (60%) than had (40%) heard of Mommy Wars.

Asked to explain what they understood "Mommy Wars" to mean, of the 53 participants who had heard the term, all but three understood what they are[7] and cited some form of "stay-at-home mothers versus mothers with paid work." Asked if Mommy Wars stories had affected their understanding of themselves as a mother (only if they had heard of Mommy Wars), 41 participants said they were not affected in any way, seven responded that Mommy Wars made them think more seriously about their own position as a mother, responses of five were unrelated to the question, and one had no comment.

Many respondents added comments[8] indicating that they felt that they have no right to judge other mothers. The first question in the rating items — "SAHM are not realizing their full potential as individual women" — was participants' first encounter with these types of questions and elicited interesting comments. One MWPW said, "Who am I to judge?," another said "I totally disagree! ...a woman shows her full potential ...in whatever role she chooses to fill in her life," while another said, "Staying at home is just as difficult as not staying at home, and I respect women who make that choice." Other respondents commented that they were hesitant to pass judgment on a whole group of mothers when they knew nothing about their situations. One respondent actually said, "Come on!!! That [question] is horrible!"

Comments reflected that SAHM did not want to judge all MWPW but rather to examine each in her own context. One said, "It's hard to answer [about] ALL mothers.... mothers handle their situations differently," and another stated her frustration with answering this question and others about MWPW:

> This is getting difficult. There are so many different scenarios for why/how women work or stay at home. Some stay-at-home moms spend less time communicating with children than paid work moms. I feel it's not so much about the job vs. no job, but more about taking the time to know your children. When I read this question I think of kids dropped off at daycare from 7am to 7pm and want to say 'yes'. But that is too simplistic.

One SAHM said, "Some of the most caring and concerned mothers I know are working parents," and another said, "I wish you had phrased your questions positively–I know what you're getting at but the way you've phrased your questions is making me mad! It's an exact microcosm of how society [sic] doesn't give moms a break, either at home or working, so we pick at each other, trying to feel better," suggesting that what difficulties there are between mothers result from immense social pressures on them.

DISCUSSION

Results constitute clear and compelling evidence that the story of Mommy Wars (Berg, 1985; Darnton, 1990; Gardner, 2002) is untrue. Neither group of mothers harshly judged the other. In fact, some respondents were actually hostile to the very idea of Mommy Wars, as revealed by their spontaneous comments, which precisely contradicted several claims from media stories, and in some cases mothers even said supportive things about mothers of the other group.

The active attempts of the mothers in this study to give mothers in situations different from their own the benefit of the doubt are consistent with both traditional female socialization to be caring and supportive (e.g., Caplan, 2000) and the feminist principle of understanding and respecting the contexts of women's lives and choices. They are inconsistent with the portrayal in antifeminist backlash (Faludi, 1991; Caplan, 2000) of women as quick to engage in "catfights" with other women.

The implicit assumption in media coverage of Mommy Wars is that most mothers are fighting among themselves. This position is consistent with the misogynist view that not just mothers but women in general are quick to demean and compete against other women (Caplan, 2000); yet according to the data from the present study, most mothers are unaware that such a war is said to be raging. One respondent considered the wars "ridiculous," and another said, "I decided what was right for myself and my children and was not affected by the press' accounts of 'warring' between working and SAHMs."

Since, as noted, society places enormous pressure on mothers no matter what they do (Hays, 1996; Caplan, 2000; Douglas & Michaels, 2004; Neal, 2006), it is perhaps surprising that the results of this study suggest that groups of mothers are not set up against one another. It is all the more surprising, given that a common response to intense pressure is to strike out against those in proximity rather to join together to combat these pressures (Caplan, 2000; Douglas & Michaels, 2004; Peskowitz, 2005).

It will be desirable to see whether similar results are obtained from a random and representative sample across the full range of socioeconomic classes and in various geographic areas, rather than a convenience sample. It will also be informative to construct questions that allow distinctions among mothers who work part-time, mothers who work full-time, and mothers who have "high-powered careers," as some respondents pointed out that the survey did not allow them to make those distinctions, and thus they found it difficult to answer for all MWPW.

NOTES

[1]These are articles that are actually about Mommy Wars rather than misusing the term or using it differently from the way it is used here.
[2]Available on request from first author.
[3]Questionnaire available on request from first author.
[4]Seeing if mothers feel negatively about their own group does not bear directly on whether mothers experience Mommy Wars but could be a cause or effect of Mommy Wars or a simple explanation for why mothers are not happy with being a SAHM or a MWPW.
[5]The race/ethnicity question was left open-ended on the survey. The few participants reporting being of mixed descent (all were half white and half something else) were counted in the non-white category.
[6]For hypotheses 1-5, respondents indicated the degree to which they agreed with negative statements about SAHM and MWPW. The rating scale ranged from 0 for "strongly disagree" to 10 for "agree strongly." The means of each group were examined to see if they fell on either the agree or disagree side of the spectrum. The split between the agree and disagree sides of the spectrum is made from 0-5 and 6-10 because a tenet of Mommy Wars advocates is that mothers in each group negatively judge mothers of the other. Thus the answer "neither agree, nor disagree" (5) is included in the lower end of the spectrum, since answers there would not be consistent with the idea that mothers of each group judge one another.
[7]Participants were regarded as understanding the notion of Mommy Wars if they mentioned some form of SAHM versus MWPW or SAHM and MWPW being against one another.
[8]The comments have been taken directly from the questionnaire of the present study.

REFERENCES

Allen, Amy 2012 "'Mommy Wars' Redux: A False Conflict." *New York Times*, May 27.

Bellafante, Gina 2006 "If Mommy Helps Baby, Who Helps Mommy?" *New York Times*, April 27, E10.

Berg, B 1985 "Mothers Against Mothers." *The Washington Post*, January 3, Pp. 5.

Bureau of Labor Statistics 2005 "2005 National Cross-industry Estimates of Employment and Mean Annual Wage for Major Occupational Groups." Retrieved from http://www.bls.gov/oes/ (cited January 2007).

Burros, M 1992 "Now is the Time to Come to the Aid of Your Favorite Cookie." *The New York Times*, July 15.

Caplan, P. J. 2000 *(The New) Don't Blame Mother: Mending the Mother-Daughter Relationship.* New York: Routledge.

Clemetson, Lynette 2006 "Work vs. Family, Complicated by Race." *New York Times*, February 9, G1.

D'Arcy, Janice 2012 "Hilary Rosen vs. Ann Romney Reaction: Mothers Are Not So Easily Divided." *Washington Post*, April 16.

Darnton, N. 1990 "Mommy vs. Mommy." *Newsweek*, June 4, 115(2): 64.

Douglas, S. J., and M. W. Michaels 2004 *The Mommy Myth: The Idealization of Motherhood and How it has Undermined Women.* New York: Free Press.

Faludi, S. 1991 *Backlash: The Undeclared War Against American Women.* New York: Crown.

Fox News. 2012 "Fox Flash: The Mommy Wars." April 16.

Gardner, R., Jr. 2002 "Mom vs. Mom." *New York Magazine*, 35(3): 20.

Hays, S. 1996 *The Cultural Contradictions of Motherhood.* New Haven: Yale University Press.

Johnston, D. D., and D. H. Swanson 2004 "Moms Hating Moms: The Internalization of Mother War Rhetoric." *Sex Roles*, 51(9-10): 497-509.

Neal, J. H. 2006 "Fearless and Fabulous: Blogger, Author and Activist Arianna Huffington on Mommy Fears and Squelching Her Inner Critic". *Washington Post.* Retrieved from http://www.washingtonpost.com/wp-dyn/content/article/2006/12/05/AR2006120500907.html (cited February 2007).

NPR 2012 "Rosen's Words About Ann Romney Fuel 'Mommy Wars.'" April 17.

Oprah 2007 "Oprah: Can Women Really Have It All?" Harpo Studios.

Peskowitz, M. 2005 *The Truth Behind the Mommy Wars: Who Decides What Makes a Good Mother?* Emeryville, CA: Seal Press.

Pleck, J. 1997 "Paternal Involvement: Levels, Sources, and Consequences." In *The Role of the Father in Child Development.* M. Lamb, ed., pp. 66-103. New York: Wiley.

Richardson, Lynda 1992. "No Cookie-Cutter Answers in 'Mommy Wars.'" *New York Times*, September 2, B1.

Spragins, Ellyn 2001 "Love & Money: Is My Mom Better Than Yours?" *New York Times*, July 1, p.10.

Steiner, L. M. 2006 *Mommy Wars: Stay-At-Home and Career Moms Face Off on Their Choices, Their Lives, Their Families.* New York: Random House.

Stolberg, Sheryl Gay 2001 "Public Lives: Another Academic Salvo in the Nation's 'Mommy Wars.'" *New York Times*, April 21, A8.

Wyatt, Edward 2004 "New Salvo is Fired in Mommy Wars." *New York Times*, November 2, E1.

Section II: On the Home Front: National Perspectives

5.

Staying At Home

Low-Income Mothers in Rural America

ANN ALLGOOD BERRY, YOSHIE SANO, MARY JO KATRAS AND JAERIM LEE

Since the passage of the Personal Responsibility and Work Opportunity Reconciliation Act (PRWORA) in 1996 in the United States, federal programs assisting low-income families have placed strong emphasis on work participation. For example, under the Temporary Assistance for Needy Families (TANF) program, recipients are required to seek, obtain and maintain employment regardless of marital or parental status. The emphasis on personal responsibility and work has created an ideological contradiction regarding motherhood (Henderson et al. 2005) in that traditional motherhood ideology assumes that women should eschew employment, staying home full-time caring for children (DiLapi 1989). Current public policies, however, focus almost exclusively on employment, thereby devaluing the role of mothering at home (Baker 2004). Unlike stay-at-home mothers in middle- or upper-income families, low-income mothers who stay at home are often viewed as deviant by popular media (Arendell 2000; Dodson 2007). Consequently, low-income mothers receiving welfare benefits must choose to be "a good mother or a good recipient" (Henderson et al. 2005:140) and often are unable to meet the expectations of either role.

In this chapter, we examine low-income women's decisions to stay at home based on previous research, which explored the patterns of employment among low-income mothers in rural America (Berry et al. 2008). In our original study, we found a sizable number of mothers who chose to stay at home despite their need to increase their financial security and the "work first" approach of the TANF. These rural stay at home mothers raise important questions regarding the intersection between their values regarding motherhood and current welfare policies. By exploring low-income mothers' perspectives, we examine how they negotiate the dominant ideology of motherhood with economic security in rural America under the umbrella of current welfare regulations.

This investigation allows us to understand the lived experiences of stay-at-home mothers in diverse socioeconomic groups and locations. Rural communities are not simply smaller versions of their urban counterparts; they qualitatively differ (Findeis et al. 2001), presenting unique challenges and obstacles for low-income populations. Due to geographical isolation, there are generally fewer jobs available, fewer educational and training opportunities, and less access to childcare, transportation, and family support services (Bauer et al. 2000; Katras et al. 2004; Weber et al. 2001). The deepest, most persistent poverty affects rural populations in particular (Weber et al. 2001). Thus, low-income mothers living in rural America are undoubtedly one of the most-in-need populations.

FAMILY RESILIENCE FRAMEWORK

Family resilience is a concept widely used in psychology and family studies and has application to studying children and families facing adversity (Masten 2001). According to Masten (2001:234), resilience is considered part of the human adaptive process and "refers to a class of phenomena characterized by good outcomes in spite of serious threats to adaptation or development." This framework suggests that researchers, practitioners, and policymakers should focus on protective factors or strengths, rather than threats or challenges, in order to create supportive policy and programs for children and families facing adversity (Masten 2001; Walsh 2002).

METHOD

Rural Families Speak Project

Data for this chapter are drawn from the Rural Families Speak Project, a longitudinal multi-state Agricultural Experiment Station research project that assesses changes in the well-being and functioning of rural families within the context of welfare reform (Bauer 2004). The original project included 413 families across 14 states and 24 counties in the U.S. Participants were primarily residents of non-metropolitan areas with populations between 2,500 and 19,000. Mothers were recruited through programs serving low-income families, including the Food Stamp program, Head Start, Women, Infants and Children Special Supplemental Nutrition Program (WIC), and welfare-to-work. The primary qualifying criteria for the project included an income below the 200 percent federal poverty thresholds and parenting at least one child 12 years old or younger at the time of the initial interview.

Baseline data (Wave 1) from 413 families were collected from 1999 to 2001. In Wave 2 (2000-2002), 326 families from 13 states were re-interviewed; the attrition rate was 21%. Because this population moved frequently, tracking the families over time was challenging. In Wave 3 (2002-2003), 263 families from 13 states were re-interviewed. All participants were mothers interviewed about various subjects such as family well-being, employment, parenting, and community characteristics. The mothers also completed surveys of specific measures during the semi-structured interviews, which typically lasted between two and three hours. Each mother was asked a standard set of questions, but given the qualitative nature of the interviews, some mothers spoke freely about topics not included in the interview protocol.

Sample

The sample for this chapter draws from our previous article, *Job Volatility of Rural, Low-income Mothers: A Mixed Methods Approach* (Berry et al. 2008). In this article, we analyzed the employment trajectories of rural low-income mothers using a sample of 245 mothers who participated in all three waves of data collection. Of these 245 mothers, the focus of the present chapter is 56 mothers who were continuously unemployed across the three waves.

According to baseline information of the continuously unemployed mothers, participants' average age was about 30 years old and they had two or three children, the youngest of whom was 3.1 years old. Approximately two-thirds of the mothers were non-Hispanic, white and were partnered by marriage or cohabitation. Eighty-four percent of the mothers completed at least high school or General Educational Development (GED) exam (Berry et al 2008).

Qualitative Data Analysis

We conducted an inductive analysis to identify emergent themes from the interview data (Berry et al. 2008). The first stage involved an initial coding of the interview transcripts; the second stage involved a more comprehensive reading of the transcripts to identify specific themes and to refine initial themes. Using the list of emergent themes, the transcripts were coded accordingly, and inter-rater reliability was performed.

THEMES AND ISSUES

Two overarching themes emerged from the inductive analysis: choice and health problems. Some women exercised choice, choosing not to work outside the home, preferring to stay home with their children. Others had health problems posing a major barrier or threat to finding and keeping a job (Berry et al. 2008).

The theme of choice was woven throughout the interviews with the mothers. The theme appeared to be aligned with their ideology of motherhood influencing how they cared for their children. Several mothers who talked about why they were not employed stated, "to stay home with my children, especially when they were young." Jeanette's comment highlighted the importance of motherhood even at the expense of earning a higher income: "So I can stay with my kids. We manage okay. I had a good salary, but it was too high of a price to pay not being home at all. I didn't want someone else to raise my kids." In a subsequent interview, Jeanette added: "I am just happy to be with the kids. We'd rather do with less than have to rely on outside care." The values of motherhood of some of the rural low-income mothers often drive their decisions not to work outside the home for their children.

The choice that these rural low-income mothers made to stay home was aligned with the motherhood ideology prevalent in dominant U.S. society. Several of these mothers believed that their job was to stay home and care for their children. When Steph was asked why she was not working, she responded, "'cause I'm a full-time mother, grandmother, and wife." Willa said of her partner, "He wants me to stay home and do the housework. And make sure I am here when they [children] get home." To support their families financially, these mothers often relied on their partner's employment or accessed pubic and/or private resources within their communities.

Although the mothers were not employed at the times of interviews, it did not mean that they would be always be stay-at-home mothers. Finding balance between work and family was a tenuous process for most of the mothers, requiring constant adjustments and negotiation. Many of these rural low-income mothers talked about waiting until their children were school age to seek employment. However, several spoke of finding employment that would allow them to balance family and work. Norine mentioned how, as a family, they negotiated that balance:

> We were talking about me staying at home right now until the baby's old enough to start Head Start. Then we're talking about me getting a part-time job so that I can be there when the kids are home from school... By then, both of the boys will be in school all day. So, I'll do a part-time job while she's in Head Start; then I can be home with her when the boys get home.

The needs and demands of motherhood changed as these rural low-income families moved across the life span, leaving families with new choices and adjustments. As Norine stated above, some families had a plan that when their children were older, they would re-enter the workforce and adjust to find work-family balance.

For some mothers, not working was not their own "choice" to make, due to inadequate support and lack of trusted care for their children. Marie described the first day she left her son at a home daycare:

> My son was five months old, and the very first day of me going to work, somehow she [daycare worker] fractured his arm. I ended up telling my case worker, "I'm sorry, I can't do this. I cannot."[...]I wanted to work just to get out of the house for my own self-esteem. I thought about it, and I said, "I can't sacrifice my child just for that." I can get out of the house and go to the library or whatever or just go back to school. At first I thought they were going to cut my benefits because I voluntarily quit my job. I told her, "I can't work with someone who is going to be that negligent towards my child." It just made me so afraid to even go to look for someone else.

If the women did not have a childcare option that they trusted, having a job was often not a choice.

Chronic and debilitating health problems, our second theme, were a major barrier to finding and keeping a job (Berry et al. 2008). For some rural low-income stay-at-home mothers, their own health problems prohibited them from obtaining and maintaining employment. Monique discussed her disability as a barrier to her ability to work and her employment as a threat to her keeping her benefits:

> I am not able to work because of the insurance and things I am on. If I earned any income, I would lose my nursing and things like that so I am not able to. I don't work because nursing. I have to have a nurse with me all the time. I am disabled and my hands do not work.

These rural low-income mothers with health problems were faced with obstacles that were not easy to overcome. They were often forced to stay out of the workforce, making the choice no longer their own to make.

It was not only the mothers' own health problems but also the children's health issues that led some mothers to stay home. Allene mentioned the high level of care that her daughter with special needs required, leaving Allene no other choice but to stay home: "Yeah, I'm still not working. With my daughter's problems, the psychiatrist said that I needed to be here [home]. . . . I need to be here around the clock for her." Several of these rural low-income mothers were faced with health issues of a child who required constant attention, making it impossible to enter the paid workforce.

DISCUSSION AND IMPLICATIONS FOR FAMILY POLICY

A mother's choice to stay home to care for her young children is a complicated decision based upon her ideology of motherhood, the family health, available community resources, and the family's economic situation, and values. The rural, low-income, stay-at-home mothers in our study illustrated that though being out of the workforce could be a threat to the financial security for their families, access to formal or informal social support and their partner's wage could be protective factors. Although the current welfare policy in the U.S. requires low-income mothers to be employed for them to receive certain benefits, the rural low-income mothers in our study chose to put their families first. This finding supports Baker's (2004) study confirming that mothers in New Zealand believed taking care of their children was their primary job, despite their country's welfare-to-work policies.

The rural, low-income mothers, who chose to stay home for their children, appeared to be resilient in managing the financial well-being of their families, were able to access the resources they needed, and stayed true to their values regarding work and caring for their children. However, other mothers who had to remain home due to either the health problems of their own or their children, faced unique challenges. These mothers' circumstances differed from those who chose to stay at home while their children are young but planned to work when children start school or reach a certain age.

The findings of the present study have implications for family policy that aims to enhance family's' economic well-being. The families in our study were all at or below 200 percent of the U.S. federal poverty thresholds at the time of the interviews. If the mothers had been in the labor force, they would have had to access childcare resources from informal networks or choose from limited childcare resources in rural areas, straining the already limited incomes of these families. Of course, nonparticipation in the workforce results in lost wages during the years a mother stays out of the workforce. This mother cannot earn retirement benefits, either through Social Security or an employer-sponsored plan. The average total cost of family caregiving on the female caregiver in terms of lost wages, foregone pension benefits, and reduced Social Security benefits is USD $324,044 in funds available for retirement (MetLife Mature Market Institute 2011). Health insurance is another benefit that may not be provided if the mother is unemployed. Under The Patient Protection and Affordable Care Act of 2010, all Americans are now required to have health insurance. This legislation will provide access to health insurance to individuals who may have never had health insurance and provide a safety net for unexpected health issues that can leave individuals and families with large amounts of debt. Unless they have a spouse working in a job with benefits, these are not being accrued, which can lead to poverty in the later life years. The Center on Budget and Policy Priorities reported that in 2012, 48.3 percent of women age 65 and over who were not receiving Social Security were living in poverty, while those in poverty receiving Social Security dropped to 10.7 percent (Van de Water and Sherman 2012).

Policymakers usually consider economic and environmental effects before they pass a law or enact a rule; however, family impact is not normally a consideration (Ooms 1990). Bogenschneider (2006:299) recommends that policymakers assess how families are affected as they develop, enact, and implement public polices by asking questions including, "What effect does (or will) this policy (or proposed program) have for families? Will it help or hurt, strengthen or weaken family life?" Given that the family is charged with providing for and developing children into competent, caring, and responsible adults, policies that support this endeavor should be enacted. Mothers who choose to stay home to perform this meaningful job should not be penalized but instead benefit from policy. Any new policy for social assistance programs should be "family-friendly" and should take into account interaction of single parent parenting (lone parenthood), poor health of either mother or child, childcare problems (i.e., lack of affordable, dependable, and quality care in rural areas), and the ability to find and keep a job. Employment opportunities in rural communities are often lacking.

Current U.S. policies support benefits to reduce the stresses of work and family life, such as limited unpaid parental leave, family services (e.g., parenting education, adoption assistance, and child support enforcement), Earned Income Tax Credit, child tax credits, and childcare subsidies. The federal government provides over USD $16 billion in subsidies for various cash and in-kind benefits to working parents putting their children in childcare facilities (Gilbert 2005). Although these family-friendly policies do address needs of low-income mothers trying to balance work and family, low-income families do not always benefit as many fail to meet eligibility criteria such as time limits and income cut-offs. For example, childcare subsidies are limited to one year after leaving welfare (Albelda 2001). Many low-income families do not qualify for the child tax credit since their annual incomes are not high enough to take advantage of this credit. Though the option of taking unpaid parental leave is available for those employed in businesses with over 50 employees, many low-income families cannot afford to not be earning wages.

Feminist economists have debated the benefits of providing support to the mothers and even fathers, who choose to stay home and care for their children. Folbre and Himmelweit (2000) argued that family policy is now a feminist issue. The cost of family care is fueling the debate over who should pay for rearing children: the next generation of workers. In some European countries, progressive family policies support stay-at-home mothers, as well as fathers, by providing in-home care to their young children. Norway and Finland have similar policies paying cash benefits to all families with children up to three years of age if the child is not enrolled in state-subsidized childcare facilities (Gilbert 2005). Germany is debating whether to give mothers a monthly income equivalent to USD $190 if they choose to stay home to care for their infants (Malm 2012). Sweden subsidizes care by the child's own parent as well as non-parental care. Blades and Rowe-Finkbeiner (2006) found that 163 countries guarantee paid maternity leave; 45 countries guarantee paid paternity leave; 37 countries guarantee paid leave for children's health; and 84 countries limit the maximum length of the work week. The U.S. does not offer any of these benefits.

Gilbert (2005) suggests changes in family policy to include tax credits and home-care allowances to full-time homemakers with children under five years of age in lieu of subsidized childcare in the U.S. He also proposes a social credit model for parents caring for their children at home similar to the veterans' benefit. Veterans sacrifice career opportunities to serve our country and, in turn, receive benefits for education and training. Perhaps social credits could be earned by parents providing in-home care for young children to be used for similar job-related opportunities. We suggest that family policies directed at supplementing family income for a limited time, rather than paying for daycare facilities, better assist rural low-income mothers who choose or must stay home to care for their young children. In addition to social credits for job benefits, credits toward Social Security for retirement could be earned as well during those years parents stay at home to care for young children.

Though policies provide assistance and support to mothers wishing to join the labor force after a few years, these will not help those mothers who have no choice but to stay home due to health problems or disability. Supplemental Security Income (SSI) and Social Security Disability Insurance (SSDI) are both current benefits for qualifying low-income adults and children. However, both of these benefits are reduced or curtailed when the recipient receives wages. Will these government benefits supply the only income to these mothers throughout their lives and into retirement? Consideration for future family-friendly policies and allocation of federal dollars must include these individuals in legislation.

Gilbert (2005) suggests support for policies that free workers to be better parents rather than emphasizing those policies that free parents to be better workers. Some believe that staying home to care for children should not be rewarded as they believe parenting is their responsibility. Many others agree that public policies can influence the conditions that make this easier or more difficult for parents to succeed. Walsh's (2002) recommendations for researchers and practitioners can be transferred to policymakers as well. Supporting the strengths of vulnerable families through policies could foster more successful parenting and family well-being. If a government chooses to provide financial incentives to low-income workers through various social supports, some of that money could be given to those caring for children. Monetary benefits could be used for monthly expenses, prepare for the transition into the workforce, save for the children's education, and to save and invest for retirement. Investing in our nation's human capital starts with investing in our nation's families. Enacting family-friendly policies that include supports for parents, particularly mothers who choose and/or must stay home to care and nurture their young children, should be at the forefront of the agenda of policymakers.

REFERENCES

Albelda, Randy 2001 "Welfare-to-Work, Farewell to Families? US Welfare Reform and Work/Family Debates." *Feminist Economics* 7(1): 119–135.

Arendell, Terry 2000 "Conceiving and Investigating Motherhood: The Decade's Scholarship." *Journal of Marriage and the Family* 62(4): 1192–1207.

Baker, Maureen 2004 "Devaluing Mothering at Home: Welfare Restructuring and 'Motherwork.'" *Atlantis: Critical Studies in Gender, Culture & Social Justice* 28(2): 51–60.

Bauer, Jean W. 2004 "Basebook Report: Low Income Rural Families: Tracking Their Well-being and Functioning in the Context of Welfare Reform."

Bauer, Jean W., Patricia H. Dyk, Bonnie Braun, Bonita Quass, Mary Jo Bartl (Katras), Sharon E. Powell, Kathy Prochaska-Cue, Sally Bowman, Sharon Seiling, Frances C. Lawrence, Leslie Richards, Corinne Corson, and Sheila Mammen 2000 "Rural Low-Income Families in the Context of Welfare Reform: Findings and Policy Issues." Paper presented at the *Annual Meeting of the National Council on Family Relations,* Minneapolis, November 8–14. http://www.cehd.umn.edu/FSoS/projects/ruralspeak/pdf/basebook.pdf (accessed January 29, 2013).

Berry, Ann A., Mary Jo Katras, Yoshie Sano, Jaerim Lee, and Jean W. Bauer 2008 "Job Volatility of Rural Low-Income Mothers: A Mixed Method Approach." *Journal of Family and Economic Issue* 29(1): 5–22.

Blades, Joan, and Kristin Rowe-Finkbeiner 2006 "Working Mothers Paying for Poor Policies." *National Council of Jewish Women, Winter.* http://www.ncjw.org/content451.cfm (accessed January 31, 2013).

Bogenschneider, Karen 2006 *Family Policy Matters: How Policymaking Affects Families and What Professionals Can Do*. 2nd edition. Mahwah: Lawrence Erlbaum Associates.

DiLapi, Elena M. 1989 "Lesbian Mothers and the Motherhood Hierarchy." *Journal of Homosexuality* 18(1–2): 101–121.

Dodson, Lisa 2007 "Wage-Poor Mothers and Moral Economy." *Social Politics: International Journal of Gender, State & Society* 14(2): 258–280.

Findeis, Jill L., Mark Henry, Thomas A. Hirschl, Willis Lewis, Ismael Ortega-Sanchez, Emelie Peine, and Julie N. Zimmerman 2001 "Welfare Reform in Rural America: A Review of Current Research." *RUPRI Rural Welfare Reform Research Panel, P2001-5*. Columbia, MO: Rural Policy Research Institute.

Folbre, Nancy, and Susan Himmelweit 2000 "Introduction-Children and Family Policy: a Feminist Issue." *Feminist Economics* 6(1): 1–3.

Gilbert, Neil 2005 "What Do Women Really Want?" *The Public Interest* 258(Winter): 21–38.

Henderson, Debra. A., Ann R. Tickamyer, and Barry L. Tadlock 2005 "The Impact of Welfare Reform on the Parenting Role of Women in Rural Communities." *Journal of Children and Poverty* 11(2): 132–147.

Katras, Mary Jo, Virginia S. Zuiker, and Jean W. Bauer 2004 "Private Safety Net: Childcare Resources from the Perspective of Rural Low-Income Families." *Family Relations* 53(2): 201–209.

Malm, Sara 2012 "Germany to Pay Stay-At-Home Parents Extra Benefits for Keeping Toddlers Out of State Daycare." *MailOnline*, August 18.

Masten, Ann S. 2001 "Ordinary Magic: Resilience Processes in Development." *American Psychologist* 56(3): 227–238.

MetLife Mature Market Institute. 2011 "Caregiving Costs to Working Caregivers: Double Jeopardy for Baby Boomers Caring for Their Parents." *New York: Metropolitan Life Insurance Company.* (accessed January 31, 2013).

Ooms, Theodora 1990 "Families and Government: Implementing a Family Perspective in Public Policy." *Journal of Religion & Spirituality in Social Work: Social Thought* 16(2): 61–78.

Van de Water, Paul N., and Arloc Sherman 2012 "Social Security Keeps 21 Million Americans Out of Poverty: A State-by-State Analysis." *Center on Budget and Policy Priorities* (accessed January 29, 2013).

Walsh, Froma 2002 "A Family Resilience Framework: Innovative Practice

Applications." *Family Relations* 51(2): 130–137.

Weber, Bruce A., Greg J. Duncan, and Leslie A. Whitener 2001 "Welfare Reform in Rural America: What Have We Learned?" *American Journal Agriculture Economics* 83(5): 1282–1292.

6.

Stay at Home Jewish Mothers

A Jewish-Israeli Perspective

DARYA MAOZ

Women's employment patterns along their life cycle are related to family events, and especially to the presence of children. During the past decades, the labor force participation of western women has increased steadily, nevertheless many of them still tend to drop out of the labor force after giving birth or turn to part-time employment (Moen and Han 2001; Spain and Bianchi 1996; Stier at al. 2001; Stier and Lewin-Epstein 2000).

Women who choose to leave their work and devote themselves to what was first termed the "mommy track" (Schwartz 1989) are inclined to be less educated, more conservative or religious, and of lower socio-economic status. Some research indicates their self-esteem is found to be low, as is their earning potential (Moore 2000, 2006). In liberal, secular societies and within highly educated groups we expect to find women who combine career and motherhood. These women are inclined to hold more liberal views and to handle a less gendered division of labor at home and have more egalitarian relations in the household (Braun et al. 2008; Hoffnung 2004; Moore 2000; Stier and Lewin-Epstein 2000; Stier and Lewin-Epstein 2006).

In light of these findings and assumptions I was interested in a growing phenomenon in Israeli society; secular, Jewish women of middle to upper-middle class, well-educated, with high potential income, who choose to leave their job for an unlimited time after giving birth. These women also choose, accordingly, a traditional and gendered model of division of labor at home.

Why do these highly educated women prefer to leave their job and choose a 'mommy track' in contrast to most women in their status who combine family and work (or working part-time)? What were the reasons and causes for their decision?

MOMMY TRACK AND THE JEWISH-ISRAELI SOCIETY

Surveys conducted in Israel in recent years indicate that after childbirth as much as fifty percent of Israeli women reduce their working hours; twenty six percent stop working altogether while others turn to part-time jobs (the Central Bureau of Statistics (Israel) 2010; Darom 2013). Thirty four percent of women in Israel were found to attribute more importance to family than to work in an Israeli research and hence to prefer a traditional and gendered family model. The majority – 51 percent – adopt a "combining pattern" and attribute high importance to both family and work (Moore and Guy 2006).

The role of national, social and cultural characteristics in shaping maternal behavior, women's choice of occupation, the division of labor at home, and the wage gap, has been investigated in the literature. Researchers have suggested that socio-cultural factors can explain differences in parental behavior of mothers from different countries (Antecol 2001; Hays 1996; Moore 2000, 2006; Reid Boyd 2002, 2005; Stier and Lewin-Epstein 2006).

Jewish Israeli mothers differ from Western mothers in two main respects: they live in a country in a state of intractable, protracted ethnopolitical conflict with neighboring Arab states and with Palestine (Ron & Maoz In press), a country which has compulsory military service and is a home for Jewish survivors of the Holocaust, and they live by familial and conservative values.

One of the most prevalent identities in Israel is the family one. Israel is a pronatalist society which encourages procreation. While in Europe we witness a decline in fertility rate (in the OECD countries - 1.71 children per woman), in Israel there is a significant rise among Jewish women (from 2.57 in 2001 to 3.05 in 2013), which places it first in fertility rate in Europe (the Central Bureau of Statistics (Israel) 2014).

Motherhood is a national duty for Jewish women in Israel and is considered a privilege and means of self-realization. A Jewish woman is seen as a mother above all or as a potential mother and some argue Israeli women's role is to be "a national womb" to ensure the demographic advantage of

Jews in a country situated in hostile surroundings (Berkovitz 1994; Donath 2010).

Israel offers a particularly interesting opportunity to examine the subject of nation-specific patterns among mothers. Israelis cannot be categorized in simplistic terms as either "Western" or "Eastern." They live in a society which, like many societies around the world, aspires to become "Western," yet Israel's location also makes it "Eastern." It is situated in the Middle East, among Arab neighbors, and many of its Jewish inhabitants originate from the Arab nations. Israeli culture shows clear signs of Middle Eastern and Arab influences, alongside the presence of Western cultural attributes. As a peripheral country, Israel constantly redefines its identity vis-a-vis its immediate Arab neighbors and its more distant European neighbors. While some studies show weakening of collective identities in Israel, others indicate an opposite trend – strengthen of collective patriarchal ideologies (Moore 2000, 2004). Accordingly, Israelis cannot be subsumed in the broader category of Western, and have indeed been considered an exceptional group (Maoz 2007). These aspects play a crucial role in the construction of mothers' motivations and behavior.

METHODS

The analysis presented here is based on in-depth interviews with 20 Jewish Israeli women who have at least one child and who dropped out of the labor force after giving birth and devoted themselves to motherhood. Interviewees' ages range from 25 to 50, with 17 of the interviewees being married. They live in Israeli towns or communities that are predominantly Jewish. All but one served in the Israeli military; they grew up in secular homes, and about two-thirds are of Ashkenazi origin. Most of them are of middle to upper-middle class backgrounds in terms of their family's income levels.

Interviews were conducted at a location chosen by the interviewee, usually their home or the researcher's. The interviews were semi-structured and included two main parts: the first part dealt with the interviewee's individual story, while the second part posed questions about the topics addressed in the study (Berg 2004; Fontana and Frey1994). Each interview lasted from one and a half to three hours. All interviews were recorded and transcribed.

The analysis proceeded by identifying meaningful themes and frames that emerged in the interviews, rather than imposing preconceived categories and classifications. Accordingly, the research tools used are qualitative (Glaser and Strauss 1967; Strauss and Corbin 1998).

FINDINGS

An examination and analysis of the researched mothers' motivations to drop out of the labor force can be summarized in one title – a conflict between home and work. Within this category two main themes were found: "a perceived conflict" (based on images of "the ideal mother") and "an objective conflict" (a "real", circumstantial conflict). Perception of gender roles was crucial in accounts of and rationales for staying at home, as was found in other studies, as well as acceptance together with ambivalence towards this decision (Reid Boyd, 2005).

A PERCEIVED CONFLICT

"...I am not feminist at all", said the most popular and famous model in Israel – Bar Refaeli – in an interview to a very popular paper in Israel. She continued "I will not have him wash the dishes, I wash the dishes and I am the one who cleans and I am the one who wants to stay home with the children at the end" (Spector 2013). Another famous model, Eve Limasov, was also cited in this paper saying: "...Career is important to me. But more important are children, their upbringing and education. The family. Clean house. Tasty food. Showered, clean and successful children, who will not be raised by some nanny" (Bar Haim 2012).

Those two famous women are as models in double meaning. They serve as socio-cultural icons; role models for numerous women (and men) who admire and look up to them. Both are young and trendy, still not married, very successful in money terms, career women who travel the world. Nevertheless, those women share the same old fashioned concepts; family and children first, even if it means giving up a very attractive job, men as the providers, women as caregivers. These women, along with other leading figures in Israel, express the message that a woman cannot be fulfilled unless she becomes a mother, and that good motherhood requires total devotion to the child/ren.

Women who drop out of the labor force after giving birth hold the same dichotomous perception of subordinate (women) and dominant (men), home/private (women) and work/public (men) (Moore 2000). Those traditional beliefs serve as motives and as justification for them to leave their jobs and to depend on their husband (or father) for economic support (Budig and England 2001). The reasons the interviewed women give in this category to leaving their job do not necessarily rely on an actual experience with combining work and home. They are based on a primary and basic assumption that those two arenas should not be combined by mothers.

This perception also goes hand in hand with the false consciousness that this is how it was meant to be; that the 'right' and 'natural' traditional order does right by women and by the whole family structure. Women go through a psychological process termed system-justification, which is contributing to the preservation of existing social arrangements even at the expense of their personal and group interest. They hold false or inaccurate beliefs that are contrary to their own social interest, which contribute to the maintenance of their disadvantaged position and justify their own subordination (Jost and Mahzarin 1994; Jost, Kay & Thorisdottir 2009; Jost and Others 2012). They are victims of gender or patriarchal systems (Bruegel 1996; McCrate 1988). As McCrate (1988: 237) argued: "A male-dominant society limits opportunities for women and men to explore and develop their identities". She continues, "Women therefore choose to *learn to prefer* mothering over auto mechanics... the expected payoff is higher" (Italics in text).

The mothers I met believe that motherhood bestows women the most profound and important meaning and satisfaction. They also believe that their child, like any child, needs his mother (more than his father) in order to be happy and healthy. Working outside home is equivalent in their eyes to abandoning a child. Mothers who do this are considered less good and even bad.

These women are not alone. In Israel many still believe that a woman's role is to take care of the children and family while men should provide for their families. Seventy one percent of Israelis believe that a mother to preschool children should work part-time or give up work altogether, while 25 to 42 percent believe that any mother who works will harm her children by doing so (TGI Survey 2009; Glickman at el. 2003).

This thinking and perception lead the women interviewed not only to leave their jobs but also to abandon other aspects of their lives, and conduct symbiotic relations with their children, whom they see as their first and sometimes only source of satisfaction.

Nira, 48, married and a mother of two daughters, left her job as a kindergarten teacher and devoted herself to motherhood. She said: " Motherhood is my self-fulfillment...I do it the best I can, moving myself aside. I cleared a lot of place for them, am like a robot, programmed to the right motherhood". Nira did not only abandon her work, but also distanced herself from her husband and says: "I disappeared, true. I moved myself aside for them".

Merav, 43, is a single mother. Unlike most mothers interviewed she does not have a husband to rely on. Her parents provide her with all her needs. She was a very successful career woman and had a good job in television. After she gave birth she decided to leave it: "...At first I felt I gave up on career...but I realized I cannot [do it] differently. If I will not be with him may hours because of the career – it will not make me happy". Her son fills her with feelings of joy, fulfillment and empowerment she says no career can. Her relations with him are so deep and intensive that she has given up dating and other aspects of her previous life: "...I have nothing without the child ...I am more dependent on him than he on me...he is like my little lover...I don't go out a lot because of him". Merav has guilt feelings if and when she does other things (such as work or date): "It is a horrible neglect...it's a shitty feeling all day and it's not worth it. I did it for four months and couldn't go on". Merav's guilt feelings, and those of other women, are related to the notion that a "good mother" is a mother who invests in her children and does not "disappear" to work. A working mother is by this perception not a 'good enough' mother (Antecol 2001; Pelham et al. 2001).

AN OBJECTIVE CONFLICT

An objective conflict stems from the difficulty in conducting two careers/shifts; inside the house and out of it (Hochschild and Machung 1990). This conflict, as opposed to the perceived one, is "real" and is related to the objective circumstances the women live in. As such, this conflict can be solved by changing those circumstances. This "objective" conflict might exist beyond the women's awareness, and they are not necessarily aware of it. As Marxists have pointed out, women may be blinded by false consciousness[1] and are unable to see that they live in an oppressed society and suffer from discrimination, inequity and exploitation.

Studies show that in Israel the model of division of labor at home is still gendered. According to OECD Better Life Index, Israelis are poor at balancing home and external work. Almost 18% of Israeli employees work very long hours, much higher than the OECD average of 9%, with 27% of men working very long hours compared with 8% of women (OECD 2013). While her husband is working long hours, an Israeli woman invests 2.5 times as much on house labor and children than her husband (Lavee and Katz, 2002). When she works – she earns an average salary of 7,244 NIS, while

Israeli men earn an average of 10,953 NIS (the Central Bureau of Statistics (Israel) 2014).

Gilit, 45, a mother to three, experienced deep disappointment with her husband when she found, upon becoming a mother, that she was expected to do all the work at home while her spouse continues with his life as if nothing has changed. Like many other women she decided to leave her job as a teacher and to devote herself to raising the children. "Our relations", Gilit says, "were very much affected by the children. It emphasized the distance between us...we didn't work together, we didn't take care of them together, he worked outside and I was with them". Gilit tried to work after becoming a mother, but she found it hard technically (with no help from her husband) and hard emotionally: "After coming back to them I decided that no work is going to take me away from them ever again, I could not leave them for even one night".

Orly, 39, is married and a mother to twins (5 years old) and a baby (1 year old). She left her prestigious job at the academy and devoted herself to raising her children. Orly adopted a traditional view only after becoming a mother and she says: "I and my husband were madly in love. Never in my life did I think I would see him as a provider, a father. This was not his role. It saddens me a bit, but I am realistic..."

As we saw with the previous respondent, her children provided her with a sense of fulfillment and joy and made her abandon or distance other supportive factors, such as her husband and job. But a few years after becoming a mother, when Orly started thinking of going back to work, she realized it will be difficult if not impossible: "I can't imagine myself working out from early morning and then hurry back home and start another job, this time with them. It is simply impossible – mentally and emotionally. I am exhausted only from raising them, so work outside?"

Orly, as other women interviewed, was to some extent a 'gatekeeper' (Gaunt 2008), who hardly allowed her husband to participate in taking care of their children, especially when they were young: "raising the twins alone, my husband worked, no nanny, whole days. It is a control thing. I can, I am fine, I do not need help". But when she asked for help and needed it, her husband, who was used to not giving it and who worked long hours declined: "He was used to being free of annoying tasks".

Orly is an example of a process in which a perceived conflict between work and family leads to an objective, real one. During the five years she stayed at home with her children two things happened: firstly, she did most of the housework and care of children, driving her relationship and division of work at home to be more and more gendered and traditional, and secondly she distanced herself from the world outside to the point she became insecure and does not believe she could find a decent job. "It totally decreases the self-confidence outside", she said, "I feel that being a mother – maybe I can't deliver the goods. All my advantages were erased".

CONCLUSION

Secular, educated Jewish women who leave their job and choose a 'mommy track' tell of a gendered division of work as a central cause for leaving work and devoting themselves to the house and children, not being able to work in two shifts; reasons which I term "an objective conflict". But most of them also express a traditional way of thinking, which is still very much apparent in Israel's culture and media. It puts the mother in the home arena with her children and sees her as the most important figure in the child's life and vice versa (the child is her whole life); a notion which I term "a perceived conflict".

This "perceived conflict" stems from the false consciousness that the "ideal mother" is a woman who devotes herself to her children and loves them constantly and unconditionally. This notion is even stronger in the Jewish culture and religion in which motherhood is considered the most important role in a woman's life and her true (and sometimes only) fulfillment. A childless woman ("akara") is seen as extremely miserable while a woman who is a mother is supposed to be happy for this reason only, especially if she has boys, as was said in the Bible; "Em Ha'banim Smeha" [The mother of the boys is happy], (Tehilim KYG, T).

The conflict in any case is real; women feel they cannot work both outside the house and in it. Their actual choice of leaving work usually stems from a traditional perception of gender roles and definitely reinforces it. As the less a woman works out of the house, the more she has to work in it, while her husband will be driven to the opposite direction, participating less and less in household labor (Gaunt 2008).

NOTES

[1]The term was first used in print by Friedrich Engels in a letter written in 1893 to Franz Mehring (cited in Guenter 1982: 3).

REFERENCES

Antecol, Heather 2001 "Why is there Interethnic Variation in the Gender Wage Gap? The Role of Cultural Factors." *Journal of Human Resources*36: 119-143.

Bar Haim, Gabi 2012 "Anashi, shehee lo Makira Omrim la barehov: 'Magia lah Yoter. Ta'azvi oto' [People she doesn't know tell her on the street: 'You deserve more. Leave him'". *Yediot Achronot, Zmanim Modernim*, August 1st, 8-10.

Berg, Bruce Lawrence 2004 *Qualitative Research Methods for the Social Sciences.* Boston, MA: Pearson.

Berkovitz, Niza 1994 "Imahut Kemesima Leumit. [Motherhood as a National Mission]." *Noga* 27: 24-27.

Braun, Michael, Noah Lewin-Epstein, Haya Stier, and Miriam K. Baumgarner 2008 "Perceived Equity in the Gendered Division of Household Labor." *Journal of Marriage and Family* 70(5): 1145–1156.

Bruegel, I. 1996 "Whose Myths Are They Anyway?: A Comment." *British Journal of Sociology* 47(1): 175–77.

Darom, Neomi 2013 "Tasbich Avot [Fathers' Comlex]." *Haaretz Magazine*, May 5th, 34-43.

Donath, Orna 2010 "Pronatalism Saduk: Nerativim shel Holada Ve'Iholada Be'Israel [A Cracked Pronatalism: Narratives of Procreation and Non Procreation in Israel]." *Sociologia Israelit* YA (2): 417-439.

Fetterman, David M. 1990 *Ethnography - Step by Step.* Newbury Park: Sage.

Fontana, Andrea, and James Frey 1994 "Interviewing: 'The Art of Science'". In *Handbook of Qualitative Research*, Norman K. Denzin and Yvonna S Lincoln, eds. Pp. 361-376. California: Sage.

Gaunt, Ruth 2008 "Maternal Gatekeeping Antecedents and Consequences." *Journal of Family Issues* 29(3): 373-395.

Glaser, Barney G., and Leonard A. Strauss 1967 *The Discovery of Grounded Theory: Strategies for Qualitative Research.* Chicago: Aldine.

Glickman, Anya Oren, Anat, and Noah Lewin-Epstein 2003 "Mishpaha Israelit Hadasha? Tafkidey Min Vehaluhat Avoda Bemishpaha Bereshit Hame'a Haesrim Ve'ahat [A New Israeli Family? Gender Roles and Division of Labor in the Family in the Beginning of the 21st Century." *Deot Ba'Am* 8. Tel Aviv University.

Guenter, Lewy. 1982 *False Consciousness. An Essay on Mystification.* New Jersey: Transaction, Inc.

Hays, Sharon. 1996 *The Cultural Contradictions of Motherhood.* New Haven: Yale University Press.

Hochschild, Arlie, R., and Anne Machung. 1990 *The Second Shift.* New York: Avon Books.

Hoffnung, Michele 2004 "Wanting It All: Career, Marriage, and Motherhood During College-Educated Women's 20s." *Sex Roles* 50: 711-723.

Jost, John T., and Mahzarin R. Banaji 1994 "The Role of Stereotyping in System-Justification and the Production of False Consciousness." *British Journal of Social Psychology* 33(1): 1–27.

Jost, John T., A.C., Kay, and H. Thorisdottir, eds. 2009 Social and Psychological Bases of Ideology and System Justification. New York: Oxford University Press. [Political Psychology series]

Jost, John T., V. Chaikalis-Petritsis, D. Abrams, J. Sidanius, J. van der Toorn, and C. Bratt 2012 "Why Men (and Women) Do and Don't Rebel: Effects of System Justification on Willingness to Protest." *Personality and Social Psychology Bulletin* 38: 197-208.

Lavee, Yoav, and Ruth Katz 2002 "Division of Labor, Perceived Fairness, and Marital Quality: The Moderating Effect of Gender Ideology." *Journal of Marriage and Family* 64: 27-39.

Maoz, Darya 2007 "Backpackers' Motivations. The Role of Culture and Nationality." *Annals of Tourism* Research 34(1): 122-140.

McCrate Elaine 1988 "Gender Difference: The Role of Endogenous Preferences and Collective Action." *The American Economic Review* 78(2): 235-239.

Moen, Phyllis, and Shin-Kap Han 2001 "Gendered careers: A life Course Perspective." In *Working Families: The Transformation of the American Home.* R. Hertz and N.L. Marshall, eds. Pp. 42–57. Berkeley: University of California Press.

Moore, Dahlia 2000 "Gender Identity, Nationalism, and Social Action Among Jewish and Arab Women in Israel: Redefining the Social Order?" *Gender Issues* 18: 3-28.

2004 "Gender Identities and Social Action: Arab and Jewish Women in Israel." *The Journal of Applied Behavioral Science* 40: 182-207.

2006 "Why Don't They Demand More? Entitlement and Work Values of Religious and Secular Women and Men in Israel." *Journal of Applied*

Social Psychology 36 (8): 1924–1960.

Moore, Dahlia, and Anat Guy 2006 "Shiluv Mishpa'cha Veavoda Vehashivuto Lesviut Razon shel Nashim BeIsrael. [An Integration Between Family and Work and its Importance for Satisfaction of Working Women in Israel]." *Sugiot Hevration BeIsrael* 2: 45-72.

OECD Better Life Index - Israel. http://www.oecdbetterlifeindex.org/countries/israel/

Reid Boyd, Elizabeth 2002 "'Being There': Mothers who Stay Home, Gender and Time." *Women's Studies International Forum* 25(4): 463 – 470. 2005 "Mothers at Home: Oppressed or Oppressors or Victims of False Dichotomies?" In *Motherhood: Power/Oppression.* Porter, M. (ed). Toronto: The Women's Press.

Ron Yiftach, and Ifat Maoz In press. "Peacemaking through Dialogue? Effects of Intergroup-Dialogue on Perceptions Regarding the Resolution of the Israeli-Palestinian Conflict." *Dynamics of Asymmetric Conflict: Pathways toward Terrorism and Genocide.*

Spain, D., and Suzanne M. Bianchi 1996 *Balancing Act.* New York: Russell Sage.

Stier, Haya, and Noah Lewin-Epstein 2000 "Women's Part-Time Employment and Gender Inequality in the Family." *Journal of Family Issues* 21(3): 390-410. 2006 "The Division of Household Labor in Germany and Israel." *Journal of Marriage and Family* 68: 1147–1164.

Stier, Haya, Noah Lewin-Epstein and Michael Braun 2001 "Welfare Regimes, Family-Supportive Policies, and Women's Employment along the Life-Course." *American Journal of Sociology* 106(6): 1731–1760.

Schwartz, Felice N. 1989 "Management Women and the New Facts of Life." *Harvard Business Review* 67(1): 65-76.

Spector, Dana. 2013 "Ani Nire't Sababa…Az Ma lo Beseder Iti?" ['I Look Great…So What Is Wrong With Me?"] *Yediot Ahronot*, 7 Yamim: 38-46.

Strauss, Leonard, A., and J. M. Corbin 1998 *Basics of Qualitative Research: Techniques and Procedures for Developing Grounded Theory.* Thousand Oaks, CA: Sage.

TGI Survey 1. 2009 Signon Haim 18-35. Ravakik mul Nesuim [*Life Style: 18-35. Single versus Married].* Le'Omek Ha-toda'a. Prisum Veshivuk Le'zeirim.

The Central Bureau of Statistics (Israel) 2010 *Collection of Data for International Woman's Day.* March 4th. 2013 *A Press Release.* March 6th.

2014 *International Women's Day*. A Press Release. March 4th.

7.

Young Mothers in the UK

Push and Pull Factors Relating to Choices to Stay at Home or Not

GERALDINE BROWN, GERALDINE BRADY AND GAYLE LETHERBY

INTRODUCTION

In the UK young motherhood is considered a social problem as it challenges what is expected of a girl/young woman in her teenage years (Aapola et al 2005). These expectations are firmly rooted in objectives around economic growth through higher education and increased female workforce participation (Wilson and Huntington, 2005). Without labour market participation young mothers are assumed likely to be socially excluded. Yet, as Graham and McDermott (2005: 26) suggest, young parents recognise 'the importance of education for future employment but do not anchor their future identities in the labour market ... futures are built, instead, around motherhood, where the opportunities for self-esteem and social respect appear more certain'. This view serves to challenge the implication that young mothers are reluctant to engage in education, employment and training yet allowing a young mother time and space to be a mother has been at odds with UK target driven strategies, underpinned by economic concerns that young mothers and their children are likely to be a drain on the welfare system, which have led to young mothers being 'pushed' out of the home and into education, training or employment.

Paradoxically, alongside being 'pushed' out of the home by policy drivers, young mothers are also 'pulled' into the home by the discourses of 'total motherhood' and 'intensive mothering' (Hays 1996). Research suggests that many young mothers equate being a 'good' mother with staying home with their child/ren until they go to school (Graham and McDermott, 2005). A good mother is there for their child and does not relinquish responsibility by 'dumping' them on a child minder or nursery or, in some cases, on the child's father.

In this chapter we draw from a number of research projects which all focused on the experience and views of young people (most of whom were mothers and fathers). We highlight the myriad factors which influence young mothers' 'choice' to stay at home or to undertake education or employment outside of the home, and the context within such 'choices' are situated.

BACKGROUND AND CONTEXT

Since the Conservative-Liberal Democrat coalition government came into office in May 2010, alongside an increased emphasis on participation in the labour market has been a reaffirmation of teenage pregnancy as a public health problem (Department for Children, Schools and Families 2010). Apparent opportunities are available to encourage/coerce young mothers out of the home but in reality opportunities are limited in terms of financial support to study for higher education qualifications and to study beyond the age of 19. Alternatively, recent policy developments in the UK, supported by the Coalition government, emphasise that 'good' mothers (and fathers) need to model good behaviour, to breastfeed, to be aware of stages of child development, to socialise children into good citizens Indeed, the value placed on good parenting underpins the current Troubled Families Programme, where we see the introduction of a framework set up to target interventions at specific families identified as a problem (Local Government Association, April 2013).

The discourse of responsibility cuts across policy and lived experience. Individuals are responsible for managing their own behaviour, well-being and for taking up opportunities and raising their aspirations. Young people are expected to 'take responsibility'. Taking up employment demonstrates responsibility but so too does taking seriously the new role of mother or father. For young mothers, decisions are further complicated by political and media discourses, which have, following the report of the Social Exclusion

Unit in 1999, positioned them as both inappropriate and inevitably disadvantaged. Motherhood is an expected identity for women but only in the 'right' social, economic and sexual circumstances (DiLapi 1989, Letherby 1994, Earle and Letherby 2003, 2007). Thus, there is a hierarchy of motherhood and teenage mothers along with lesbian mothers, older mothers, disabled mothers, non-biological mothers and so on are defined as 'inappropriate'. As Kent (2000) notes the legal and social concept of the 'child' which has developed in modern society became divorced from sexuality and this has meant that it is particularly difficult to acknowledge the emotional and physical capacity of teenagers for sexual activity. Young mothers are not only stereotyped as a burden on the state (see for example Phoenix 1991) but despite evidence to the contrary (Phoenix 1991, Ussher 2000) teenage mothers are stereotyped as bad mothers and their children as severely disadvantaged.

Duncan and colleagues (2010) recent edited collection which challenged the construction of the problem of 'teenage pregnancy' offers a wide range of evidence which draws attention to gaps between current policy and the lived experience of young parents. Young mothers are aware of the contradictions and have 'aspirations to create a family with themselves at the centre, and to carve out an independent and rewarding life' (Owen et al 2008: 300). They are of course influenced by what they see and know around them and by what they feel is right for their child which sometimes means that their experience challenges the expected lifecourse timeline (Cotterill 1994) in that they do not follow the contemporary expected trajectory of school to university to career to family, more associated with middle class values and opportunities (Carabine 2007). Young women operate with realistic and pragmatic understandings of their position, trajectory and likely opportunities (Carabine, 2007:970).

OUR APPROACH

Drawing on the sociological concept of the lifecourse in order to understand the experiences of young pregnant women and mothers (Letherby, 2002) we argue that teenage pregnancy and young motherhood 'disturb the chronological order of lifecourse and create individual lives and family forms which differ from the ideal' (Cotterill, 1994:112). The lifecourse approach 'encompasses social and demographic changes which affect all our lives, as well as the personal biographical events in each individual's lifecourse' (Cotterill, 1994:112):

> ... using this approach we can see that an individual's journey from birth to death is not a simple unidirectional trip, but one which has 'false starts, changes in direction and hidden obstacles' (Hockey and James, 1993:50).

Between 2001 and 2013 we (research teams always including some of the authors of this article, sometimes plus others) completed seven research projects focusing specifically on the experience of teenage pregnancy and young parenthood all in the Midlands of England plus three additional projects which although wider in focus include young mothers as respondents. Two of these projects focused on housing needs and experiences; one was concerned particularly with the pregnancy, birth and post-natal experiences of young women; one with 'young' fathers' experiences; one with support prior to and following termination and miscarriage and one focused on the presence of power and control in the lives of pregnant teenagers and young mothers, and one on young mother's educational and work needs and experiences. The broader focused projects included an evaluation of a local theatre's arts and health project and a project exploring young people's aspirations. All except one of these projects exclusively used qualitative methods – and respondents included pregnant teenagers and young parents (including at least 250 young mothers in total), informal supporters (e.g. parents) and formal supporters (e.g. health and social care professionals) and individuals with strategic level responsibilities (e.g. members of the local and regional Teenage Pregnancy Partnership Board). In this paper we draw on data from the following projects:

- Housing in Warwickshire (HiW) 2003
- Fathers' Experience (FE) 2004
- Lifelong Learning and Young Parents (LL) 2005
- Power and Control in the Lives of Young Mothers (PandC) 2006
- Young People's Aspirations (Aspire) 2011
- Arts and Drama Evaluation (AandD) 2013 (See Appendix I).

Our aim has always been to present data from the perspective of young mothers (and fathers) and not to suggest a linear, ideal, lifecycle-type series of events and experiences (Letherby et al, 2002). This chapter is a further example of this.

TO STAY-AT-HOME OR NOT

An over-reliance on quantitative research as evidence for policy has led to teenage pregnancy being identified as a route to social exclusion (Graham and McDermot, 2005). Concern arises amongst professionals when young mothers do not respond positively to the offer of education. Yet our research shows that professionals often show a lack of awareness of how being a mother can impact on the learning experience, for example, in terms of acceptable childcare provision, travel arrangements and finances:

> It's a clicky village because you either live there all your life and know everybody, or you come in and nobody wants to know you ... I mean there's public transport, but when you've got a toddler and then a new born baby, a pushchair, a carrier bag, it's just impossible, and nobody helps you get on and off the bus. . . . So I found myself just staying in and not doing anything, I got into quite bad depression (young mother HiW).

> When I'm on the bus with the baby and they say 'look how old she is and she's got a baby'. . . . they look at you funny and stare (young mother LL).

> Sometimes I think working doesn't benefit you as when you are working you've got to pay half of your rent, childcare and by the time you've done that you've only got left what you would have got on income support anyway (young mother LL).

Finding oneself pregnant and becoming a mother (or father) can also lead to other issues and concerns taking priority. Young people have aspirations that include having a child at what they feel is the right time:

> I've always said that if I was going to have a kid I wouldn't never wait until anywhere over like 25 or something, you want to be younger than 25 to have a kid. . . because I don't want to be one of them old dads and that, be about 40 and your kid's about 12 (young man Aspire).

> She [partner's mother] thought that she [partner] should get her career sorted out first and all the rest of it but it wasn't

> what [partner] wanted so she didn't get it done. But her mother was like really pressuring her at the same time saying 'get it done [termination]' but after a while [partner] just said 'No' I'm not doing it and then her mum was like happy as anybody else. I think her mum just wanted her to make the right decision for her life, because it is a big decision to have a kid or not (young father FE).

As Wilson and Huntington (2005) note the socially accepted order of events; education, job, marriage/steady relationship, children is generally more associated with a middle class linear transition to adulthood where adult responsibility can be delayed whilst young people undertake further or higher education. Our respondents take their adult responsibilities seriously and this often means staying at home and devoting themselves to their children's needs:

> When I'm older, if I've lived my life and done what I want to do then yeah. But if I haven't like lived my life and if I ain't going somewhere and I haven't got a good career then no because I wouldn't want to be bringing kids into something where I can't do nothing that they want. . . I wouldn't want to be one of those mothers who have children when they're like so busy doing their own thing, and then not have time to spend with their children (young women Aspire).

> I want to stay at home until the baby is old enough to go to nursery and then I'll get a job (young mother LL).

> I'm going to wait until my little girl grows up and then do a course and get a job like a nurse or something like that (young mother LL).

Thus, young mothers feel that they can pause their own education and employment paths whilst their children are young and pick these up later:

> I'm going to be a mum, but when she's older, when she's in school, maybe I can still go back and do it again so it never really stops you. It just makes you think 'later', rather than 'never' really (young mother Aspire).

> I can always do what I want to do when she gets a bit older (young mother Aspire).

On the other hand some of the young people we have spoken to would rather take the expected route (to college) and then have children shortly after establishing themselves:

> She [sister] hasn't been to college yet, she had a baby straight from school. I don't really want to do that. I obviously want to start college so that I have actually got a place (young woman Aspire).

The very fact that young mothers have engaged with us and our work, many over a period of years, is evidence, we suggest, of aspiration. In addition to the traditional research work we have undertaken we have designed and co-delivered several development programmes. Working with young mothers over a period of time has highlighted the push and pull of home and work that young mothers' feel. For example the involvement of young mothers in the development and delivery of various presentations and training programmes is not only governed by practical pressures and deadlines but also framed within broader political drivers. For example in Leicester the Teenage Pregnancy Partnership's commissioning of a training project was influenced by a concern to meet NEET to EET targets, that is, move young mothers who were NEET (not in education, employment or training) into EET (in education employment and training), in line with the political conceptualisation of 'support' for young mothers. Throughout the consultation phase of this project and the developmental workshops young mothers identified a number of challenges to simplistic understandings of the transition from NEET to EET, as highlighted in the examples above. During delivery of the training programme to practitioners some young mothers spoke about their desire to take time to establish themselves in their new role as a mother before thinking about EET. As the project was being delivered at our university, a mobile crèche with childcare workers was central to delivery of the project.

Decisions to stay at home are also related to young mothers' wish to be a 'good mother' and 'good motherhood' is equated with stay-at-home motherhood in their child's early years:

> It's all about her, nothing to do with me. When you have a baby you see that your life don't matter, your child's does, and

> I want to make the most of her while she's a baby because I'm only going to have the one chance and when she starts school then think about myself (young mother Aspire)

That these expectations are gendered is not surprising:

> When he was first born she wanted to get back to work more than what I did so it was like the first, I think it was seven to eight months, of him being born I was the one that was staying at home looking after him. I was quite happy to do that (young father FE).

> Everyone says I should stay at home and look after the children and [partner] should be the one out working and supporting his family. I've actually only just come out of work. I've had to finish because I'm pregnant. I did heavy lifting jobs because I worked in care I couldn't carry on. So I've only been out of work myself for only six weeks and [partner] has actually been at home for the last 12 months with the kids and I went back to work pretty much as soon as I had my son so it's been really nice. It's been a nice 12 months for me to have a break from the kids. . . [partner] said to me all he ever wanted to do was go back to work because he was sick of hearing people say 'Why do you let your girlfriend work, why don't you get a job?' and he says 'She works and she wants to work and it's not you know 1946 its 2004 and we'll do what we want', but people never understand why he would want to stop at home with his children and that's why the children actually bond a lot better with [partner] than they do with me (young mother FE).

However, respondents were keen to tell us that staying home did not mean doing 'nothing', thus challenging the stereotype that teenagers get pregnant so that they can stay home, claim benefits and not contribute to wider society. Speaking of her involvement in a drama-based project aimed at working with an isolated group of individuals a young mother said:

> . . . when this came along it felt like a wonderful opportunity for me because I did used to do amateur dramatics a long time ago and really enjoyed it but back then . . . so when I heard

> about this, I thought well I give it a try, and I've really, really enjoyed it and I'm dreading it finishing because I'm wondering – well it will actually give me time to catch up on what I've not been able to do over the past few weeks – but when I have caught up with myself around the house, I'm just worried I'm going to be back to where I started, I want something to occupy my mind that isn't just connected to the house or to my garden . . .(AandD)

As we have written elsewhere (Bailey et al 2002, Brady et al, 2012) as members of a group that are often demonised, criticised and looked down upon by wider society young mothers strive to distance themselves from the stereotypical 'teenage mother'. Knowing that others judge them they regard it as important to make plans to engage in work or education, to be a positive role model:

> If they [children] see their mum and dad do nothing, or their mum do nothing, they think they're going to do nothing. That's why if I try and do something and then at least even if it's just a job, no matter what job it is at least they know that 'my mum works' so maybe they think that they should get a job (young mother Aspire).

Young mothers internalise discourses and policy drivers that imply the transmission of a cycle of deprivation throughout generations. Those young mothers who do stay at home often experience financial and practical hardship.

> They said they were going to give me a house but I ended up with this flat, I can't move until June 2004. I had to take this place. There is a dealer who lives opposite and a druggie who lives along the corridor. I think housing put me here because I was young and single with a kiddie. All the people who live here are young with kids or druggies. I want to live in an area where I feel safe (young mother HinW).

And such conditions can lead to emotional and psychological distress:

> Often these girls are depressed, that's a medical ground, and they are often depressed because of the situation they are living in, the isolation, the lack of support and the lack of facilities (health professional HinW).

Sometimes financial insecurity and/or the age of the women necessitates them living their parents or in-laws which in turn can lead to additional practical and emotional struggles:

> . . . it was really hard for me because sometimes I would feel that they would treat me like a child and I just want to be an adult, and other times they would completely forget that I was a child and treat me like an adult and I would miss out on things, like stupid things like an ice cream, I still felt like a kid and wanted one. They should have balanced it out and it was really hard (young mother PandC).

Our data demonstrates the difficulties (grand)parents may have mediating between young mothers different identities; as daughters, teenagers and mothers, knowing when and when not to provide support and perhaps feeling a lack of recognition in their attempts to be supportive. Health and social care professionals often believe that those young mothers who have the support of parents and in-laws are the most fortunate but this perspective does not recognise that family dynamics can have a negative impact on a young mothers' experience:

> There is one young person I know of that said when she was living with her mother, her mother would say, 'that is the way to do it'. Now she feels that she doesn't know how to do it, and he [her child] is so badly behaved that she has requested to go on a course to deal with his behaviour. She has asked for this because she doesn't know how to be a mother and the child is 18 months old. She has lived at home and now she has no confidence . . . (health professional PandC).

The choice to stay at home or not may be determined by others: partners, in-laws, parents:

> I was living with his family at the time and it was almost like I was invisible . . . no one would ever ask me what I wanted to do. They would just sit there conversing with each other. I would just sit there thinking 'Hello, I do exist!' . . . Her view was because I was married, and had a child my place was inside the house (young mother PandC).

And when (grand)parents are willing and able to help health and social care professionals may see this an interference/taking on the young mother's responsibilities:

> She was saying that when Kate went back to school she would have to get up to feed the baby and that. She goes to school at 8 o'clock in the morning. If she has to get up at night . . . I will be there for her. But she [health visitor] was criticising me for that (grandmother HinW)

When subsequent pregnancies are achieved and children born this is often regarded by policy makers and some practitioners as a negative outcome. Young mothers are seen to be making another mistake, yet young parents' rationale is often to have their children close together and to resume study or a career after this.

SOME REFLECTIONS

Far from living 'shattered lives and blighted futures' (Tony Blair, SEU 1999:4) and being 'trapped in a cycle of despair' (1999:4) our data illustrates how becoming a parent can be a route to social inclusion for some young women (and men) (Brown et al 2009; Duncan et al 2010) despite the push and pull to both be a 'good' mother, which is often articulated through the stay at home discourse, and to become independent and contribute to economically to wider society. Our findings are illustrative of the ways in which normative discourses of 'good' motherhood impact on the lived maternal experience of young women. This is unsurprising as parenting has come to be seen as a cause of and solution to a range of social problems, and teenage mothers have been particularly singled out as posing a threat to the social order:

> Teenage mothers are less likely to finish their education, less likely to find a good job, and more likely to end up as single parents and bringing up their children in poverty. The children themselves run a greater risk of poor health, and have a much higher chance of becoming teenage mothers themselves' (Blair, 1999:4).

Despite the challenge it provides to such external discourses, becoming a mother is a realistic and achievable option for some young women (and men), which demonstrates that the transition to adulthood, independence and responsibility is varied and should be viewed as such. The journey is neither linear nor chronological, whilst young mothers (and fathers) are making choices and negotiating their present and future they are also limited at times by structural constraints. However, economic activity is often regarded as the only way to participate productively in society. For many of our young mother respondents becoming a mother was, despite the problems they faced, the best thing that had ever happened to them:

> It's just made me realise I didn't do a bad thing getting pregnant at 16. Yeah it was bad to some people but to me she saved me you know. I wouldn't be the person I am today if I didn't have her. It's as simple as that (young mother AandD).

Author's Note We write 'young' fathers in single quotation marks to acknowledge that young is often a misnomer as male partners can, and in a significant minority of cases are, much older than the young woman.

APPENDIX OF REFERENCED PROJECTS

Housing in Warwickshire (HiW) 2003 Letherby, G. Brown, G. Butler, C. (2003) *Housing Needs of Young Parents in Warwickshire*, Centre for Social Justice, Coventry University.

Fathers' Experience (FE) 2004 Letherby, G., Brady, G. and Brown, G. (2004) *Experience and support needs of 'young' fathers in Warwickshire* Centre for Social Justice, Coventry University.

Lifelong Learning and Young Parents (LL) 2005 Reid, K. Letherby, G. Mason, L. Burke, E. Taylor, C. Gough, A. (2005) *Research on Lifelong Learning for Pregnant Young Women & Young Parents in Sandwell* JCJ Solutions and Centre for Social Justice, Coventry University.

Power and Control in the Lives of Young Mothers (PandC) 2006 Brown, G. Brady, G. and Letherby, G (2006) *Issues of power and control in the intimate and familial relations of pregnant teenagers and young mothers* Coventry University.

Young People's Aspirations (Aspire) 2011 Newby, K. Brady, G. Bayley, J. and Sewell, A. (2011) *Exploring the aspirations of young people at risk of teenage pregnancy: findings and recommendations* Coventry University.

Arts and Drama Evaluation (AandD) 2013 Savin Baden, M. Brady, G. Wimpenny, K. and Brown, G. (2013) *Evaluation of the Belgrade Theatre's Creative Gymnasium project* (Esmee Fairbairn Foundation). Learning Innovation Research Group/SURGE: Coventry University.

REFERENCES

Aapola, S., S. Gonick and A. Harris 2005 *Young Femininities: Girlhood, Power and Social Change.* Basingstoke: Palgrave Macmillan.

Arai, L. 2009 *Teenage Pregnancy: The Making and Unmaking of a Problem.* Bristol: Policy Press.

Bailey, N., G. Brown, G. Letherby and C. Wilson 2002 "The Baby Brigade." *Journal of the Association for Research on Mothering,* Spring/Summer 2002 4(1): 101-110.

Brady, G., G. Brown and C. Wilson 2012 "Young Mothers' Experiential Knowledge and the Research Process." In *Critical Perspectives on User Involvement.* M. Barnes and P. Cotterell, eds. Bristol: Policy Press.

Brown, G., G. Brady, C. Wilson and G. Letherby 2009 "Teenage Pregnancy and Young Parenthood: Questioning the Inevitability of 'Risk', Lone Motherhood and Social Exclusion." In *Evaluating the Political Achievement of New Labour since 1997: Social policy and the Public Trust.* N. Johns and A. Barton, eds. Ceridigion: Edwin Mellen.

Brown, G., G. Brady and G. Letherby 2011 "Young Mothers' Experiences of Power, Control and Violence within Intimate and Familial Relationships." *Child Care in Practice Special Issue: Effective Interventions with Children and Families Exposed to Domestic Violence* 17(4): 359-374.

Carabine, J. 2007 "New Labour's Teenage Pregnancy Strategy." *Cultural Studies* 21(6): 952-973.

Cotterill, P. 1994 *Friendly Relations?: Mothers and their Daughters-in-Law.*London: Taylor and Francis.

DiLapi, E. 1989 "Lesbian Mothers and the Motherhood." *Hierarchy Journal of Homosexuality* 18: 101-121.

Department of Communities and Local Government 2012 *Working with Troubled Families, A Guide to the Evidence and Good Practice.* Crown

Copyright: London.

Department for Children, Schools and Families 2010 *Teenage Pregnancy the Strategy: Beyond 2010.* Crown Copyright: London.

Duncan, S., R. Edwards and C. Alexander, eds. 2009 *Teenage Parenthood: What's the Problem?* Tuffnell Press: London.

Earle, S., and G. Letherby, eds. 2003 *Gender, Identity and Reproduction: Social Perspectives.* London: Palgrave.

Earle, S., and G. Letherby 2007 "Conceiving Time?: Women Who Do or Do Not Conceive." *Sociology of Health and Illness* 29(2): 233-250.

Graham, H., and E. McDermott 2005 "Qualitative Research and the Evidence Base of Policy: Insights from Studies of Teenage Mothers in the UK." *Journal of Social Policy* 35(1): 21-37.

Hays, S. 1996 *Cultural Constructions of Motherhood.* New Haven: Yale University Press.

Hockey, J., and A. James 1993 *Growing Up and Growing Old: Ageing and Dependency in the Lifecourse.* London: Sage.

Kent, J. 2000 *Social Perspectives on Pregnancy and Childbirth for Midwives, Nurses and Caring Professions.* Buckinghamshire: Open University.

Letherby, G. 1994 "Mother or Not, Mother or What?: Problems of Definition and Identity." *Women's Studies International Forum* 17(5): 525-532.

Letherby, G., G. Brown, H. DiMarco and C. Wilson 2002 *Pregnancy and Postnatal Experience of Young Women Who Become Pregnant Under the Age of Twenty Years Report.* Centre for Social Justice: Coventry University.

Owen, J., G. Higginbottom, M. Kirkham, N. Mathers and P. Marsh 2008 "Ethnicity, Policy and Teenage Parenthood in England: Findings from a Qualitative Study." *Social Policy and Society* 7(3): 293-305.

Phoenix, A. 1991 "Mothers Under Twenty: Outsider and Insider Views." In *Motherhood: Meanings, Practices and Ideologies.* A. Phoenix, A. Woollett and E. Lloyd, eds. London: Sage Publications.

Social Exclusion Unit 1999 *Teenage Pregnancy.* London: The Stationery Office.

Ussher, J. M. 2000 *Women's Health: Contemporary International Perspectives.* Leicester: The British Psychological Society.

Wilson, H., and A. Huntington 2005 "Deviant Mothers: The Construction of Teenage Motherhood in Contemporary Discourse." *Journal of Social*

Policy 35 (1): 59-76.

8.

Mothering from a Caribbean Perspective

Challenges, Determination, and Survival

JANET M. HAYNES

INTRODUCTION

Like many mothers throughout the world, Caribbean mothers have always sought ways to improve their family's economic well-being. Opportunities leading to home ownership, access to higher education for their children, secured income at retirement, and quality health care are goals that many women throughout the Caribbean strive to achieve. Unfortunately, abject poverty and ongoing economic subordination are also realities for many Caribbean women. The desire to transcend poverty has motivated many single mothers to seek employment, often as live-in nannies or domestics, in England, the United States of America or Canada. Single mothers often made the heartbreaking decision to leave their children and family members behind, in their home countries, with the hope that their temporary employment abroad would lead to permanent residency, which in turn would reunite them with their children as well as create a better future for their family.

In this chapter I provide a qualitative analysis of experiential narratives shared by seven single mothers who emigrated from the Caribbean to Ottawa, Canada as temporary workers between 1977 and 2000. Special attention is paid to their experiences as they sought to acquire permanent residency and be reunited with their children. These mothers shared their perspectives of motherhood and the factors affecting their decisions to be either 'stay-at-home' mothers or 'working' mothers. Such factors often intersected to produce harsh realities for certain women. In this chapter I share and validate these seven mothers' strengths, determination, perseverance and power to redefine the concept of motherhood within a non-European context without generalizing their voices and mothering roles to all Caribbean women.

Finally, this chapter provides an insider's view of the multiple intersecting barriers some Black Caribbean women faced in Canada. The term 'insider' is used in a context where both the researcher and the participants share a Caribbean culture. Although I do not share in their domestic experiences in Canada, I nonetheless bring an analysis to this project that is deeply rooted in much of the Black Caribbean women experience in Canada of which I am familiar. Thus, I am able to explain the ways in which many of the barriers simultaneously produced differences in the multiple roles of many immigrant mothers who began as domestics and their struggle to achieve upward social mobility. The Caribbean within the context of this chapter refers to the English speaking Islands of the Caribbean.

RESEARCH METHODOLOGY

> Qualitative researchers want to enter the worlds of the people they study, get to know them and ultimately represent and interpret these worlds. It follows that qualitative writing tends to be rich with quotation, description, and narration, as researchers attempt to capture conversations, experiences, perspectives, voices and meanings. This is research, it could be said, with words instead of numbers. (Hull, 1997)

The statement above captures the spirit of the research project on which this chapter is based. In other words, through mutual trust and respect, the women in this research project were able to share their individual and collective experiences openly and honestly with me. More importantly, qualitative research generally examines people's words and actions in narrative or descriptive ways more closely representing the situation as experienced by the participants (Maykut and Morehouse 1994). Utilizing a qualitative methodology enabled participants to reflect on their past life experiences in their homeland and share not only their reasons for coming to Canada, but also to speak candidly about their pre and post Canadian experiences as domestics and nannies.

ACCESS AND DATA COLLECTION

Twelve women met regularly at a community center to discuss issues pertaining to immigrant women. In preparation for international women's week, the Executive Director of the Center asked the women to share stories of their early years in Canada. A series of three two-hour sessions were held over a three-week period. The first session was used to explain the research process and permissions were obtained. Individuals were given the option to have their stories published and as such, seven of the twelve women consented to share their stories as part of this research.

The women made the decision to tell their stories as part of a collective group experience as opposed to individually. They felt their collective struggles and experiences could serve as a source of strength to the group and to other third world immigrant women who may be experiencing similar struggles in Canada. According to bell hooks (2003), "working class Blacks are not ashamed or afraid to talk about class oppression; they simply have little or no public venues in which to air their views" (bell hooks 2003 in Haynes 2005:80). They also believed immigration officials ignored the many ways Canadian employers exploit domestic workers and nannies. Silvera stated:

> The Canadian Employment and Immigration Commission considers employment visas a 'temporary solution' to the domestic labor shortage, and thus feels quite justified in exploiting the labor of Third World women and turning a blind eye to the inhumane working condition that have become synonymous with domestic work. (1989:8)

The sessions were audio taped and the names of the women were changed to protect their identity. As such, I will be using fictitious names in citing the participants. In addition, the women told their stories with the aid of an interview guide. Although several themes emerged in their stories, I focused on the aspects of their stories that described how they came to be in Canada and the factors that affected their roles as mothers, particularly in terms of being working or stay-at-home mothers.

PROFILES OF THE FAMILIES FROM THEIR NARRATIVES

> I did every type of job to make two ends meet. I had four children to feed and I was both mother and father to them. I got a job in one of the hotels in St. Lucia hoping to meet someone who could help me find a job in Canada. I wanted my children to go to university and have a better life than me – tell me how was I going to send four children to university on a chambermaid's salary and no father to help? I was determined to give them the opportunity I never had and I did not see any way out of poverty in my situation at that time. (Barbara Grant, Janet Haynes, March 1, 2005)

Barbara's profile is reflective of the mothers who participated in this project and to some degree could be considered typical of a large portion of domestic workers from the Caribbean. Like Barbara, prior to entering Canada, all the women were single mothers and came from the English speaking Caribbean. The women had varying levels of education ranging from some high school, high school, to college.

The table below includes the individual demographics of each participant. The mothers are identified using fictitious names to protect their confidentiality.

'Table 1' clarifies that each of the seven women left children behind in their respective countries. It also illustrates the age of each child when the mothers left their islands, including how long it took them to acquire permanent residency, whether they had blended families and whether they worked or stayed at home.

It took approximately two to four years for the mothers to transition from temporary workers to permanent residents of Canada. The mothers also reported that it took them approximately two to three years after gaining residency before they could be reunited with their children. For example, Bernice left Trinidad and Tobago at the age of 30 to work as a domestic in Canada in 1975, leaving Joey, her 5-year-old son with her parents. She received her landed residency in 1977, but was not able to reunite with Joey until two years later, when he was nine years old. Similarly, Bernice spent two years transitioning from contract worker to permanent resident, and another two years going through the immigration process and preparing for her son's arrival.

The participants reported that they did not all gain their residency through independent sponsorship. On the one hand, Lisa, Sandra and Marjorie, the youngest of the seven women, reported that they gained residency through marriage, which offered them the opportunity to quit their domestic jobs. On the other hand, Bernice, Barbara, Charmaine, and Sarah gained residency status after completing their work contract but continued to only have access to low-waged and low-skilled jobs.

FINDINGS

The following themes emerged from the data:

Being a Domestic/Nanny in Canada

Life in Canada as a domestic or nanny carries a cold, harsh and severe reality that for the most part was marred with silence. All seven mothers reported that the dream of working abroad was not how they had imagined life to be once they arrived at their employers' home in Ottawa. Sandra and Sarah were forced to change employers three times during the employment contract due to employment-related violations and sexual abuse. As a consequence they had to work an extra year before qualifying to file for permanent residency.

The women reported that their employers violated their contracts by either giving them less salary than was stated on their work contracts; or by requiring them to work almost twice the number of hours in their contract, without overtime pay. They were also subjected to sexual harassment, intimidation, isolation and verbal abuse. According to Barbara:

> I had to work from 6 in the morning to 9 at night and I know that was wrong, but I did it and I did not complain. They abused me, knowing that I had no one to talk to and nowhere to go, so I prayed and continued to ask God to make a way out for me, and that is when I met my husband. I was able to escape the hell I found myself in. (Barbara Grant, Janet Haynes, March 8, 2005)

Sandra indicated that shortly after she arrived to work as a nanny, her employer requested that she do domestic chores because her cleaner had just left. So, she had to work longer hours to take care of the house as well as the children for the same salary. She talked about the isolation and the shame she experienced because she could not let her family know that her opportunity to work was only an opportunity for her employers to exploit her labor. The women's experiences were identical to the issues raised by Silvera (1989):

> Employment and Immigration Canada has established certain minimum standards to be used as guidelines by people who employ workers on the Temporary Employment Visas.... On the contrary, what is most common is that the employer does not follow these guidelines... They have, in fact, a free hand in setting wages because Immigration does little to enforce its regulations. So, duties, hours of work and salaries are often changed unilaterally by the employer. (1989:9)

Violations and abuse were not limited to long hours and extra work duties. The mothers also reported stories of rape and sexual intimidation by their male employers. For example, Lisa reported that her employers' friend, who came to visit at a time when he knew his friends would be at work and knew that she would be alone in the house, raped her. She reported the incident to her female employer but was told that she must have agreed to have sex with the family friend because he was a good man and would never do such a thing. Lisa stated that her female employer told her that if she continued with the accusation she would have no choice but to end the work contract and send her home.

The participants agreed that when poor women leave their country to seek a better life for themselves and their children, they don't expect to be abused. As a result they become isolated, fearful and vulnerable because they do not want to lose their jobs. Charmaine noted:

> We were made to believe that we had to take whatever our employers did to us. They paid us low wages, we worked long hours and some of us even got abused. I knew two domestic workers who got raped on the job and one of them got pregnant by the employer. Instead of helping her, the wife accused her of sleeping with her husband, then fired her. We come here thinking we have found a way out of poverty; instead, many of us found hell instead. But, we endure whatever happens to us in silence because our families are depending on us to send financial help back home. It is a price we pay to better

> our lives as women, and to provide for our children. (Charmaine Little, Janet Haynes, March 8, 2005)

The narratives in Silvera's 1989 book echo the experiences of the seven women regarding their isolation, fears, physical and sexual abuse, and their determination to succeed.

> Ten West Indian women talk about their lives as domestic workers in Canada, the bitter-sweet memories of family back home, the frustration of never having enough money and the humiliation of being a legal slave. They tell of working overtime for no pay, of sharing their rooms usually with a baby or the family pet, of shaking off the sexual advances of their male employer, and in the case of Hyacinth, of being raped. They talk about the experiences of being manipulated and degraded by female employers. (1989:12)

Six of seven women reported they endured much of the abuse because they neither lost sight of the children they left behind, nor forgot the reasons they came to Canada in the first place: to improve the life chances of their children and support their mothers who were caring for the children in their absence. However, Marjorie reported that she had decided to return to her native Dominica just before she met and married her husband:

> I hated my job and I was getting ready to go back home. They worked me like a slave. Imagine, I had to work round the clock for the same pay. If their children got sick I had to stay up with them all night while the mother and father slept. I got no rest, worked all day and night and I could only leave the house half days on Sundays although the contract said I got the weekend off. I was very lucky to meet Jules shortly after I got here. So Jules and I got married almost immediately after we met and he sponsored my son and I. (Marjorie Jules, Janet Haynes, March 15, 2005)

Except for Marjorie, the women reported that the mentoring they received from the nannies and domestic workers who came before them was crucial. Charmaine, Barbara, and Sarah explained they connected with other mothers they called their 'sisters from yard' with the term 'yard' referring to 'back home'.

The Mentoring Role

The mentoring relationships that developed between the domestic workers and newer arrivals were critical for not only the survival of these women in Canada without any family support but also for the mentoring that helped them navigate the immigration processing system. Most importantly, the relationships between these two groups of women created a 'sisters in the struggle' type of bonding whereby they looked out for each other by sharing information that normally would not have been accessible to newcomers. The women believed these relationships were especially important in the first year of their employment given the level of exploitation and abuse they were subjected to. Additionally, it was through these relationships that they became educated about their rights as temporary visa workers and the actions they could take if they encountered abuse with the families employing them.

All seven mothers believed that coming to Canada was a once in a lifetime opportunity to improve their economic life but they were also keenly aware that it was only a temporary opportunity; they needed to figure out a way to become permanent residents. Their mentors helped them to understand what they needed to do in order to increase their chances of success in the immigration process. For example, their mentors explained that they needed to demonstrate they had taken active measures to improve themselves during the period of their temporary residency. One such measure suggested was furthering their education through the continuing education program. Consequently, all seven women took either high school courses or health care aid courses, thereby increasing their chances of success when they applied for their permanent residency. They also knew that paying to take these courses was demonstrating initiative, which also looked good on their application for residency. This strategy proved to be very effective because all six women successfully applied for and were granted permanent residency status in Canada.

Transitioning from Domestic Worker to Permanent Resident

Transitioning from temporary foreign workers to permanent residents of Canada proved difficult for the women after receiving permanent residency. Six of the seven women recalled how eager they were as new Canadians to finally have the opportunity to apply for employment. Marjorie stated:

> Initially, when I got my papers, I thought I would now be able

> to choose which jobs I wanted or if I wanted to work in the east end near my home or in the west end of Ottawa. After applying for several jobs, I quickly found out that people only saw me as a domestic. They only saw me with a mop and a broom in my hands and with a college education I am more than that. (Marjorie Jules, Janet Haynes, March 8, 2005)

Sarah stated, "I thought that now I can finally get a job where I actually get paid for the hours worked. I felt like a freed woman" (Sarah, 2006). The mothers' voices were unmistakably strong in identifying the challenges they faced after becoming permanent residents of Canada, and they recaptured those memories in their statements:

> I realized after getting my residence that I did not have the "Canadian" experience. Although I had a college education from home, and I could do other types of work, all I could get was domestic work. I go into the stores and there were only white people; but when I applied they would tell me that the job is taken or that I did not have Canadian experience. I had to go back and do domestic work. But now I had to pay my own rent, buy my own food, pay the light and heat and still send money back home. I realize I was worst off now because of racism. (Bernice Smith, Janet Haynes, March 15, 2005)

> When I first arrived in this country, I kept thinking about the life back home and how hard it was for my family and me. I am their hope and they are depending on me, so I could not forget that. Then when I got my papers, I cried because of the silent suffering I endured for my children. I can now work three jobs so that my children can be with me. (Charmaine Little, Janet Haynes, March 15, 2005)

All seven women reported they saved substantially for their transition to permanent residency and the costs associated with sponsoring their children. The mothers reported that as Canadian residents, they began to realize the differences between living on a tropical Island and living in a four season's climate. Barbara said although she was used to paying for lights and water she had not thought about the high cost of heating an apartment, and buying winter clothing for four children.

The women added that children not being required to wear school uniforms created an additional burden on them. Their children had to have different clothing each day for school, compared to the Islands where students had to wear uniforms. As the women began to assess their living expenses for their households including childcare costs, they realized having one minimum wage job was not sufficient for their families' survival. Now they required more than one job, as explained by Barbara:

> Reality hits you after you get your papers. You realize you have no family here. You cannot go to the corner store to buy three eggs, a pound of sugar or a pound of flour. You have to buy the entire package. Back home I could go to the store and buy half a dozen eggs and half a loaf of bread. If I did not have the money, I could pay the storeowner later but not here, I have to pay on the spot or go hungry. When I saw how things run here, I realize that what I thought was paradise was not paradise after all. (Barbara Grant, Janet Haynes, March 15, 2005)

So, the excitement of job hunting was short-lived for Charmaine and Lisa as both women discovered that the only jobs that were available to them were low-wage domestic jobs. Both women realized that as the heads of their household, the wages they were being offered could not support the cost of housing, food, clothing, and transport for them and their children. In addition, they both reported that having multiple children severely affected their ability to work multiple jobs. For example, Lisa reported that because her children were young she was unable to work multiple jobs. Yet, the minimum wage jobs available to her were insufficient to cover her childcare and living expenses. Charmaine, on the other hand, reported that because one job could not cover her costs she attempted to work multiple jobs. She reports:

> Because I had to work two jobs, my kids were home alone sometimes because I did not have a car and would miss my bus sometimes. One day, my neighbors called Children's Aid on me. I had no idea who they were because I had never heard of them before. When they came I found out that they could take my children. They did not care that I had to work two jobs. That was my problem. I had to give up my second job, forcing me to stay home and finding another way out or losing my children. I did not struggle to bring my children here

> so people could take them from me. (Charmaine Little, Janet Haynes, March 15, 2005)

For Charmaine and many other women from the Caribbean, the idea of Youth Protection workers being able to remove their children from their care was a new concept for them because there was not a formal child welfare structure in the Caribbean. They themselves had been raised in the extended family structures that included friends and neighbors, relatives and immediate family members. Therefore, from a Caribbean perspective, Charmaine would have been able to work multiple jobs without facing the threats of having her children removed due to parental 'neglect' as defined by youth protection laws in Canada. However, despite the extended family networks existing in the Caribbean, Jamaica passed its Child Protection Law in 2003 and Lisa Hanna, the Minister of Youth and Culture, launched a Child Protection Database in June, 2012.

Once the jubilation of being reunited with their children subsided, the reality of their situation and the forthcoming challenges quickly emerged. Though Canada was the land of opportunity for these women, it was also a place of stringent regulations with respect to parenting standards, standards that were unfamiliar to Caribbean mothers. Meeting parenting guidelines was not the only challenge. These mothers also had to cope with the intersecting barriers of being single, poor, Black, immigrants, with children, all of which affected their ability to secure a well-paying job outside the field of childcare or domestic work. The mothers who were suddenly thrust into situations for which they were ill prepared soon found themselves having to make yet another heartbreaking decision. This time it did not involve leaving their children, but rather whether to be a work at home mother or a work outside of the home mother.

Caribbean Mothers' Decision to Work Inside or Outside the Home

> It is said that it takes a village to raise a child, but what happens to those women who do not live in a village? Who will take care of the children while I am at work? How can I afford childcare when my pay is less than what it cost for childcare? (Lisa Hill, Janet Haynes, March 15, 2005)

These were central considerations for the mothers when deciding whether to work at home or outside the home. Being single, having multiple children, and lacking extended family support affected both Charmaine's and

Lisa's decision to stay home. Although Lisa was married, she became separated after experiencing domestic violence. She was now raising her family alone as a single mother, and living below the poverty line due to the size of her household and her family's income. In addition, not having family support, Lisa had to quit her job to stay home with the children because she was not able to cover her childcare costs.

However, although Sarah and Sandra also had multiple children, they had established partnerships, which provided dual incomes and additional family support for their families. Both Sarah and Sandra reported that having financial and childcare support enabled them to work outside the home and attend school, which they felt increased their chances of achieving upward social mobility. Sarah had the opportunity to complete her college degree in accounting, which she had started in Jamaica, whereas Sandra was training to become a registered nurse. Though they worked as domestics and nannies in other women's homes, they rejected the idea of being a mother who worked at home. Sarah and Sandra each pointed out:

> I know I spent a lot of time away from my children. I wish I had my family here to look after them with my boyfriend. But I saw how these Canadian women lived. The women I worked for when I first came to Canada worked all day and went out in the evenings. Sometimes they only saw their children at breakfast, but the kids were happy. These women have so much. Their families were happy as any other family back home. So I made the choice to work and achieve my goals too. I made sure to tell my children that they have to work hard like me. (Sarah Bell, Janet Haynes, March 8, 2005)

> When I worked as a nanny, I saw how the Mrs. lived. She had a job that kept her away from the family for long hours, but the family lived so well. They had a beautiful house. The children had everything they wanted. This is the life I wanted for myself and my children. (Sandra Clarke, Janet Haynes, March 15, 2005)

Although both Sarah and Sandra acknowledged the difficulties in being absent from their children for extended periods, they justified their decisions by using their previous female employers as role models. Though their working experiences were quite negative, these women regarded the lifestyle of their employers as something to attain. These unlikely role models for Caribbean mothering demonstrated that working mothers could have it all: happy family, well-adjusted children, marital equality and financial stability.

The mothers who worked outside the home described a sense of empowerment and pride, and together with support, their goals became attainable. However, Marjorie's attitude towards mothers who worked at home differed: "If I worked in other people's home and took care of their children, why would I not work in my own home and take care of my own children, if I had the choice?" (Marjorie Jules, Janet Haynes, March 8, 2005). Marjorie rejected the term 'staying at home' and argues that when she is at home she is working. She further argues that her husband's financial stability enables her to choose whether to work at home or work outside the home. However, the other mothers' decision to work at home was not a choice, but resulted from a lack of options due to their status as Black, single immigrant female, head of households and lacking kinship care for their children.

Stay-at-Home Mothers: Perceptions of Self Through a Cultural Lens

The women individually shared stories of the significant impact they experienced in losing their kinship support. When living in their Islands, they could call upon family members to watch over the children while they went to work, shopped, or attended an appointment. In Canada, their support systems were lost when they immigrated. On the Islands, it took a village to raise a child, and the 'village' consisted of your family members, friends and neighbors. Such villages were not available to the mothers in Canada, and without such support, working low-end jobs made survival a challenge, particularly for those with single incomes. Barbara stated:

> Back home I would have had my mother, sisters, aunts, friends and neighbors to watch out for my children while I am at work. Here, I have no support system and at the same time the Children's Aid social workers did not understand that my minimum wage job could not cover my bills and it looks like they did not really care. They were ready to take my children. Luckily I had a cousin here to come and help me so that I could continue to work my jobs, otherwise I would have been forced to stay home and struggle. For me, staying home meant strug-

> gling just like when I was back home because who can afford to stay home when there are mouths to be fed? And I am not a lazy woman. (Barbara Grant, Janet Haynes, March 8, 2005)

It is critical that the word 'lazy' be noted in Barbara's statement. When I asked her why she felt that staying home could be perceived as her being lazy, she noted that poor people do not get rich staying home. She said that staying home is for people who like being poor. Similarly, Lisa also had a very negative image of mothers who worked at home due to her own economic subordination. She states:

> We had no man in the house, so life was hard for my mother. But she refused to bring a man in the house with her daughters because she feared he might get tempted to touch her girls or abuse her. She told me constantly that she did not want to go to prison, so she would rather 'work her skin to the bones' than have a man provide for her and think her daughters would be available for his pleasure. So the burden was on me, the oldest girl, to help my mother provide food, clothing and an education for my two younger sisters. So I went to work at an early age and I have been working ever since. All I know is hard work. Now I have to stay home because I can't pay to look after my children. I can imagine what my family is saying about me, 'she's gone to foreign and turned worthless'. (Lisa Hill, Janet Haynes, March 8, 2000)

Consequently, some mothers felt ashamed of their decision to work at home because they feared that they may be perceived as not taking advantage of the opportunities that are available to them in Canada. As such, Lisa viewed her situation as a failure because of her inability to work outside the home. Some Caribbean families considered working at home to be the natural role of mothers. Therefore, work at home is neither recognized nor valued as 'real' work. The working-class mothers who felt forced to work at home or who had to work multiple jobs felt that the only way out of poverty was to work outside the home.

CONCLUSION

Very few women, regardless of culture, would deny the physical and mental demands of rearing children and maintaining a home. Yet, financial recognition and validation for the work of mothers at home remains but a dream for most women. Black working-class immigrant mothers who work at home are viewed negatively by family members and society, which further subordinates their role as working mothers. The mothers made a very persuasive argument that when Black mothers work at home there is a generalized perception that they are lazy and want to live off the system, an image that they struggle to reject. However, they identify the Children's Aid structure, the lack of an extended family support system, and their marginalization within the workforce that relegates them to the domestic and childcare end of the labor market, as impediments to achieving upward social mobility. It is critical to remember that for some of these mothers, the decision to work at home arose not out of some altruistic calling, but rather, due to an economic necessity. Ironically, the perception that a real opportunity existed in Canada for meaningful economic advancement was, for many of these mothers, replaced by a reality that impeded their ability to achieve financial stability for themselves and their children.

REFERENCES

hooks, bell. 2003 "Teaching Community: A Pedagogy of Hope". In *The Impact of Race and Class on the Educational Experiences of Black Students in Ottawa's Educational System*, thesis by Janet Haynes, McGill University, 2005. http://www.law.yale.edu/rcw/rcw/jurisdictions/caribbean/jamaica/frontpage1.htm,

Hull, G. 1997 "Research with Words: Qualitative Inquiry" http://www.ncsall.net/index.php@id=468.html

Maykut, P., and E. Morehouse 1994 *Beginning Qualitative Research: A Philosophical and Practical Guide*. London: TheFalmer Press.

Silvera, M. 1989 *Silenced*. Canada: Sister Vision, Black Women and Women of Colour Press.

Name	Age	Country of Birth	Type of Visa (Temporary/ permanent)	Children Born in Home Country	Children Born in Canada	Working vs. Staying Home
Bernice Smith	30	Trinidad & Tobago	Domestic 1975-77 (2 years)	1 (5 yrs. old)	1	Working
Barbara Grant	38	St Lucia	Domestic 1971-73 (2 years)	4 (3, 5, 9, & 11 yrs. old)	0	Working
Charmaine Little	31	Jamaica	Nanny 1974-77 (3 years)	2 (5 & 7 yrs.)	3	Stay-at-home
Lisa Hill	25	Jamaica	Domestic 1979-82* (3 years)	3 (2, 4 & 8 yr)	2	Stay-at-home
Sandra Clarke	24	Barbados	Nanny 1982-86* (3 years)	1 (6 yrs.)	2	Working
Sarah Bell	33	Jamaica	Domestic 1980-84 (4 years)	3 (8, 5, 4 yrs.)	1	Working
Marjorie Jules	26	Dominica	Domestic/ Nanny 1975-77* (2 years)	1 (7 yrs.)	3	Stay-at-home

*Indicates permanent residency through marriage

Table 1: Participants' Background Characteristics

9.

Mediating the Mommy Wars in Contemporary Germany

VALERIE HEFFERNAN

INTRODUCTION

In a *New York Times* article published in 2006, appropriately entitled: "Chick Lit: The Sequel", columnist Lizzie Skurnick drew attention to a new phenomenon in popular fiction for women. Skurnick pointed out that many of the best-loved and most widely-read authors of chick lit had grown up and graduated to a new kind of women's fiction popularly referred to as 'mommy lit'. Helen Fielding's romantic heroine Bridget Jones had just given birth to a son in the British newspaper *The Independent*; the protagonist of Sophie Kinsella's bestselling shopaholic series was all set to reappear on bookshelves in *Shopaholic and Baby* (2007); and other big names from the chick lit Hall of Fame, including Jennifer Weiner, Jane Green and even *Sex and the City*-creator Candice Bushnell had all apparently decided that motherhood was cool. It was time for their heroines to 'settle [...] down with Mr Right and swap [...] their stilettos for Bugaboo strollers'. Accordingly, Skurnick summarizes the new heroine of popular women's fiction as follows: 'Mom lit's prevailing aesthetic is Carrie Bradshaw, with a carriage' (Skurnick 2006).

It is interesting to note that these authors, many of whom used to write about sisters and best friends, have taken to writing about mothers; it suggests a trajectory through their own lives and possibly also those of their readers. At any rate, mommy lit has begun to play an important role in popular perceptions of contemporary motherhood. In bookshops, mommy-lit is often shelved next to parenting manuals, and as Heather Hewitt points out in her analysis of the emerging genre, it can often offer more guidance and comfort to the new mother than they can (2006: 120). Contemporary mommy lit is popular because it reflects the balancing act that defines many women's lives: the difficulty of combining a career and motherhood and of doing both reasonably well; the impossibility of living up to a media-conceived and media-fuelled ideal of what makes a good mother; and the difficulty of hanging on to some sense of one's own identity in the process.

Opinions are divided on whether mommy lit is a step forward for women's writing. While Kate Arosteguy praises mommy lit for providing "a lens through which we can study the intense anxiety that contemporary pressures of motherhood produce in women" (2010: 409), other critics have raised questions about the extent to which mommy lit can actually help mothers to deal with those pressures. In her analysis of Alison Pearson's bestseller *I Don't Know How She Does It* (2002), for example – a novel which incidentally was made into a movie in 2011, starring, ironically, Sarah Jessica Parker of *Sex and the City* fame, who is now herself a mother of three – Heather Hewitt points out that though Pearson's novel 'effectively mirrors the anxieties many middle-class women experience surrounding motherhood, [...] it does not provide any answers or get us closer to thinking about work and family in new ways' (2006: 130). It might even be argued that mommy lit exacerbates those anxieties by caricaturing new mothers and making light of their genuine struggles. And yet, the popularity of the genre among its target audience would suggest that that is not how it is read.

This chapter seeks to look more closely at the emerging genre of mommy lit and to interrogate the question of where it fits in, how it relates to contemporary anxieties about motherhood and what it can say and do for mothers. Focussing its attention on German author Kerstin Gier's bestselling *Mütter-Mafia-Trilogie* and its place within the German popular fiction market, it will consider in particular how mommy lit both enacts and subverts media-driven debates about motherhood. A key question that it will seek to answer is whether mommy lit can represent a subversive space that allows us to contemplate other ways of looking at motherhood and alternative strategies for coping with the anxieties associated with it.

'MOMMY LIT' IN GERMANY

Given the omnipresence in the German media landscape of debates about motherhood, it is surprising that mommy lit has not made a bigger impression on the popular fiction market. The media obsession with motherhood is rooted in the worryingly low birth rates in the country; since the early 1990s, Germany's birth rate has hovered around a total fertility rate of 1.3, a rate that implies a halving of the stable population every 45 years (Kohler et al. 2002: 642). Researchers, policy makers and media pundits alike have sought to understand the reasons why Germans are not having babies, and it is not unusual for them to refer to the correlation between the low birth rate and the high level of female employment in Germany. In an attempt to encourage German men and women to produce more children and stay home to raise them, the German government has sought to make family-friendly policies a priority. Between 2007 and 2013, the conservative Christian Democratic Union party, spearheaded by the former Minister for Family Affairs, Ursula von der Leyen, introduced a number of new initiatives to improve parental leave, to increase financial support for new parents and to broaden access to state-sponsored childcare. Although these measures have improved the situation for stay-at-home mothers significantly, they have not as yet had their desired impact on the low birth rates in Germany.

Legislation in the political arena has been matched by a large volume of popular and critical publications on the topic of demography more generally and motherhood and feminism in particular. Two of the more divisive contributions to the debate came in 2006 and 2007, with the publication of Eva Herman's bestselling *Das Eva-Prinzip* [The Eve/Eva Principle] and Alice Schwarzer's *Die Antwort* [The Answer]. Herman's book, labeled anti-feminist by the media, laid the blame for the decline of the German population and the dissolution of the nuclear family in Germany squarely at the feet of working women. The book's subtitle, 'For a new femininity', highlights its call to German women to remember their femininity and return to a traditional family structure, focusing on looking after the home and raising children. Within a year of its publication, well-known German feminist and public figure Alice Schwarzer responded to Herman's claims with a book in which she advocated that men are just as capable of looking after children as women. Unsurprisingly, both books provoked controversy and debate across the media and amongst all strata of the German population. The fact that both also spent weeks on the bestseller list indicates the divided views amongst the German public on this contentious issue.

Despite this widespread interest in mothers, mothering and motherhood, mommy lit has not yet had the same impact on the German literary market as it has in other countries. Popular writer Kerstin Gier, however, is an exception to this rule; Gier is a prime example of the kind of chick-lit-turned-mommy-lit novelist that Skurnick refers to in her article. She began writing in 1995 and now has a long list of popular bestsellers. Virtually all of her novels – and there are over twenty, some published under pseudonyms – have had high sales figures, establishing Gier as one of the foremost writers of women's popular fiction in contemporary Germany. The three volumes of her *Mütter-Mafia* [mother mafia] trilogy were published in 2005, 2006 and 2009 respectively, and between them, they have sold over a million copies.

Gier's mother mafia trilogy tells the story of Constanze, who at the beginning of the first novel is a 35-year old mother of two whose lawyer husband Lorenz has decided after 15 years of marriage to replace her with a younger model. While Lorenz stays on in the family's trendy loft apartment in the city, he sends Constanze and the children to live in the suburban house of his recently-deceased mother. The move to the suburbs brings Constanze into contact with the Mother Society, a group of mothers living in the housing estate where Constanze's new home is located. This elitist group, which comprises both high-powered working mothers and even more high-powered stay-at-home mothers, rules the roost in the residential area. The Mother Society is very protective of its territory and very choosy about who it invites into the group and who is excluded from membership. Constanze is intimidated and ultimately repulsed by these über-mothers, who seem to care more about appearance than the realities of mothering. Despite her initial shock at Lorenz's betrayal and some initial difficulties adjusting to her new circumstances, Constanze soon finds her feet, a new set of friends, and even a love interest in the shape of her divorce lawyer, the gorgeous Anton.

At first glance, Kerstin Gier's novels do not seem to offer much more than a distraction and a bit of comic relief from the trials and tribulations of motherhood. However, I would argue that they feed into debates about the meaning of motherhood in contemporary German society in important ways. As the following analysis will show, Gier's popular mother mafia trilogy both enacts and subverts media-driven debates about motherhood in Germany.

CHARACTERS, CARICATURES AND CLICHÉS OF MOTHERS

The various mothers in Gier's mother mafia novels are one-dimensional caricatures who are more notable for their entertainment value than for their psychological depth. Constanze, for example, is clearly an exaggerated representation of a stay-at-home mother: She fell pregnant with her first child while still at university, and she was quite content to give up her studies and her chance of a career to stay home and care for her child. For 14 years, she has been a full-time wife and mother; thus, her confidence and self-perception are closely linked to this role. Constanze's friend and neighbor Mimi, on the other hand, is representative of many contemporary would-be mothers, who, having spent their twenties focusing on their studies and their thirties focusing on their careers, suddenly find when they decide to have children that nature is no longer willing to play ball. 'It just won't work', Mimi sobs. 'Although I'm not stressed any more, it just won't work! I'm not used to that: I'm famous for the fact that my plans always work out. But this just isn't working out!' (Gier 2005: 96). On the other side of the divide is Sabine, the bitchy, hard-nosed working mother who heads up the Mother Society. Sabine is the stereotypical absentee mother whose commitment to her job means that her two children see far more of their Eastern European nanny than they do of her; notably, Sabine goes to great pains to justify her life choices by undermining everyone else's. And then there is Mama Gitti, the token single mother in the Mother Society. Gitti is caricatured throughout the trilogy as silly, naïve and generally a little bit flaky; she doesn't have a full-time job, but tries to make some extra money by convincing the other mothers in the Mother Society to sign their children up for her arts and crafts classes. The other mothers make no effort to hide the fact that they only tolerate her out of sympathy for her circumstances, and their general attitude towards her is one of disdain and mild annoyance.

These are only a few of the assortment of mother-figures presented in Gier's novels, and it is evident even from those mentioned here that they are all based on stereotypes that have become common currency in media-driven discussions about contemporary mothers. In the introduction to her book *Mediating Moms*, Elizabeth Podnieks offers an overview of just a few of the overwhelming array of images of motherhood that confront us:

> They [moms] are alpha, beta, slacker, slummy, and yummy, as well as being martyr mommies and sanctomomies; they are summed up in acronyms like MILF (Mothers I'd Like

> to Fuck), SMUMs (Smart, Middle-Class, Uninvolved Mothers), SCAMs (Smart, Child-Centered, Active Moms), SMCs (Single Mothers by Choice), and WAHMs (Work at Home Moms). (2012b: 4)

A glance at the German media landscape confirms that it too has a tendency to classify mothers according to stereotypes. For example, a 2009 study carried out by the Germany's future institute, the Zukunftsinstitut, analyzed lifestyle trends amongst mothers in Germany today and found that nine distinct 'types of mothers' emerged. These included the predictable Professional Mom, but also "new" types such as the Pippi-Longstocking-Mother, the Latte-Macchiato-Mother and the Mommaddy (Horx 2009: 24).

On the one hand, the fictional world of the mother mafia trilogy can serve as a lens through which to view the anxieties that underlie contemporary visions of motherhood in Germany. Constanze's plight, for example, and her struggles to regain her financial and emotional stability after her husband leaves her may cause us to reflect on the vulnerable position that many full-time mothers find themselves in. Similarly, Gitti's precarious financial situation and her dependence on her parents for help with her daughter may well represent the reality of life for many single mothers who do not receive support from the fathers of their children. Furthermore, Mimi's miscarriage and her struggle with infertility across the three novels no doubt strike a chord with many contemporary readers.

On the other, the overt stylization and caricaturing of the mothers in the novels undermines any possibility that the reader might identify with them or take them as genuine reflections of "real" mothers. Rather, they are obviously reflections of stereotypes of mothers similar to those propagated by the media. The fact that they are so obviously caricatures, distorted representations that bear little or no relation to the lived reality of mothers' lives, offers the writer and her readers space to poke fun at them. Thus, the very one-dimensionality of the mothers depicted in Gier's novels in fact enables the subversion of these stereotypes.

CHALLENGING THE MOMMY FORUM

Current theoretical literature on contemporary motherhood activism highlights the enormous importance of online networks and support communities. As Elizabeth Podnieks notes, 'mothers have taken to blogging auto/biographical narratives to a staggering degree, with personal blogs complementing and often accompanying networking sites' (2012b: 4). Modern-day mommy blogs and online forums that claim to offer women advice and companionship have replaced the community of female family members and female friends that, according to nostalgic accounts of time past, used to rally round the new mother. As Rachel Cusk remarks, 'In those days, the story goes, mothers were told what to do by their mothers … Like the great library of Alexandria, a world of knowledge has gone up in flames' (2004: 117-8). For the new mother in particular, but also for the more experienced mother, online communities can offer support and assistance, a chance to share experiences and learn what worked for others in a similar situation. Moreover, online forums such as those offered by Babycenter.com, EUMom.com and others are often divided into sub-forums – 'moms of preemies', 'toddler moms', 'TTC', and so on, making it even easier for browsers to connect with other moms who are dealing with similar issues. Certainly, the simplicity of being able to get a rapid answer to any question, as well as the temporary relief offered through the feeling that we are not alone in this, have no doubt contributed to the popularity of online forums.

This is not to suggest that online communities and forums are always a positive influence. In fact, the possibility of being able to compare her child's progress, to evaluate how her child measures up to others of a similar age, can often cause anxiety for the mother who would otherwise have gone on with her life in blissful ignorance. In addition, quarrels can often break out between mothers who have opted for different choices in matters of, for example, breast or bottle feeding, home birth versus hospital birth and so on. The competition between mothers that seems an integral part of contemporary mothering can often be exacerbated when mothers take to the internet.

The mommy forum of the Mother Society is a case in point. The group claims to represent "a network of joyful, open and tolerant women" and proclaims: "Here, we talk about topics of relevance to the modern woman and mother and support each other with love" (Gier 2005: 7). The mommy forum is actually an integral part of the text, and the chapters of all three novels are interspersed with excerpts from the Mother Society's forum. The mothers' posts to one another on the forum comment on the events in the narrative and offer an insight into how the other mothers view Constanze and her situation. However, alongside this, their posts reveal the rivalry and antagonism within the group, and we see plenty of snide comments and examples of subtle one-upmanship. This particular forum is clearly driven more by competition than by support.

What is noteworthy, however, is that the language of the Mother Society's forum mirrors the language of many online forums. It might be argued that Gier uses her novels as a vehicle to pose a challenge to the mommy forum and the assumption of its cultural value. Sure, the mothers in this group are a especially insidious bunch, and in line with the caricaturing of the mothers, their website is exaggerated and ridiculous. However, as the following section will show, Gier's novels privilege a more tradition type of bond amongst women that, I argue, reveals the synthetic quality of many online forums.

BAND OF MOTHERS

In the black and white mediated images of mothers, there is a line drawn in the sand between those mothers who choose to go back to work – and the question of the extent to which this actually constitutes a choice is seldom debated – and those that opt to give up work, either temporarily or permanently, and stay home to devote themselves to the business of raising children. This dissection of all mothers into two neat categories is particularly popular in the media; talk shows in particular are very fond of pitting the stay-at-home mothers against the working mothers, each group sitting on opposite sides of the TV studio, and watching them fight over the issue of which group make the better moms. Miriam Peskowitz, author of *The Truth Behind the Mommy Wars* takes issue with this neat division of women into two categories:

> Nowadays, all over the media it's the Mommy Wars: Mothers are either working full-time and are uninvolved, absentee parents, or full-time homemakers, non-intellectual, hovering, and provincial. In the Mommy Wars version of motherhood, the women in each group have nothing in common with the women in the other; they share no values. Instead, battles rage. (2005: 20)

As Peskowitz is keen to point out, mothers today often belong to neither group; they work part-time or full-time or stay home part-time or full-time at various junctures of their lives, and their decisions are often made for them by their financial situation or their families' needs at any given time.

> Far from helping us understand the social and political stakes of motherhood, the media's Mommy Wars obscure the issues facing us. They transform parenting into a style war. [...] They prevent mothers from feeling empathy for each other. They diminish the parent problem by expressing it in the trivial terms of catfights. (2005: 6)

The division between mothers that is so present in the media has moreover made its way into literature. In time with the increased pressure on mothers to parent their children excessively, a trend identified by Susan Douglas and Meredith Michaels as the 'new momism' (2004: 4), Imelda Whelehan argues that the antagonism between mothers is more evident in contemporary mommy lit than in previous incarnations of the genre. Comparing it for example to mommy lit from the 1970s, where mothers banded together to form a collective, she finds that, 'The mothers of contemporary mum lit are depicted as oppressed by their peers – other moms who seem to be succeeding where they fail' (Whelehan 2012: 149-50).

This oppression by one's peers, fuelled by competition between mothers, is also given exaggerated expression in Gier's mother mafia novels, both in the criminal imagery behind the titles of the three novels and in the hostile confrontations between the mothers in the Mother Society and those of mother mafia, a group conceived to compete with it. One run-in is described in particularly evocative terms: 'Frauke and Sabine also quickened their pace when they saw us coming. When we pulled up alongside each other, it was a little bit like the chariot race in *Ben Hur*. The only thing that was missing was for us to start snorting and neighing and shaking our manes' (Gier 2005: 297).

However, there is one aspect of the conception of the mother mafia group that is particularly significant and which opens up a space for exploring alternative ways of looking at contemporary mothers and mothering. The decision to form the group is certainly instigated by the idea of creating a counter-group to the Mother Society; however, it is noteworthy that of the four members of the group, only two are actually mothers. 'We're our own Mother Mafia. You and I and Mimi. She'll make a great mother. And your friend Trudi belongs as well, of course. She told me yesterday that's she's already had a bunch of kids in her past lives. The four of us make a really great network!' (Gier 2005: 273). Rather than motherhood per se, the membership of this group is focused on a model of mothering that emphasizes practice rather than status. In other words, to return to a distinction proposed by Adrienne Rich, mothering as practice is understood as separate from motherhood as institution. In proposing an alternative to media-conceived ways of dividing and classifying mothers, Gier's novels refuse to subscribe to their categories and thus take back control of mothering.

CONCLUSION

As emphasized by Heather Hewitt in her analysis of various incarnations of mommy lit since the 1950s, the genre has a long history of irreverent humor that can be linked to subversive attempts to rewrite the script of motherhood. As this chapter has shown, Kerstin Gier's novels continue that tradition. To return to Hewitt's assertion that '[mommy lit] does not provide any answers or get us closer to thinking about work and family in new ways' (2006: 130), one might argue that it can offer a space for the subversion of cultural and media-driven images of mothers. In laughing at the absurdity of the stereotypes and divisions that pervade cultural visions of mothering, our laughter represents a challenge to those norms.

REFERENCES

Arosteguy, Kate 2010 "The Politics of Race, Class, and Sexuality." *Contemporary American Mommy Lit. Women's Studies* 39: 409-29.

Cusk, Rachel 2008 *A Life's Work: On Becoming a Mother*. London: Faber & Faber.

Douglas, Susan, and Meredith Michaels 2004 *The Mommy Myth: The Idealization of Motherhood and How It Has Undermined Women*. New York: Free Press.

Ferris, Suzanne, and Mallory Young, eds. 2006 *Chick Lit: The New Woman's Fiction*. New York: Routledge.

Gier, Kerstin 2005 *Die Mütter-Mafia*. Cologne: Bastei-Lübbe. 2006 *Die Patin*. Cologne: Bastei-Lübbe. 2009 *Gegensätze ziehen sich aus*. Cologne: Bastei-Lübbe.

Herman, Eva 2006 *Das Eva-Prinzip. Für eine neue Weiblichkeit.* Munich/Zurich: Pendo.

Hewitt, Heather 2006 "You Are Not Alone: The Personal, the Political, and the 'New' Mommy Lit." In *Chick Lit: The New Woman's Fiction*. Suzanne Ferris and Mallory Young, eds. Pp. 119-39. New York: Routledge.

Horx, Matthias 2009 *Modern Moms – Lebenswelten zwischen Kindern, Karriere und Konsum. Fanta- Trendstudie.* Kelkheim: Zukunftsinstitut.

Kohler, Hans-Peter, Francesco C. Billari, and José Antonio Ortega 2002 "The Emergence of Lowest-Low Fertility in Europe During the 1990s." *Population and Development Review* 28(4): 641-680.

Peskowitz, Miriam 2005 *The Truth Behind the Mommy Wars. Who Decides What Makes a Good Mother?* Emeryville, CA: Seal.

Podnieks, Elizabeth 2012 *Mediating Moms: Mothers in Popular Culture.* Montreal: McGill-Queen's.

Schwarzer, Alice 2007 *Die Antwort.* Cologne: Kiepenheuer & Witsch.

Skurnick, Lizzie 2006 "Chick Lit, the Sequel: Yummy Mummy." *The New York Times*, 17 December. University Press. 2012b "Introduction: Popular Culture's Maternal Embrace." In *Mediating Moms. Mothers in Popular Culture.* Elizabeth Podnieks, ed. Pp. 3-32. Montreal: McGill-Queen's University Press.

Whelehan, Imelda 2012 "'Shit and String Beans.' Boredom and Babies. Bad Mothers in Popular Fiction since 1968." In *Mediating Moms. Mothers in Popular Culture.* Elizabeth Podnieks, ed. Pp. 147-66. Montreal: McGill-Queen's University Press.

10.

Integrating Choices

'Being There for My Children' and 'Being a Citizen Worker': Irish Survey on Stay-at-Home Mothers

NOELIA MOLINA

INTRODUCTION

> The feminine mystique permits, even encourages, women to ignore the question of their identity (Friedan 1963, 53)

Half a century after the groundbreaking publication of *The Feminine Mystique* it is important to re-consider discourses that surround stay-at-home mothers in the twenty-first century. Today, women who intentionally embrace domestic life as a fulltime option, function with motivations, feelings, challenges and choices that are deeply rooted in the social, cultural, economic and political fabric of contemporary society. A feminist perspective/approach will be applied throughout this paper with the aim of establishing the mutation, evolution or decline of the feminine mystique.

BACKGROUND AND METHODS

This study surveyed 100 stay-at-home mothers in Dublin, the capital city of Ireland. These mothers are over 18 years of age, Irish residents and from a middle-class socioeconomic background. The survey was available online in stay-at-home mums' forums and parenting organizations. It used twelve questions with five to nine parts each to better elucidate on what grounds these mothers are making the decision to stay at home. The various themes behind the decisions to stay at home are: number of children and their age, sources of income, reasons or influences for staying at home, plans to return to paid work and their feelings, and beliefs about the choice to stay at home. Empirical data analysis was carried out using SPSS. Descriptive analysis was performed, and frequency and percentages were obtained showing the statistical trends in demographic variables.

Ireland is an exceptional country with the high birth rate. *The Irish Perinatal Statistics Report* (IPSR 2011)[1] reported Ireland's birth rate is 2.03, the highest total fertility rate of the 27 European Union countries. Global patterns of total fertility rates in the developed and developing world today show 2.1 as the upper limit and 1.1 as the lower limit. Much of Europe is located in the middle or lower half of that range. Ireland's birth rate has always been closer to that of the United States, Canada and New Zealand, which are located in the upper end (Fahey 2001:176). Another important figure in the IPSR (2011) is that women aged between 30 and 34 years had the highest number of babies. Some 3,673 babies were born to Irish mothers aged 40 years and over in 2010. The average age of Irish women giving birth was 31.5 years, up from 30.3 years in 2001.

In this survey, the majority of women (70 percent) were 35 plus years old and married/cohabiting (91 percent). Forty percent of women had one child, with almost thirty percent reporting two children, twenty percent reporting three children and the rest reporting four to seven children. The majority of women have at least one or two children in the 3-6 years category, with almost seventy percent of women caring for pre-school children. The participants are well educated with fifty percent holding a degree and forty percent have finished postgraduate education at a Master and PhD level. The source of income for the majority at eighty-seven percent is their partner's salary with ten percent receiving State benefits as their main income.

This profile is consistent with the maternal literature. Having fewer financial constraints, middle-class women tend to wait to have children until they have achieved the 'right relationship, career and personal sense of self' (MacMahon 1995:91). This social and demographic trend is well developed in the Western world with white middle-class women delaying motherhood and obtaining a good level of education and career profile. The ability of women to control when and by what means they will become pregnant is all part of this social change (Morgan 1996; Wu and MacNeill 2002; Becker

2000). Unique to this phenomenon is that an increasing number of women nearing the end of their reproductive cycle are resorting to assisted reproductive technologies (Friese et al 2008).

The findings show that mothers spend around ten years in unpaid caring work though as the number of children increases so too does the length of time. The main reasons for staying at home are a 'duty to care' for young pre-schoolers. There is an ideology of 'need for the mother' in those years in the responses of the participants, exposing intense feelings of maternal separation anxiety. The majority of the women in this survey had put their career on hold and planned to return part-time to the labor force. These mothers wish to achieve a balance between work and family. The results are compared with the different efforts of Irish governments in reconciling work and family with the current European Union (EU) equality legislation.

WOMEN AS 'CITIZEN WORKERS': HOLDING AMBIVALENCE BETWEEN TWO SPHERES.

There have been substantial changes in Irish legislation in the past thirty years. A wife's income used to be her husband's for taxation purposes and women did not have entitlements to unemployment benefits. A man was expected to provide for her (See Scannell 1988). In 1973, the Marriage bar was abolished, enabling women to work after being married. After that, *The Maternity Protection Act* (1988) protected employees expecting babies (Reynolds and Healy 2008).

Therefore, the male breadwinner model in Ireland was insured in welfare and tax provision and the Irish Constitution drawn up in 1937 valued the role of women in the home: "The State shall therefore endeavour to ensure that mothers shall not be obliged by economic necessity to engage in labour to the neglect of their duties in the home." (Article 41.1.2). Since then, there has been an appeal for the government to call a referendum to amend the Constitution and refer to the 'parent in the home' instead of the 'mother'. The Irish government is embracing the new European agenda for a new vision of the 'European social model' by building 'an active welfare state'.

Work and family reconciliation have been on the agenda of social policies in the European community since the 1957 Treaty of Rome. Recently, the Lisbon European Council statement, issued in 2000, aimed for 60 per cent of women in paid employment by 2010 (Council 2000a:2)[2]

This model is based on the 'adult worker identity', and a 'new constellation of work-and-welfare variables' (Goodin 2001:39). The obligation of every citizen is to be in paid work. This has created a whole re-structuring of work and welfare relationship in a gender neutral language.

As a consequence, women as well as men are 'citizen workers' (Lewis 2002; Lewis and Giullari 2005). Women are an untapped labor reserve. The 60% goal was adopted as the best measure to ensure higher female labor market participation. The aim was to create a competitive tax base of the European social insurance welfare states (Ferrera et al 2000; Esping Andersen 2001). The Irish Government is committed to achieving this model of independence and self-sufficiency for all individuals in the labor market (Coakley 2005:6).

Feminist researchers have argued that this model narrows conceptualizing gender equality in the labor market only. They have pointed out that the unequal gender divisions in the family are not addressed (Hoskyns 2000; Woodward 2003; Walby 2001) and that the work/family relationship is often 'fitted' into the business case of gender quality (Dex 2003) and into a 'malestream' as most concepts in the labor market are based on male working patterns (Russell and Gannon 2002).

The economic development of Western Europe changed radically during the Enlightenment and the Industrial Revolution. The general European consensus was that a new era was created on what they called individuality, personal freedom, citizenship, intrinsic uniqueness and a sense of responsibility for one's self (Simmel 1913). Working patterns radically changed after that. There was growing reliance on formal markets and a change in production toward the factory system (Mokyr 2007).

The Spanish philosopher, Celia Amoros developed a philosophical feminism in which she clearly stated that: "Men have captured the entire significance of the generic human values since the Enlightment" and that women, instead of "embracing those generic human values", are 'fit into' the male (Amoros 1992). The conceptualization of equality for women is not about 'becoming equal to men' in a 'rationalized male market'. This public endorsement of the 'adult worker model' for the family is not replaced by new gender models (Pascall and Lewis 2004). Women are left holding this economical and cultural ambivalence of society unaided. On the one hand, they are urged to be 'citizen workers' in these 'active welfare states' and on the other hand, they are expected to carry the 'private caring work' unequally. Since the Industrial Revolution, a cultural model of a rationalized market society coexists in tension with the cultural model of intensive motherhood (Hays 1996:97).

In Ireland, stay-at-home mothers are highly valued and yet mothers are under pressure to be employed full-time (Daly 2004:38). It has been argued that if paid work is a citizenship obligation, then unpaid work, voluntary, community or caring work is devalued (Lister 2002). Unpaid family care is still the dominant form of childcare in Ireland (DJELR 2003).[3]

A recent book: *Mother Ireland: Why Ireland hates motherhood* criticized what the author called: 'the ideological war' in Irish society that is about how children are to be reared and the complete maximization for both parents to be in full-time work when the majority of Irish parents believe that ideal childcare is carried out by parents in the home (White 2010:72).

There are two mixed, polarized messages given in Ireland about the value of staying at home and yet the importance of being employed outside the home. This illustrates the dilemma feminists have called attention to about the paradoxical place of women in the fabric of society.

Motherhood, as an enforced identity and a political and economic institution, is described clearly in the literature (Rich 1976). Maternal writings have consistently addressed the issue of how work/family policies are represented by normative assumptions regarding gender order and gender differences (Mazey 2000; Bacchi 2004). These gender institutionalized features of the family structure and social relations of reproduction will therefore be perpetuated by the generation that follows (Chodorow 1978).

REASONS AND INFLUENCES FOR STAYING AT HOME

The duty to care: "Staying at home is fulfilling and makes me a happy mother"[4]

Forty percent of the participants chose fulfillment and happiness as a reason for being at home. This answer is intrinsically related to the 'duty to care' for the family. Women who stay at home do not inhabit the dichotomy of two spaces: the work and the maternal. They are not in this struggle as they devote all their work and space to children's needs. They have made this decision according to their cultural, financial, political and economic context. The relationship between autonomy, individualism and choice is a complex one. These mothers have made the choice to be mostly engaged in the maternal space and feel 'happy' in relation to their ethic of care (Miller 2012).

Mothers are directed by an ethic of care as much as, or more than, an ethic of work or self-development (Williams 2004). This duty of care originally was proposed as an integral component of women's moral development (Gilligan 1982). The relationship between gender, power, care and ethics is an intricate and multi-faceted issue. Writings in feminist ethics have argued that this duty of care relied on a mythical image of 'woman' and a 'motherly metaphor'. It has been proposed that this duty of care is the extension of un-chosen and conflicting moral obligations (Mendus 1993). Such obligations have persisted for too long in moral texts and failed to realize the diversity of experiences of real-life mothers (Sevenhuijsen 1998).

When mothers are in the public domain, they are seen as one-dimensional, either as careers or earners (Kennedy 2002). There is no integration between the public and the private as mothers are not permitted to bring the maternal into the public space or the public into the maternal space. How the family should carry out its caring tasks is embedded in the dominant family model around the socio-cultural constructions of gender relations (Pfau-Effinger 2004).

> 'I put my children's needs first'; 'I want to have a strong bond with my children'; 'Nobody will do this work better than me'.[5]

Forty percent of the participants chose one of the reasons above. They are related to children's needs. Mothers seem to feel primarily responsible for the well-being (emotional, physical and spiritual) of children. Women's responsibility for their parenting is consistent and unchangeable in that mothers remain the primary careers of children. Among the six countries in the United Nations Research Institute for Social Development (UNRISD) project, the mean time spent by women on unpaid care work is more than twice the mean time spent by men (Razavi 2008). A comparative study of 400 men and women with dependent children in Ireland, France, Italy and Denmark on work-life balance issues found out that in all four countries, mothers are in charge of most of the domestic and childcare duties in the home. Only a minority of mothers view themselves as 'primarily workers' in combining motherhood and paid work (Fine-Davis et al 2002).

Intensive mothering is a concept that is well researched in the literature. It has been argued that middle-and upper-middle class mothers are most likely to engage in this to the extreme (Hays 1996:115). The sentiment that paid caregivers can never substitute for the mother is a very common one (Hays 1996:100).

Extensive research has been carried out about these socio-cultural maternal constructions (Miller and Brown 2005; Douglas and Michaels 2004; Petrassi 2012; Choi et al 2005). These discursive research articles argued that although the domestic and caring gendered division still exists, women also engage in a gendered language that perpetuate the meaning of their unequal power relationships.

Many responses in this survey relate to this kind of gendered language. Mothers thought of caring as her domain in the family structure:

> I strongly believe that, where possible, it is important to be at home with my children. I think the children feel the absence of the mother if they work full-time. I could not bear to be parted from my baby.

In having to choose between caring and working in such a polarized manner, one mother puts it like this:

> My husband's work is all-encompassing and if I also work in a high-powered job, there really would be no point in having children.

There is also a sense of ambiguity in women regarding what influences they think affect their decisions. When the mothers were asked about what influenced them to stay at home, thirty-three percent thought they were influenced by their family and partner. Twenty-five percent of the women specified influences as strong feelings of sadness at being separated from their children that interfered with, their value system and philosophy of parenting. An important aspect of this question was the reluctance of the participants to answer it. Forty percent of them did not want to comment on what influenced them to stay at home.

The majority of mothers in this survey (seventy percent) stated that staying at home was the best decision for the family in contrast with the twenty six percent who declared that they do not mind staying at home but they wish they could work outside the home. Only two percent answered that they do not want to stay at home and they wish that they worked outside the home. These decisions are deeply embedded in assumptions about women's lives and maternal capacities (Miller 2005). The gendered constructions of family life do still exist in Ireland and women are faced with tough choices around earning and caring for their families (Daly 2004).

THE PART-TIME UTOPIA

> A mother of three talking about finances and childcare stated: Financially it wouldn't be worth it for me to go to work even if I wanted to.

According to this survey, women tend to leave paid work for a period of five to six years with the first child. This period will be extended with the arrival of the second and third child. In all, these mothers can be out of the workplace for more than ten years and the majority clearly stated that they wish to come back on a part-time basis. These mothers considered their employment decisions linked with their responsibilities to their children. It has been noted in the literature that the EU members face a great challenge to integrate women into this individualized worker model (Hobson 2003).

The reality is that stay-at-home mums surveyed here felt they wanted and needed to care for their children at least until they go to school. After that transition, they still want to combine paid work on a part- time basis with caring for family. Studies corroborate these findings (Duncan 2003; Sevenhuijsen 1998; Dean 2001).

In Ireland, among those who had never given birth, participation peaked at age of 30-34 with a rate of 92.6 percent compared with a participation rate of 73 percent for those of the same age who had given birth. For mothers, rates will consequently decline by age 40-44 years before climbing to 69.2 percent participation at age 45-49 (CSO 2011).[6]

On average 70 percent will enter part-time employment each year and the main reason given was childcare and domestic work (Russell et al 2002:114). Part-time work is highly feminized in that three-quarters of part-timers in Ireland are female. The higher incidence of part-time employment among women contributes to the overall gender wage gap (Barry 2006; McGuiness 2009).

WHAT PRICE IS TO BE PAID FOR BEING OUT OF THE WORKFORCE FOR ABOUT TEN YEARS AND THEN COME BACK ON A PART-TIME BASIS?

Part-time positions are more flexible but low-paid and often insecure. Any professional career will definitely suffer if left on 'stand-by' for that period. Labor market outcomes have revealed women's disadvantages in any career prospects by working part-time (Blossfeld 1997; Duffy 1992; Gornick 1996).

Analysis of the economic activity of part-time workers has revealed invisibility both in the market place and the household. Research has demonstrated that, whereas full-time employment contributes to equality in household work and responsibilities, part-time has no different effect than unpaid work (Stier 2000).

In view of these arguments, part-time is seen as the ideal option to have the best of 'both worlds'. It is important to challenge this notion as this idealization can also contribute to the intensive mothering and the perfectionism that mothers put themselves in.

THE WORLD OF DUALITIES AND THE DESIRE FOR INTEGRATION

Despite many attempts to expose these socio-cultural understandings of gender, intensive mothering has survived feminism's second wave of activism. Feminist researchers pointed out a 'return to the romanticization of motherhood' in third wave feminism (Press 2012). It has been suggested that third wave feminism's fertility and motherhood personal narratives contribute to the mythology of motherhood that second wave feminism tried to destroy. However, third wave feminists, now in their thirties and forties, construct a framework which permits simultaneous critique and embracing of motherhood (Crawford 2011).

This survey reveals that mothers' value time spent with young children but they wish to go back to work after their children are in school. They desire an integration of family and work responsibilities in a non-polarized scheme. They want to combine the public and the private. The participants' views on mothers who work outside the home reveal that wish. Seventy percent stated that they feel admiration of mothers who manage to balance family and work. Most of the participants recognize the difficulty of juggling the multi-dimensional aspects of motherhood.

The National Women's Council of Ireland (NWCI) highlights that women in low-paid, part-time employment are there as the direct consequence of Irish society's failure to value caring, and unfriendly family policies (NWCI 2002, 2003).[7] Many studies show that women in general bear this unpaid caring work and are at a disadvantage in a world that values money (Elson 2005).

CONCLUSION

At the outset I remarked that half a century has passed since the groundbreaking *The Feminine Mystique* was published. In the above essay I have, as promised, re-considered the discourses that surround stay-at-home mothers in the twenty-first century. It seems that stay-at-home motherhood is still embedded in the language of mystique, but today the mystique has deeper cultural and economic challenges than in previous generations. The gender cultural construction around power and the economy construct a system in which it is difficult for women and of course, children and men to have the best life they can.

Societies that support families cannot be only reduced to only issues of childcare or getting women back to work. The needs of the economy undermine not only the values and desires that women have for their lives but the future lives of children.

This survey shows that these women want to combine and balance family and work as an important part of their identity. Once confronted with this dichotomy of motherhood (without cultural or economical support in contemporary society), many mothers are still choosing to sacrifice their careers and stay at home with their young children.

NOTES

[1]For more information about the IPSR see : www.esri.ie.

[2] Lisbon European Council 2000a Towards a Europe of Innovation and Knowledge: Employment, Economic Reform and Social Cohesion. Luxembourg: Office for Official Publications of the European Communities.

[3]DJELR (Department of Justice, Equality and Law Reform).2003. *Developing Childcare in Ireland; a Review of progress to end 2003 on the implementation of the EOCP 2000-2006*.Dublin: DJELR.

[4]This sentence was an option on the survey.

[5]These quotations are options given in the survey.

[6]Central Statistics Office, more information see: http://www.cso.ie/en/index.html.

[7]National Women's Council of Ireland 2002 Valuing Care Work. Dublin: NWCI. National Women's Council of Ireland 2003 A Woman's Model for Social Welfare Reform. Dublin: NWCI.

REFERENCES

Amoros, Celia 1992 "Feminismo, Ilustración y Misoginia Romantica [Feminism, Enlighnment and Romantic Misogyny]." In *Filosofía y Género [Philosophy and Gender]*. Fina Birules, ed. Pamplona: Pamiela Publishing.

Bacchi, Carol Lee 2004 "Policy." In *A Companion to Gender Studies.* Philomena Essed, David Goldberg and Audrey Koboyashi, eds. Pp. 181-191. London: Blackwell.

Barry, Ursula 2006 "Gender Pay Gap in Ireland." *UCD School of Social Justice Working Papers Series* 6(1): 1-34.

Becker, Gay, Anneliese Butler, and Robert Nachtigall 2005 "Resemblance Talk: A Challenge for Parents Whose Children Were Conceived with Donor Gametes." *The US Social Science and Medicine* 61(6): 1300 - 1309.

Blossfeld, Hans-Peter, and Catherine Hakim 1997 *Between Equalization and Marginalization: Women Working Part-time in Europe and the United States of America.* Oxford: Oxford University Press.

Chodorow, Nancy 1999 *The Reproduction of Mothering: Psychoanalysis and the Sociology of Gender.* Berkeley: University of California Press.

Choi, Precilla, Carole Henshaw, Sarah Baker and Joanne Tree 2005 "Supermum, Superwife, Supereverything: Performing Femininity in the Transition to Motherhood." *Journal of Reproductive and Infant Psychology* 23: 167-180.

Coakley, Anne 2005 *Mothers, Welfare and Labour Market Activation.* Dublin: Combat Poverty Agency.

Crawford, Bridget 2011 "Third-wave Feminism, Motherhood and the Future of Feminist Legal Theory." In *Gender, Sexualities and Law.* Jackie Jones, Anna Groer, Anne Fenton and Kim Stevenson, eds. New York: Routledge.

Daly, Mary 2004 *Families, and Family Life in Ireland; Challenges for the Future. Report of Public Consultation Fora,* by Mary Daly. Dublin: Dept. of Social and Family Affairs.

Dean, Hartley 2001 "Working Parenthood and Parental Obligation." *Critical Social Policy* 21:3.

Dex, Shirley 2003 *Families and Work in the Twentieth-First Century.* York: Policy Press.

Douglas Susan, and Meredith Michaels 2004 *The Mommy Myth: The Ide-*

alization of Motherhood and How it has Undermined All Women. New York: Free Press.

Duffy, Anne and Morene Pupo 1992 *The Part-time Paradox: Connecting Gender, Work and Family.* Toronto: McClelland & Stewart Inc.

Duncan, Simon, Edward Reynolds and Pam Alldred 2003 "Motherhood, Paid Work and Partnering; Values and Theories." *Work, Employment and Society* 17(2): 309-330.

Elson, Diane 2005 "Unpaid Work, the Millennium Development Goals, and Capital Accumulation." Paper presented at the *Conference on Unpaid Work and the Economy: Gender, Poverty and the Millennium Development Goals.* Levy Institute of Economics. Annandale-on- Hudson, New York.

Esping-Andersen, Gosta 2001 "A Welfare State for the 21st Century.' In *The Global Third Way Debate.* Anthony Giddens, ed. Pp. 134-156. Oxford: Polity Press.

Fahey, Tony 2011 "Trends in Irish Fertility Rates in Comparative Perspective." *The Economic and Social Review*32(2): 153-180.

Ferrera, Maurizio, Anton Hemerijck and Martin Rhodes 2000 *The Future of Social Europe. Recasting Work and Welfare in the New Economy.* Lisboa: Celta Editora.

Fine-Davis, Margaret, Jeanne Fagnani, Dino Giovannini and Lis Hojgaard 2004 *Fathers and Mothers: Dilemmas of the Work-Life Balance - A Comparative Study in Four European Countries.* London: Academic Publishers.

Friedan, Betty 1963 *The Feminine Mystique.* New York: Norton.

Friese, Carrie, Gay Becker, and Robert Nachtigall 2008 "Older Motherhood and the Changing Life Course in the Era of Assisted Reproductive Technologies." *Journal of Aging Studies* 22: 65–73.

Gilligan, Carol 1982 *In a Different Voice: Psychological Theory and Women's Development.* Cambridge: Harvard University Press.

Goodin, Robert 2001 "The New Social Question: Rethinking the Welfare State." *Economics and Philosophy* 17(1): 121-145.

Gornick, Janet and Jerry Jacobs 1998 "Gender, The Welfare State, and Public Employment: A Comparative Study of Seven Industrialized Countries." *American Sociological Review* 63(5): 688-710.

Hays, Sharon 1996 *The Cultural Contradictions of Motherhood.* New Haven: Yale University Press.

Hobson, Barbara 2003 "The Individualised Worker, the Gender Participatory and the Gender Equity Models in Sweden." *Social Policy and Society* 3:1.

Hoskyns, Catherine 2000 "A Study of Four Action Programmes on Equal Opportunities." In *Gender Policies in the European Union.* Marigrazia Rossilli, ed. Pp. 43-59. New York: Peter Lang Publishing.

Kennedy, Patricia 2002 *Motherhood in Ireland.* Cork: Mercier Press.

Lewis, Jane, and Susanna Giullari 2005 "The Adult Worker Model Family, Gender Equality and Care: The Search for New Policy Principles and the Possibilities and Problems of a Capabilities Approach." *Economy and Society* 34 (1): 76-104.

Lewis, Jane 2002 "Gender and Welfare State Change." *European Societies* 4(4): 331-357.

Lister, Ruth 2002 "Citizenship and Changing Welfare States." In *Changing Labour Markets, Welfare Policies and Citizenship.* Per Jenson and Jorgen Goul Andersen, eds. Bristol: The Policy Press.

MacMahon, Martha 1995 *Engendering Motherhood: Identity and Self-Transformation in Women's Lives.* New York: Guilford Press.

Mazey, Sonya 2000 "Women, Power and Public Policy in Europe." *Journal of European Public Policy* 7(3): 149.

McGuinness, Seamus, Elish Kelly, Tim Callan and Philip O'Connell 2009 *The Gender Wage Gap in Ireland: Evidence from the National Employment Survey* 2003. The Equality Authority and the Economic and Social Research Institute, Dublin.

Mendus, Susan. 1993 "Different Voices, Still Lives: Problems in the Ethics of Care." *Journal of Applied Philosophy* 10(1): 17-27.

Miller, Dorothy and Wendy Brown 2005 "Determinants of Active Leisure for Women with Young Children an 'Ethic of Care' Prevails." *Leisure Sciences* 27: 405-420.

Miller, Tina 2005 *Making Sense of Motherhood: A Narrative Approach.* Cambridge: Cambridge University Press.

Miller, Tina 2012 "The Narration of 'Choices' around Returning to Work after Becoming a Mother." Paper presented at *Motherhood in Post-1968 European Literature Network: Mothering and Work: Employment Trends and Rights.* Institute of Germanic and Romances Studies, London, October 26.

Mokyr, Joel 2007 "The European Enlightenment, the Industrial Revolution and Modern Economic Growth?" Paper presented at Max Weber Lecture, European University, Florence. March 27.

Morgan, Philip 1996 "Characteristic Features of Modern American Fertility." *Population and Development Review* 22: 19 - 63.

Pascall, Gillian and Jane Lewis 2004 "Emerging Gender Regimes and Policies for Gender Equality in a Wider Europe." *Journal of Social Politics* 11(3): 373-394.

Petrassi, Daniela 2012 "For Me, the Children Come First: A Discursive Psychological Analysis of how Mothers Construct Fathers' Roles in Childrearing and Childcare." *Feminism & Psychology* 22: 518-527.

Pfau-Effinger, Birgit 2004 Development of Culture, Welfare States and Women's Employment in Europe. Aldershot: Ashgate.

Press, Andrea 2012 "The Price of Motherhood: Feminism and Cultural Bias." *Communication, Culture & Critique* 5: 120–125.

Razavi, Shahraand and Silke Staab 2008 *The Social and Political Economy of Care: Contesting Gender and Class Inequalities.* United Nations Research Institute for Social Development (UNRISD) Division for the Advancement of Women Department of Economic and Social Affairs United Nations, New York.

Reynolds, Brigid and Sean Healy 2008 *Making Choices-Choosing Futures: Ireland at a Crossroads.* Dublin: CORI Justice.

Rich, Adrienne 1995 *Of Woman Born: Motherhood as Experience and Institution.* New York: Norton.

Russell, Helen, Dorothy Smyth, Maureen Lyons and Philip O'Connell 2002 *Getting out of the House: Women Returning to Employment, Education and Training.* Dublin: Liffey Press.

Russell, Helen, and Brenda Gannon 2002 "The Male/Female Wage Gap in Ireland." In *Impact Evaluation of the European Employment Strategy in Ireland. Department of Enterprise, Trade and Employment,* ed. Pp. 61-79. Dublin.

Scannell, Yvonne 1988 "The Constitution and the Role of Women." In *De Valera's Constitution and Ours.* Brian Farrell, ed. Pp. 129. Dublin: Gill & Macmillan.

Sevenhuijsen, Selma 1998 *Citizenship and the Ethics of Care.* New York: Routledge.

Simmel, George, and Donald Levine 1972 *Freedom and the Individual.* London: Chicago Press.

Stier, Haya, and Noah Epstein 2000 "Women's Part Time Employment and Gender Inequality in the Family." *Journal of Family Issues* 21(3): 390-410.

Walby, Sylvia 2004 "The European Union and Gender Equality: Emergent Varieties of Gender Regime." *Social Politics* 11(1): 4-29.

Williams, Fiona 2004 "Rethinking Families, Rethinking Care." Paper presented at *Irish Social Policy Association Conference: Families, Children and Social Policy - Ten Years on from the Year of the Family*. Croke Park, Dublin.

White, Victoria 2010 *Mother Ireland: Why Ireland Hates Motherhood.* Dublin: Londubh Books.

Woodward, Alison 2003 "European Gender Mainstreaming: Promises and Pitfalls of Transformative Policy." *Review of Policy Research* 20(1): 65-88.

Wu, Zheng, and Lindy MacNeill 2002 "Education, Work, and Childbearing After 30." *Journal of Comparative Family Studies* 33(2): 191-213.

11.

The Mommy Curve

Stay-at-Home Mothers in Australia

ELIZABETH REID BOYD AND ANN-CLAIRE LARSEN

INTRODUCTION: THE M(OMMY) SHAPED CURVE

Over the last fifty years, the large scale entry of women into the paid labour force has been one of the most significant changes to women's childcare patterns. In 1954, women made up just 23 percent of the Australian labour force (ABS 1998). At the time of my PhD study (completed in 2000) on mothers at home, the percentage had almost doubled to 43 percent (ABS 1998). By 2006, this figure reached 58 percent (ABS 2008). In contrast, the proportion of men who were employed declined marginally from 74 percent in 1979 to 72 percent in 2006, a fall that has been linked to changing employment industries and increasing male involvement in family and child caring (ABS 2006; ABS 2008).

There are stark differences between coupled and lone women in employment. The proportion of partnered women in employment has continued to increase more than the rate for non-partnered women. The proportion of partnered women in paid employment rose from 39 percent in 1979 to 56 percent in 2004, in contrast to the proportion of non-partnered women from 41 percent in 1979 to 48 percent in 2004 (ABS 2006). These changes involving lone mothers in particular must be seen in the context of the events of 1975, when the Labor Prime Minister Whitlam introduced the no-fault divorce legislation (see Swain and Thornton 2011). Important also were developments that flowed from the feminist movement's demands for equal pay for women, free childcare and paid maternity leave (Swain and Thornton 2011). Though I am not suggesting causative links can be traced to political reforms and women's work place participation, I am suggesting that these events have correlative bearing on mothers' capacity and need to enter and leave the paid workforce.

The ebb and flow of partnered mothers joining and leaving paid employment resembles an 'M' shaped pattern. For many years, the normative pattern for these women has two peaks in paid employment coinciding with their age group of 20-24 and 34-44 years. The interim years, the 'prime child bearing ages' of 25-34 years, represent the trough of the 'M' (ABS 1998). I refer to this as the M(ommy) shaped curve. By the 1970s, the floor of the trough had begun to rise. In 1968, 32 percent of married women aged 25-34 years were in paid employment, but by 1998 this figure had increased to 66 percent (ABS 1998). The erosion of the M shaped pattern of partnered and non-partnered women's participation rates continued in the last decade, and in 2004, the trough was much less marked. Notably, it also shifted to the age groups between 30 and 39 years, reflecting the trend towards women having children later in life.

Another factor in women's employment is the age of their youngest child. Stay-at-home mothering is particularly acute in the pre-school years. In 1997, 46 percent of partnered mothers with children under five years were employed mostly in part-time jobs (ABS 1998). Partnered women with children in this age range were more likely to be employed than single women with children under five (ABS 1998). By 2004, mothers were employed in 45 percent of families (both partnered and single) whose youngest child was under five years (ABS 2006). Of the 45 percent of women with children under 5 who are employed, 31 percent are employed part-time (ABS 2006). Single mothers are more likely to stay at home than partnered mothers, given the difficulties associated with combining both roles without a partner's support. In 2004, a higher proportion of 60 percent of partnered mothers with children under 15 years were employed than lone mothers with children at 46 percent (ABS 2006).

Once their children start school, in line with the M-shaped curve, the number of employed women rises. Mothers are also working longer hours, but this does not mean they are embracing this change wholeheartedly (Breusch and Gray 2004; Qu and Weston 2005). Part-time employment is also paralleled with the M-shape, with increasing hours of paid work as children grow older (ABS 2006; ABS 2008). Part-time work appears to be the main way that Australian mothers combine work and care (Breusch and

Gray 2004).

For mothers of pre-school children in Australia, then, approximately half, incorporating both partnered and single mothers, continue to stay at home for some or all of the time. A raft of labour market and social changes, along with government policies encouraging women, married, single or separated into the paid work force, has shifted, shallowed and shortened the M(ommy) shaped curve, but not caused the curve to disappear.

RECENT STUDIES ON AUSTRALIAN STAY-AT-HOME MOTHERS: PICKETED AND PAIRED

There is limited research specifically on stay-at-home mothers in Australia and indeed on the Australian parental experience of managing work and care (Alexander and Baxter 2005).[1] Betsy Wearing's (1984) *The Ideology of Motherhood: A study of Sydney suburban mothers* remains a landmark study, which I followed in my qualitative examination of mothers at home in Western Australia in the 1990s (Reid Boyd 2000; Reid Boyd 2002). Many other relevant studies and papers to date examine stay-at-home mothers as part of a pair, as well as one side of the picket fence in the ongoing Australian childcare debate. A selection of the last decade's relevant research reveals contrasts between stay-at-home mothers and other mothers in a number of contexts.

Liz Van Acker's (2005) paper, 'The Howard Government's Budgets: Stay-at-home mothers good - Single mothers bad' in *Hecate* critiqued the preferential policies of the conservative Coalition Australian government led by Prime Minister John Howard for "the traditional 'white picket fence' type of family, where the husband works full-time and the wife is a stay-at-home mother" (Van Acker 2005). Van Acker demonstrated the double standard for mothers expressed in the 2004/2005 national budget, which with punitive welfare to work social security measures 'encouraged' single mothers into paid work, though partnered mothers were encouraged to stay at home through increased payments. The effect of these policies, Van Acker claims, is to "reinforce choices already made, as opposed to enticements to think about other alternatives" (Van Acker 2005). Furthermore, what is obscured is the commonality between the two groups: 60 percent of single mothers are stay-at-home mothers (ABS 2006).

In their study 'Good Mothers, Bad Mothers' Paula McDonald, Lisa Bradley and Diane Guthrie found that traditional normative beliefs about motherhood and being available to children full-time still shaped women's experience, regardless of the fact that most paid employment arrangements do not accommodate simultaneous full-time child rearing (McDonald, et al. 2005). In their sample, mothers at home viewed all non-maternal care as unacceptable; part-time working mothers saw some non-maternal care as unacceptable though mothers in full-time work were more positive about non-maternal care. However, a substantial amount of ambivalence and guilt was expressed. Comparisons of good mothering were internalized and externalized.

It was Catherine Hakim's contentious British research that was to have the most direct and powerful effect on Australian social and economic policies in the first decade of the 21st century.[2] In a speech in Australia in 2003, Hakim (2003) found a substantial minority of women, 20%, remain home-centered and family-centered in their values and lifestyle preferences. Roughly 20% are work-centered and careerist in the same way that men are said to be work-centered and careerist. Around 60% of women are adaptive.

At the time, Hakim's research was taken up by the Australian Federal Liberal Coalition government under Prime Minister John Howard:

> Howard's use of Hakim's work was strategic ... Hakim had established herself as a leading critic of feminism as early as 1995, accusing feminist academics of privileging work over family and of ignoring the vast majority of women for whom motherhood would always be paramount. Howard's use of Hakim's work was notable because he was self-consciously engaging with this emergent narrative, which blamed feminism for all women's difficulties. The implication was that the Howard government now had a mandate to right the wrongs done by 1970s feminists by giving women what they really wanted: the opportunity to experience stay-at-home motherhood. (Campo 2009)

According to Natasha Campo, a further side effect was to delay paid maternity leave in Australia, which was viewed as benefitting mothers in paid employment. The battle lines between stay-at-home (supported by familialists and the Australia Liberal party) and working mothers (supported by feminists and the Australia Labor party) remained drawn.

LOOK WHO'S TALKING TWO: RESISTANT DIVISIONS IN THE AUSTRALIAN MEDIA 'MOMMY WARS'

> "If you picked up a newspaper last week, you might have noticed the news of a new outbreak of fighting in a very old war ... It's the war between stay-at-home mums and working mums...". (Brown 2010)

In the Australian media, a discernible divide separating mothers at home (and familialists) and mothers at work (and feminists) has persisted over the last decade. Federal Labor Prime Minister "Rudd's first Budget splits stay-at-home and working mums" headlined *The Daily Telegraph* when the Family Tax Benefit paid to stay-at-home parents became means tested, whereas the childcare rebate paid to parents in paid work was not (Dunlevy 2008). The next skirmish was in 2010 in the run-up to the Federal Election when funding for paid parental leave was viewed as advantaging mothers in paid work at the expense of stay-at-home mothers (see Calligeros 2010; Shanahan 2010).

There was no doubt that the issue hit home, as a letter to the editor of *The West Australian* newspaper reveals:

> Kevin Rudd said "a stay-at-home mum's job is absolutely critical". Not as critical as the working mum who will from January 2011 receive a whole lot more. What a slap in the face for stay-at-home mums. The feminist driven policy is all about getting women into the workforce. ... Feminists talk about choice being their motivation, but what about the 54% of mums who care for their children at home? (Pike 2010)

The 'slap in the face' policy referred to by Ms Pike is maternity leave payment, which she situates as opposing mothers at home. Below, I discuss further the provision of different financial support mechanisms through social security and taxation currently provided to mothers in Australia, and how these contribute to this perceived division. However, what is notable here is that stay-at-home mothers are placed implacably against working mothers even though, as I also argue, maternity leave funding enables more women to stay at home with their children.

In Ms Pike's terms it is a "feminist driven policy" which she opposes. Further on in her letter, she names herself as a feminist who was happy to fight for equality, though is now resentful for what was given up (presumably the opportunity to stay at home). In my previous research, being a feminist but 'not with a capital F' was the case for a number of public and media advocates for mothers at home, who nevertheless saw themselves as opposing (capital F) feminists who supported paid work and publicly funded childcare.

Pike's letter forms part of a 'failing feminism' narrative that according to Natasha Campo:

> [H]ad, by the mid-2000s, become common sense and any future discussions of motherhood, feminism and childcare would be framed by its terms ... The 'failing feminism' narrative ... brought into existence a new mythology of motherhood that held that what women really wanted was the opportunity to stay at home and mother. (Campo 2009)

As Campo suggests, whereas the mommy wars make a particularly acute sound bite, a glance beneath the surface chatter reveals the complexity, ambivalence and disguises of the debate. A further unfortunate effect of these divisions is that child caring remains a female issue, one fought out in the media between women of various feminist and non-feminist stripes.

An example is an exchange between leading Australian feminists following the publication by journalist and social philosopher Anne Manne (2005) of her book *Motherhood: How Should We Care for Our Children?* Manne explored her experiences as a mother at home, examined the various sides of the mommy wars, in particular problematising the positioning of pro-natalists versus feminists, and concluded that flexible family practices and parental leave were vital policy planks. Manne's book spiked controversy. The Australian Commonwealth Sex Discrimination Commissioner Pru Goward, took Manne (who she described as a 'maternalist feminist') to task in a 2006 book review: "Manne's horror of childcare is undisguised ... [S]he accuses women of putting very young children into childcare knowing in their hearts that this is harmful ... Maternal guilt might be considered a defence in some quarters; but not, I sensed with disappointment, in the righteous world of Anne Manne" (Goward 2006). Ironically, however, their conclusions were the same: it was Pru Goward who tirelessly championed paid maternity leave for women, situating it primarily as a means of assisting working mothers.

ANOTHER LADIES' CHOICE: LOTS OF MONEY FOR MOTHERS IN FEDERAL ELECTIONS

In parallel to bipolar media representations, childcare remains a divisive and partisan political issue in Australia. In my research a decade ago, I found family and childcare policy reflected a dualistic political ideology. Today, the more things change, the more things remain the same. In the Federal Elections in 2010 and 2013, childcare and parental leave was a 'barbecue stopper' and a hot policy topic for both the incumbent (centrist-left) Australian Labor party and the (Liberal/conservative) Coalition opposition.

The childcare pendulum began to swing wildly in the early 1990s between public childcare provision and private parenting choice. The Federal Labor party and government's commitment to 'available, affordable' public childcare in the early part of that decade contrasted with the policy and provision for private parenting 'choice' of the liberal Coalition Federal party and government in the latter part of the decade. In essence, this resulted in providing, in Labor's case, for childcare through the public social security system, and for the Liberal Coalition through the private taxation system. As a consequence, currently there is a raft of childcare policies and provision with remnants of both these policy emphases.

Various government and welfare provisions are available to stay-at-home mothers in Australia. The Government of Australia (2013) webpage provides information about the following schemes. The Baby Bonus, which is paid to families following the birth or adoption of a baby, was introduced in July 2004 and is paid in 13 fortnightly installments. From 1 July 2013, the Baby Bonus is A$5,000 for the first child and A$3,000 for other newborn or adopted children. Families may also receive Family Tax Benefits (A&B). Family Tax Benefit A is a two part payment (income tested) that helps with the cost of raising each dependent child or secondary student under 20 not receiving a pension, payment, or benefit. Single parent families benefit from the Family Tax Benefit B where single parent families stay at home and work part-time, depending on the age of the youngest child. Single parents and guardians with a child under 8 years and couples with a child under 6 years may also be eligible for Parenting Payment.

To assist parents and full-time custodians with the costs of childcare services, the Child Care Benefit, the rates of which are means-tested, is available providing the child is in registered childcare and outside school hour care. In 2005, the Child Care Rebate was introduced that offers a return of 50 percent for out-of-pocket childcare expenses, 'up to a maximum amount per child per year'. Finally, the former Labor party's Parental Leave Pay provides financial support for up to 18 weeks on minimum wage to help eligible parents take time off work to care for a newborn or recently adopted child. Work and income tests apply. The Coalition government, which was elected in September 2013, has promised to amend the paid parental leave scheme to 'give mothers six months leave based on their actual wage' (Liberal Party 2013).

Though long awaited the Paid Parental Leave scheme has been largely viewed as benefitting paid working mothers, since only employed women are eligible (Baird 2004; Baird and Cutcher 2005; Brennan 2007; Brennan 2009). It has, however, also enabled more women to stay at home after giving birth. As such, I suggest it is a rare policy that can be construed as a win on both sides of the mommy wars and perhaps, a way forward.

THINKING WIN-WIN: WAYS OUT OF THE MOMMY WARS

The M(ommy) shaped curve has remained remarkably persistent in Australia. Though it has shifted and shallowed, it has not disappeared. It remains marked. Whereas it may have been expected that it will erode further, the latest Australian research on gender attitudes suggests this may not be the case. Australians remain conservative in their views, including a preference for mothers to stay at home (Horin 2010). Interestingly, more conservative views are also held by younger cohorts (Generation 'Y' or those born after 1980) (Horin 2010).

Barbara Pocock predicted in 2003 that Australians were heading for a 'work/life collision' (Pocock 2003). This is reflected in studies such as Alexander and Baxter's (2005) research into the impact of work on family life among partnered parents of young children using data from the current Longitudinal Study of Australian Children (LSAC). They found negative work-to-family strain and spillover associated with employment that lacked family friendly practices, such as being able to change working hours, included long or non-standard hours and offered low levels of autonomy (Alexander and Baxter 2005). They noted the preference of mothers with young children for part-time work along with their finding that self-employment and casual work was considered beneficial for mothers at that stage of their working life (Alexander and Baxter 2005).

This resonates with research on paid work preferences of lone mothers who as a group are in less full-time employment than coupled mothers. In a consideration of labour force status of lone and couple mothers, Gray, Qu, Renda and de Vaus (2006) make the point that given that mothers with higher levels of education will, on average, have more job opportunities, their finding that lone mothers with higher levels of education experienced the largest falls in full-time employment but the largest increases in part-time employment, suggesting that there may be an element of choice in working part-time. Media reports also claim that numbers of "well-educated and work-ready mothers" are choosing to work part-time, casually or not at all (Cleary 2010).

Though part-time work persists as the main way that Australian mothers combine work and care for their children, even a temporary period of workforce detachment may serve to reduce permanently their life-long earnings (Breusch and Gray 2004). 'Market failure' for working mothers can force acceptance of low quality employment in favour of caring and household responsibilities (Arun, et al. 2004). Representation among higher status occupations in part-time employment is poor (Baxter and Gray 2006). Poverty, especially in later life, is also a consequence of having interrupted their careers (OECD 2008). A finding by Baxter, et al. (2007) is notable, however, in that there are relatively small differences in economic hardships reported by dual income and single couple families. However, families where the single parent is unemployed experience the most hardship (Baxter, et al. 2007); that is, single parenting rather than staying at home has greater economic penalties.

Various explanations have been proffered for Australian women continuing to support the trend of staying at home and part-time employment in the face of such economic costs. These include limited access to flexible full-time work, insufficient affordable quality full-time childcare and the uneven sexual division of labour. The Australian Bureau of Statistics puts it succinctly: 'in 2006, women spent almost twice as much time on household work as men did. The opposite was true of paid work' (ABS 2009). However, these do not fully explicate the case. There must be, as Gray, et al, (2003) contend, more exploration of the reasons why women are continuing to favour part-time work, and I would add, staying at home.

Preference theory has been argued as having sufficient explanatory reach. Construing stay-at-home motherhood as an unproblematised preference (eg Hakim 2000; Hakim 2003; Hakim 2007) has been critiqued for its limitations in the light of social and gender role construction, let alone economic necessity. However, it is equally problematical to argue that social construction is sufficient cause (Duncan 2006). It might be tempting to view the persistence of mothers staying at home as a form of insidious conservative backlash. Instead I suggest it might be viewed as a form of female resistance. Australian women are resisting attempts to shape their working and childbearing lives into a neat bell curve, and are willing to face the emotional, social, and economic ups and downs of the Mommy curve instead. With these thoughts in mind, I support the notion that 'there is considerable scope for more creative policy thinking as well as more substantial public investment in order to support both carers and those in receipt of care' (Brennan 2007) that better reflect and recognise the persistence of the Mommy curve. These must go beyond political point scoring. In 2014, parental leave is still a political football. Child care remains a site of continued conflict: between parents over the sexual division of labour; between paid and unpaid work; between mothers at home and mothers at work, between various kinds of feminists, and between bipolar political agenda and policies.

Such divisive conflicts played out within and without, both personally and politically, distract from the continued public/private dichotomy and the dual burden of work and care with which many contemporary mothers continue to struggle. In such conflicting circumstances, women have been striking (sometimes poor) bargains to meet dual demands of work and home. Regardless of their so-called choices, mothers continue to be 'framed' as oppositional good or bad mothers, rather than mothers doing their best. The mommy wars continue to disguise the continuities and commonalities across the life course between women. Understanding and valuing stay-at-home mothering in terms beyond dichotomies and debates is a necessary step towards new ways of caring for children, for women and men, in private and public, at work and at home.

NOTES

[1]Alexander and Baxter (2005) point out that while there has been a plethora of research on the impact of women's employment internationally; there is still relatively little Australian research in this area. The current Australian Longitudinal Study of Children has begun and will continue to garner valuable data in this area. See also Baxter (2009).

[2]Catherine Hakim's research started such an intense academic debate. In 1995, her publication of 'five feminist myths' of women's employment in the British Journal of Sociology was responded to by ten academics debunk-

ing her claims. Her follow-up book in 2000, however, had significant policy effects, particularly in Australia.

REFERENCES

ABS 1998 *Australian Social Trends* Vol. Cat. No. 4102.0. Canberra: Australian Government Publishing Service. 2006 *Trends in Women's Employment* Vol. Cat. No. 4102.0. Canberra: Australian Government Publishing Service. 2008 *Labour Force Participation Across Australia* Vol. Cat. No. 4102.0 Canberra: Australian Government Publishing Service. 2009 *Australian Social Trends* Vol. Cat. No. 4102.0 Canberra.

Alexander, Michael, and Jennifer Baxter 2005 "Impacts of Work on Family Life among Partnered Parents of Young Children." *Family Matters* (72): 18-25.

Arun, Shoba V , Thankom G Arun, and Vani K Borooah 2004 *The Effects of Career Breaks on the Working Lives of Women.* www.borooah.com/papers/MS00.014R5Borooah

Australian Government 2013 *Department of Human Services.* http://www.humanservices.gov.au/customer/services/centrelink/

Baird, Marian 2004 "Orientations to Paid Maternity Leave: Understanding the Australian Debate." *The Journal of Industrial Relations* 46(3): 259 – 273.

Baird, Marian, and Leanne Cutcher 2005 "'One for the Father, One for the Mother and One for the Country': An Examination of the Construction of Motherhood Through the Prism of Paid Maternity Leave." *Hecate* 31(2): 103.

Baxter, Jennifer, and Matthew Gray 2006 "Paid Work Characteristics of Mothers with Infants." *Family Matters* (74): 34-41.

Baxter, Jennifer, et al. 2007 *Mothers and Fathers with Young Children: Paid Employment, Caring and Wellbeing.* Department of Families, Community Services and Indigenous Affairs.

Brennan, Deborah 2007 "Generations of Care: Demographic Change and Public Policy in Australia." In *Generational Change and Social Policy Challenges: Australia and Korea.* R. Phillips, ed. Pp. 115-140. Sydney: University of Sydney Press. 2009 "Australia: The Difficult Birth of Paid Maternity Leave. In *The Politics of Parental Leave.* S.B. Kamerman and P. Moss, eds. Pp. 15-33. Bristol: The Policy Press.

Breusch, Trevor, and Edith Gray 2004 "New Estimates of Mothers' Forgone Earnings using HILDA Data." *Australian Journal of Labour Economics* 7(2): 125-150.

Brown, Jessica 2010 "Working Versus Stay-At-Home is not the Mother of all Battles." *The Age*, 25 May.

Calligeros, Marissa 2010 "At-Home Mums Deserve Parental Pay Day." *Brisbane Times,* March 29.

Campo, Natasha 2009 "FEMINISM FAILED ME: Childcare, Maternity Leave and the Denigration of Motherhood." *Australian Feminist Studies* 24(61): 325-342.

Cleary, Paul 2010 "The Cautious Mother Who Stays At Home." *The Australian*, 4 September.

Department of Human Services 2013 *Parenting Payment.* Department of Human Services, ed: Australian Government.

Duncan, Simon 2006 "Mothers' Work-Life Balance: Individualized Preferences or Cultural Construction?" In *Gender Divisions and Working-Time in the New Economy.* D. Perrons, Fagan, Colette, McDowell, Linda, Ray, Kath & Ward, Kevin, ed. Pp. 127-319. Northampton: Edward Elgar.

Dunlevy, Sue 2008 "Rudd's First Budget Splits Stay-At-Home and Working Mums." *The Daily Telegraph*, May 15.

Government of Australia 2013 *Family Payments and Allowances.* Canberra: Government of Australia.

Goward, Pru 2006 *Oh No Children, We Forgot Motherhood, Did We?* http://www.australianreview.net/digest/2006/01/goward.html.

Gray, Matthew, et al. 2003 *Changes in the Labour Force Status of Lone and Couple Mothers.* Australian Institute of Family Studies.

Gray, Matthew, et al. 2006 "Changes in the Labour Force Status of Lone and Couple Australian Mothers, 1983-2005." *Australian Journal of Labour Economics* 9(4): 395-416.

Hakim, Catherine 2000 *Work-Lifestyle Choices in the 21st Century.* Oxford: Oxford University Press. 2003 "Competing Family Models, Competing Social Policies." *Family Matters* No.64 Autumn 2003. Canberra: The Australian Institute of Family Studies. 2007 "The Politics of Female Diversity in the Twenty-First Century. In *The Future of Gender* J. Browne, ed. Pp. 191-227. Cambridge: Cambridge University Press.

Hall, Eleanor 2010 *Study Shows Less Support for Working Mums.*

http://www.abc.net.au/worldtoday/content/2010/s3034880.htm.

Horin, Adele 2010 "Attitudes Harden Towards the Lot of a Working Mother." *The Age*, October 11, 2010.

Liberal Party 2013 *Media Release* August http://www.liberal.org.au/latest-news/2013/08/18/tony-abbott- coalitions-paid-parental-leave-scheme

Manne, Anne 2005 *Motherhood: How Should We Care For Our Children?* Crows Nest, NSW: Allen & Unwin.

McDonald, Paula, K., Lisa Bradley, M., and Diane Guthrie 2005 "Good Mothers, Bad Mothers: Exploring the Relationship Between Attitudes Towards Nonmaternal Childcare and Mother's Labour Force Participation." *Journal of Family Studies* 11(1): 62.

OECD 2008 *Babies and Bosses: Balancing Work and Family Life.* Policy Brief OECD.

Pike, A. 2010 "Forgotten Mums." *The West Australian*, 22 June, 22.

Pocock, Barbara 2003 *The Work/Life Collision: What Work Is Doing To Australians And What To Do About It.* Annadale, NSW: Federation Press.

Qu, Lixia, and Ruth Weston 2005 "A Woman's Place? Work Hour Preferences Revisited." *Family Matters* (72): 72-77.

Reid Boyd, Elizabeth 2000 *'Being There': Mothers Who Stay At Home.* Murdoch University. 2002 "'Being there': Mothers Who Stay At Home, Gender and Time." *Women's Studies International Forum* 25(4): 463-470.

Shanahan, Angela 2010 "Coalition Betrays Stay-At-Home Mothers." *The Australian*, March 17.

Swain, Shurlee, and Danielle Thornton 2011 "Fault, Gender Politics and Family Law Reform." *Australian Journal of Politics & History* 57(2): 207-220.

Van Acker, Liz 2005 "The Howard Government's Budgets: Stay-at-Home Mothers Good - Single Mothers Bad." *Hecate* 31(2): 90.

Wearing, Betsy 1984 *The Ideology of Motherhood: A Study of Sydney Suburban Mothers.* Volume 21. Sydney: George Allen & Unwin.

Section III: New Angels and Old Demons: Manifestations of Mothers at Home

12.

Cyber-Mothers

Mothers at Home, Online

PAMELA WEATHERILL

INTRODUCTION

Mothers have two universal experiences. They are mothers twenty-four hours a day, and they are mothers within whatever geographical space they currently inhabit. Whether a mother is a stay-at-home mum or chooses to spend time in the paid workplace, mothering knows no temporal or geographic boundaries, with women speaking of being mothers twenty-four hours a day and anywhere they or their children are. Throughout the ages, across generations, and as we have seen in other chapters of this book, across cultures, mothers freely share their mothering knowledge with others in social spaces. The history of mothering wisdom being handed from one to another is alive and well. Mothers choosing to remain in or re-enter the public workplace provide one another with information about childcare options and dealing with 'working mother guilt'. Stay-at-home mothers swap techniques for getting through the late afternoon 'mum's taxi run' and affordable children's activity options. Mothers take part in this experience-swapping at home, at work, and now in a third space: the virtual world or cyberspace.

When sociologist Ray Oldenburg (1991) explained the concept of 'The Third Space' in his classic community building book *The Great Good Place*, he described a free space to inhabit, which was neither the first place (home) or the second place (work), but an informal community space for human interaction and growth. Oldenburg argued that this place would feel like a home away from home, where new friendships could be created through supportive conversation and old friends could spend time together easily on a regular basis. With the advent of the internet, and communication possibilities and social spaces created since the arrival of Web 2.0 digital technologies, scholars have extended Oldenburg's definition of the third space to include digital communities (Kendall 2002; Soukup 2006). What happens then, when mothers meet in this third space - not work nor home? When they inhabit this third space knowing that there might be a social divide between their experiences in the other two spaces as either at home, or out to work mothers?

On-line communities provide a virtual third space that is similar to geographical community spaces inhabited by mothers at home. Once internet connections are established, most virtual communities are free to participate in. Participants feel it is a home away from home where they can interact with other like minded mothers, regulars become old friends and new comers are welcomed. Like geographically based social spaces where mothers might gather in parks, community centers or toddler-gym, regular virtual community members assist newcomers to understand social mores and expectations. Mothers join groups relevant to their experiences, backgrounds and hobbies. Conversations of support and story sharing happen with the use of digital communication as does the stay-at-home versus go to work debate.

It must be remembered however that not all mothers at home will have affordable access to the internet. The digital divide is alive and well across the globe and non-access for mothers at home can be seen as a social issue related to inequity of access to medical and practical sources of information and services. The divide between cyber-connected mothers and non cyber-connected mothers is an important one for scholars and service providers alike. This chapter explores the experiences of at home mothers who do have internet access, and may assist with future examination of what at home mothers miss out in if they are on the poor side of the digital divide.

Online, mothers at home may breach temporal and geographical boundaries without the challenges faced when attempting socializing with toddlers in tow, getting prams into vehicles with hands full of diaper bags and picnic food, and fitting all this in between naps and school runs. Though not all stay-at-home mothers inhabit the virtual third space, many of these spaces have stay-at-home mothers present as virtual world avatars, bloggers, wiki experts and social media participants.

Though parents are visible on the internet across blogs, discussion groups, virtual reality spaces and wikis as well as following parenting hash tags on Twitter, there is little research examining the specific experience of internet use of mothers at home. Research indicates that mothers use the internet for actively seeking parenting information and health information from online clinical sources; yet, they prefer to get their parenting advice from other parents and tap into each other's wisdom (Bernhardt and Fetler 2004; Zaslow 2012). Another common research theme is mothers using the internet as a social activity. More formal social support is seen in research around online support groups where the anonymity of the space can be helpful for participants (Miller, 2006 as an example).

To introduce how mothers at home inhabit the internet as a space, this chapter will provide qualitative insights into their experiences of cyberspace. It will provide a peek at the world of cyber mothers, and the rich support they find in the third space, as well as highlight the challenges they face in its use. Most importantly, this chapter will give voice to a group of mothers at home who access this empowering third space, with all its complexities and social nuances. We have seen in earlier chapters that there is no single experience as a stay-at-home mother - with changes across cultures being the norm. Cyberspace provides as much variety of experience - with different blog spaces, chat rooms and discussion boards having their own cultures and dominant views on staying at home versus going to work.

VOICES FROM CYBERSPACE

A short on-line survey was undertaken to encourage mothers participating in cyber communities to help identify and explain their experience of being online mothers at home. The survey link was sent to a number of influential Mommy bloggers (based in United Kingdom, Australia, Canada and United States of America). They subsequently re-posted it on other internet sites. The survey was left open for a period of two months.

Four hundred and forty (n=440) Mothers from United Kingdom, Australia, Canada and United States of America responded to the survey. The majority of respondents (65%) identified themselves as at home mothers or worked part-time, and a further seven percent (7%) worked from home. The following discussion refers to these mothers. The children of these respondents ranged in age from three months to 20 years with the majority (66%) having pre-school and primary-school aged children. Though the majority had between two and four children (60%), 35% had one child and 5% had more than four.

All the participants had used Facebook as a mechanism for socializing online with other mothers. Other sources for social interaction online included blogs, parenting forums and discussion boards, Pinterest, Twitter, Google Plus, Flickr, YouTube, and LinkedIn as well as the use of email and video conferencing (Such as Skype or Facetime) communication between mothers, or messaging services such as those attached to Facebook. Mothers interacted both synchronously and asynchronously across the internet. The vast majority of mothers (87%) used internet sites to meet other mums, with the remaining mothers saying they only used it to keep in touch with other mothers they already knew offline. Their other internet activities include shopping (89%), getting advice and information (87%), corresponding with friends and family (87%), videoconferencing with family and friends (41%), studying online (33%), watching television or films (28%) and listening to music (25%). While some mothers identified themselves as either 'online' or 'cyber' mothers, and this appeared to be a significant differentiation for them, none of the mothers considered the difference between being at home or at work as a major distinction while on the internet.

Any examination of the internet will produce articles about good and bad mothering. This includes media debates about where the "good" mothers might be. In cyberspace, this third space appears to allow discussion about these different parenting experiences, without it being a defining factor for women about themselves, the way it might offline. Mothers who did identify as being at home and who did comment on this differentiation, thought it was one that the media promulgated online, with only a "minority of women caring enough to respond to the debate online". The concept of the third space being one where you only entered, and definitely only continue to participate in, where there is a values match, being more important. "There are plenty of spaces for mothers of all kinds to go on the internet, there is no need to take the debate online" summarised one mother, who had also suggested the debate on mothers at home or going to work was only "fiery in the media, not amongst real women doing the drudge of the twenty four hour job that mothering is".

BENEFITS OF SPENDING TIME ON THE INTERNET

As a third space, the internet provides mothers at home (who have access), with a tool to use for many of the challenges that motherhood brings. All the mothers in this survey described many benefits to spending time on the internet, or simply having it available. One mother saying: "Thank god for the internet really. Even if I don't use it, just knowing it is there 24/7 gives me confidence -and stops me going a little crazy". Mothers described the many benefits they derived from their cyber-social interactions.

In keeping with the research that tells us mothers enjoy peer support, the most common benefit of accessing the internet identified was the gaining of knowledge, tips and advice from other parents, as well as providing support to others.

- "I love talking to other mums that have children that are similar age to my daughter, there are always good tips to pick up on what hot toys are coming out, new clothing labels, music, schooling... heaps of cool and useful topics."
- "I don't use the internet to meet new people but primarily to get information and advice, and to spread the word about matters I think are important."
- "I use forums ... and other parenting websites to raise issues I am having and seek ideas from other people who have been through a similar thing. Also to find expert opinion through articles, publications etc, although the net is not always a reliable source of accurate information!"
- "I always get tips on shopping sites for kids and find support and advice on 'mumming'"
- "Being able to get advice at 2am when you have a new baby is invaluable. As the kids grow older it is also a great place to get different perspectives on issues."
- "It is just great for sharing helpful information, links to blogs and useful sites for parenting and education have often been a savior to a sticky situation".
- "If your child is unwell, or even struggling with school, there is nothing like the information and support you can get from others on the internet. Then you pay it forward when someone else needs advice."

Peer support for mothers on the internet can also be one of comparing and sharing about the mothering experience with others who are going through a similar experience. There were numerous responses around sharing family milestones and what is going on in the lives of friends as well.

- "It gives me a useful way to keep in touch with people who don't live locally. Great for sharing photos of important events with them."
- "It makes it so easy to share pictures with family through Facebook and Skype. It is great as it allows you to stay in touch with family and for them to see the baby growing. My youngest daughter calls my mum 'Nan iPad'! to distinguish her from my husband's mother whom she sees regularly."
- "I can keep up with what is going on, social inter-action with friends I would otherwise find very difficult to catch up with."
- "It's a great way to find out about things that I'm not actively looking for - eg: Saw a friend with a daughter the same age took her daughter to her first swimming class last week which prompted me to book my daughter in."

The third space also provides a social setting, where like minded mothers can gather. Many mothers identified cyber participation as a way of relieving social isolation, without the usual distractions of face to face meet-ups.

- "It relieves the isolation of being home with kids. I can socialize when it suits me. Can choose who I talk to (as opposed to mother's groups where you might not fit in). Can socialize with mums without having to tolerate their annoying kids."
- "I use it to just feel connected occasionally. I especially like inclusion in social groups organized online, where everyone is an at home mum and you are all going through such similar things. You don't feel so alone in your parenting. You can actually participate without junior tugging at your leg. Well most of the time anyway!"
- "I felt totally disconnected to my old job when I had Aleisha. At least with email, Twitter and Facebook I could keep up with what was happening with the old crew."
- "Sometimes it is about simply sharing joys as well as sorrows with others. It's affirming as well as social."

Social isolation is a challenge faced by many at home mothers. Meeting like-minded people on virtual forums and social networking sites was deemed a benefit of being a cyber mother.

- "I keep in touch with those I know in The Real World, but also get to meet others who share my (sometimes) idiosyncratic passions."
- "My child has a rare disease- without the internet we would have missed out on so much information, but more importantly we would have missed out on such wonderful support from others in the same situation and medical people all over the world".
- "I was a bottle feeder. That makes me a social outcast in many settings in this community. Finding a forum of others from around the world really eased my guilt and made my life easier."

Like offline social gatherings, online mothers gravitate towards people with similar experiences for peer support. For mothers who were not working but were undertaking study while raising their children, cyber participation appeared to provide a further type of advice and support

- "Without the internet I would have drowned in mothering and study. I found I could always get some support from other mothers at Uni. on the forums."
- "I am studying my first degree. I am way behind other women in my cohort who already have one. Finding and keeping in touch with other mums coming to study late, juggling family, finding childcare and the simple act of clawing away time to study was a lifesaver for me. I don't have time to go out and socialize."

Communication with others in similar situations, geographic areas or life stages is the core of any peer community. Computer-mediated communication via the internet such as email, using community building spaces such as meet-ups and forums provides another mechanism for organizing time together face to face.

- "It just makes things easier. It saves time in coordinating social and community meetings and events. It's not like you're online all the time - you're online working out how to get together more."

- "It is just plain easier to set up play dates online. You can leave a message for multiple mums and everyone gets back when they have the chance around doing stuff for their kids."
- "We organize local meet-ups on the internet. A group of four of us started this a year ago, and now we have anywhere up to 20 mums rock up to chat while the kids play. It's a great way to find mothers at home who might otherwise be isolated. We make a point of greeting newcomers warmly. We joke and call it our 'anti-playgroup group'!"

The cyber world inhabited by at home mothers provided a solution to the time paucity many at home mothers feel. One of the main benefits mothers found from spending time online was being able to attend to parenting roles as well as socializing. The removal of temporal constraints was a common theme.

- "I can be at home with child asleep and still able to connect with the outside world."
- "Waiting for Alex to go back to sleep after his midnight feed can take ages. I use that time to quickly read a couple of parenting forums. It seems there's always someone awake somewhere in the world with screaming babies."
- "Email is really useful with the unsocial hours I keep as a mum. I am often emailing friends and family (or shopping online!) at 11pm. I certainly wouldn't ring anyone at that time."
- "The net was a crucial source of support for me in the first few months of having newborn twins - I was able to email / Facebook people when I was up at 3am and never could have phoned anyone. Because we were all on different schedules with our babies it was really hard to catch up any other way."

Not all time spent on the internet was directly related to their experience as mothers at home, or even as women. Time spent on the internet for some mothers was also seen as relaxing or time for themselves.

- "I don't have to be a mom online! I get to be whomever I want. I have an avatar of me as a male CEO on Second Life. Talk about contrast to my Real World experience."

- "It's my me time. Me, the computer and a coffee is my usual activity when the kids are napping. By the time they wake up I feel human again."
- "I find it relaxing. Whether I check a couple of Mummy blogs or shop, it relaxes me. Even if I only get 5 minutes uninterrupted to check some emails."
- "You know laughter is a great relaxer - and I always find someone says something or shares a story that gives me a good belly laugh. That's time well spent in my book."

CYBER-CHALLENGES AND CONCERNS

No different to being a mother in the first or second sphere, cyber mothers were also clear that the internet was not without its concerns or challenges. One mother claimed: "Don't think it's all good though. Get in an argument with another mother on line and it is there for everyone to see. You have to be careful." On the topic of the at home versus go to work debate, while most mothers surveyed had little to say about this, and most who did have an opinion made it clear it was a "media beat up", one mother did suggest: "Sometimes I feel like I have to hone in what I say, as there are some less conservative parents out there that would quickly tell you that you're a drain on the economy because you choose not to go out to work".

In contrast, a number of mothers claimed there was no negative experience interacting with others online.

> "Look there are no issues if you are careful. I usually only interact to the ones that I have established some kind of trust with eg: mums that are from schools, or social clubs, kids sports clubs and are on the same social networks, which is usually only FB [Facebook] and Meet up."

Online communities have social mores not unlike face to face ones. The need to be present online was a burden for some mothers, in the same way peer pressure can influence offline groups.

> "There is a responsibility with being part of an online community, like any community, and I am so inconsistent with my internet access that they would feel like I wasn't really interested. But in reality sometimes I am just too busy."

Though mothers appreciated the support and advice from others, a few noted that online support is limited.

> "Sometimes you meet people and you can't really do much to help them. They might live on the other side of the world and there is no way you can offer practical support then."

Time spent on the internet was seen by some as time difficult to control or access.

- "I get on the internet in the afternoon and next thing I know it's time to pick up the kids. Time has its own pace on there. You seem to lose it."
- "I don't get enough quiet time to access the useful sites or take part properly. It's either my kids or my husband needing me in the evenings and once they are in bed I'm too tired."
- "Some people report the minutia of their lives. Boring and worrying that they have nothing better to do. Internet is a time sapper at times."
- "People aren't always online at the same time - hard for impromptu meetings (though iPhone technology is helping bridge that time lag)."

Like communication amongst any group of peers, the issue of misunderstanding the written communication of others used in many online sites was seen as a challenge and something to be cautious about.

- "The tone of some people's communication can be misread, leading to problems. Then you feel like your lovely little community is no different to the clicky mothers at the school gate."
- "Sometimes it's hard to get a feel for people you haven't met in real life and it's easy to misinterpret tone in messages and get the wrong idea about someone. People can misrepresent themselves but that's rarer."
- "Some people aren't careful about what they write and some get offended and write back emotively. Online arguments because of a simple lack of understanding or miscommunication due to poor written communication skills frustrate me!"

- "Although I don't eat a lot in front of the computer, I also don't exercise much, and I get less sleep than I ought. But it is easier to believe that everyone else is perfect when I only know them online: our honesty is harder to question. Well, we have time to paint a pretty picture, or word things more gently and carefully when we are typing in our own time..."

Cyber communication is virtual. The lack of face to face contact, and the associated use of paralanguage when communicating, was raised as a challenge by a few mothers.

- "Sometimes it feels a bit impersonal, you know when only the real thing will do!"
- "I think it's sad that a lot of people are using the net as a primary source of socializing. The richness of spending time with a friend in person, or talking on the phone, can't be matched online."
- "I am conscious of the shallowness of this communication, and want to maintain real friendships using direct communication, phone, face-to-face social time. Internet social sites can be a time waster."

Some mothers were concerned that it was easy to get incorrect information or poor levels of advice, especially from unmoderated forums.

- "I choose my sites carefully when I need medical advice. I use ones that have professionals on them as well as mums. It is too easy to be led up the garden path."
- "Sometimes other mums put up information that is just plain incorrect. That can be dangerous. There's as many crazy people on the internet as in real life I say!"

THE ROLE OF THE INTERNET IN MOTHERS' LIVES

Though some mothers said the internet was not a major part of their life, all shared the benefits they felt. For some mothers, the internet played a clear and important role in their lives as mothers at home.

- "It's VERY important to me. It's been a lifeline."

- "The internet is very important as it provides me with networks while at home with the kids. It helps me to feel connected even if I don't get out."
- "It is where I start and end each day. In between I am run off my feet though."
- "The internet is my recipe book, my counselor, my medico and my mother all rolled into one."
- "I'd say it's reasonably important. If I didn't have the internet, I'd probably go out a bit more so I don't feel so lonely. From my online 'relationships' I get to have fun, companionship, a feeling of connection without the effort of going out."
- "It is very important. Keep in touch with school websites, for all sorts of information, emailing for friends and chores like internet banking social networking information, school projects, endless kid questions that I don't have the answers for! Like a concierge for mums."
- "It was crucial, as I didn't "click" with the other local baby-group or play-group mums, and my own was 3 hours drive away."

While it might be thought that the at home mothers who use the internet identify as cyber mothers per se, this is not the case. For some at home mothers, the internet was more of a useful tool to use now and then rather than a critical part to their role as mothers.

- "It isn't important at all to my role as a mother but important to my personal development which in turn relates to my motherhood (but not directly)."
- "I'm not a cyber mother at home. I'm a mother at home who uses the internet for stuff!"
- "I spend lots of time on my computer now, but it doesn't really define me as a mother as I still prefer human contact catching up for coffee and swapping ideas."
- "Online time as a mother to me isn't important. It's only a distraction from your family. I mostly just use it to keep in contact with family and friends."

- "It's not that important now, although it was in the first six months of being a new mother. I think my social life would actually be better if my friends and I DIDN'T use it - i.e. if we phoned each other instead! Online shopping is quite important, though, as with twins it's really difficult to get the shopping done."

MOTHERS-AT-HOME – INHABITING CYBERSPACE

The internet appears to provide a space that is neither work nor home for mothers to congregate, seek advice and socialize. The debates between mothers about parenting styles are played out on the internet as much as they are in their physical communities, though as some women mentioned, this is often on media sites, not sites where women gather per se. What the internet provides is a mechanism for connection between cyber at home mothers. It enables women to connect and support one another, should they seek it, any time of the day and from any part of the globe with an internet connection.

Connection between at home mothers on the internet does not come without the many challenges that face anyone using computer-mediated communications for relationship building. It provides a space, the third space, in their at home lives. And like the space they inhabit in their communities, they navigate this space knowing there is difference between and amongst mothers who stay at home, and also inhabit cyberspace. It can highlight the many differences in experiences for mothers at home - and yet provide an extended form of peer support. It is a virtual home away from home. Cyberspace is easily added to the list of places mothers congregate for support, gossip, exchange of ideas and advice, although it does not allow for much practical support. Cyberspace provides a virtual community for mothers, and though it is without the temporal and geographical boundaries of these physical spaces, it exists with its own culture(s). It must be remembered however that there is still a digital divide, where not all mothers at home have access to affordable or reliable internet connections. The third space, where accessible, is inhabited by stay-at-home mothers on the internet appears to be a valuable asset to their mothering role - albeit virtual. Perhaps this third space also provides opportunity for the at home, at work differences between mothers to be less visible, and less important than their similarities.

REFERENCES

Bernhardt, Jay, and Elizabeth Felter 2004 "Online Pediatric Information Seeking Among Mothers of Young Children: Results From a Qualitative Study Using Focus Groups." *Journal of Medical Internet Research* 6(1).

Kendall, Lori 2002 *Hanging Out in the Virtual Pub.* Berkley CA: University of California Press.

Miller, Pam 2006 "Benefits of On-Line Chat for Single Mothers." *Journal of Evidence-Based Social Work* 3(3-4): 167-181.

Oldenburg, Ray 1991 *The Great Good Place.* New York: Marlowe & Company.

Soukup, Charles 2006 "Computer-Mediated Communication as a Virtual Third Place: Building Oldenburg's Great Good Places on the World Wide Web." *New Media Society* 8(3): 421-440.

Zaslow, Emile 2012 "Revalorizing Feminine Ways of Knowing." *Information, Communication & Society* 15(9): 1352-1372.

13.

Are Stay-at-Home Mothers Really at Home?

U.S. Mothers' Volunteer Work in Schools

BETH ANNE SHELTON AND REBECCA DEEN

The juxtaposition of stay-at-home mothers and working mothers dominates the discussion of the 'mommy wars' (Douglas and Michaels 2005; Johnston and Swanson 2006). The two groups of mothers are presumed to adopt different styles of mothering, with the former labor intensive and the latter less so. Mothering typically is described as involving time spent in the home. In another publication, we document the amount of mothering that occurs in the public sphere, specifically in and around children's schools (Deen and Shelton 2012), but public parenting rarely is included when comparing stay-at-home and working mothers. Just as in the home, the ideology of intensive parenting (Hays 1996) and the construct of the 'good mother' (Arendell 2000; Goodwin and Huppatz 2010; Gorman and Fritzsche 2002; Johnston and Swanson 2006) allow us to understand mothers' activities more fully. The expectation that good mothers are available and there for their children forms the backdrop of the 'mommy wars,' but rarely have social scientists examined the public practice of intensive mothering (for exceptions see Landeros 2011; Griffith and Smith 2005).

Stay-at-home mothers exemplify the dominant discourse surrounding the expectations women face in the era of intensive mothering (Hays 1996). Intensive mothering is generally assumed to be practised in women's own homes and with their own children (Douglas and Michaels 2005). In fact, intensive mothering may occur in the public sphere, especially the schools, and involve women in their communities (Gallagher and Gerstel 2001; Garey 1995; Landeros 2011). Rotolo and Wilson (2007) find that children, contrary to common perceptions, have a positive effect on both the likelihood of volunteering and time spent volunteering (see also Gallagher and Gerstel 2001). Moreover, employment has the same positive effect on mothers' volunteering (Musick and Wilson 2008). These findings suggest the stay-at-home mother and working mother dichotomy has, in fact, been oversimplified, especially in terms of participation in the public sphere (see also Reid Boyd 2002).

In this paper, we explore the ways that stay-at-home mothers actually participate quite actively in unpaid work outside the home, as well as how, in some contexts, employed mothers may behave in ways quite similar to stay-at-home mothers. Through this assessment we hope to uncover the ways that the rhetoric of the mommy wars obscures commonalities between groups typically characterized as representing different orientations to mothering (Garey 1995).

SETTING AND DATA COLLECTION

To understand more fully how mothers spend their time and how they think about their choices, we gathered qualitative data from a sample of seventeen mothers of pre-school age and school age children living in a mid-size city in the Southwest area of the United States and through participant observation at formal and informal parent-school functions from 2009-2013. Interview data were collected at three public schools (one for students in grades seven and eight and two for students in grades nine through twelve) and at one preschool serving approximately one hundred children from infants to age five. We included a private preschool because there is no publicly available preschool system, although we chose one that is moderately priced and serves a diverse group of children who eventually enter both public and private schools in the area.

We used a modified snowball sampling technique, beginning with lists of school volunteers and branching out to others who volunteer in the schools. Interviews ranging from one hour to three hours were conducted with all mothers in our sample and each was recorded and transcribed. Participant observation at parent-school functions evolved from casual invitations to help with various programs. At these events we talked informally with mothers about their parenting practices and listened to conversations about mothering, working and the schools. For all respondents we use pseudonyms to protect their identity.

Our sample of mothers includes seven who work full-time, five who work part-time and five who are not employed. The women's ages range from 30 to 54, with a median age of 38. The median age of mothers in all three categories is thirty-eight and the median number of children for mothers in all three groups is two. There is some variation in children's ages among the three categories of mothers. Just over half of women employed full-time had preschool age children and the others had school age children, while three of the five women employed part-time had at least one preschool age child and four of five of stay-at-home mothers had preschool children.

We analyzed our data using open coding, working from transcribed interviews and notes. We identified themes noting their presence in the transcriptions of interviews and observations. Once we identified themes, we re-examined the transcriptions to ensure our coding was comprehensive. This paper focuses on some of our unexpected findings that emerged in later stages of analysis when we looked for differences among mothers employed full-time, part-time and not at all. Surprisingly, we uncovered unexpected similarities among the three groups and it is on these similarities that we focus in this paper.

A NOTE ON DEFINITION

In our sample of self-described stay-at-home and working mothers, we expected to contrast the experiences of these two groups. Upon review of the interview transcriptions, however, we noticed that many of the stay-at-home mothers spent the equivalent of a part-time, and sometimes a full-time, job in their children's schools doing a variety of volunteer tasks, ranging from fundraising to office support to tutoring. At the same time, some of the women who referred to themselves as employed mothers described their volunteer activities in much the same way as the stay-at-home mothers. These unexpected results led us to explore more fully the ways that mothers, both employed and stay-at-home, involve themselves in their children's schools. We are interested in this subject both because schools depend on volunteers' labor to operate (Brent 2008), and because the patterns we observe suggest that employed and stay-at-home mothers represent overlapping rather than mutually exclusive groups (Garey 1995).

WHEN IS A STAY-AT-HOME MOTHER NOT AT HOME?

Examining aggregate volunteer hours and trends provides useful generalities but obscures a pattern we gradually uncovered in our interviews. Specifically, when arranging interviews with stay-at-home mothers, we found that some of these mothers were rarely at home, even though their children were in school. Instead, we had to resort, in some instances, to interviewing the women who volunteered at their children's schools as they worked. Terry, a stay-at-home mother who we interviewed while she was selling concessions to fund a school function, describes her involvement in some of the school-related activities:

> [In the beginning we had to] build a gym floor, get a marquee...get an awning [for protection when it rains].

She continued to characterize the meetings where these projects were planned:

> ...meetings were four hours long... [because we were] building a brand new school...trying to finance projects the school wasn't able to do.

Terry left the paid labor force for fourteen years to support her children while they were in school and typically spends the equivalent of at least a part-time job volunteering in the schools. She recalled that she used to:

> ...wonder what women [who] didn't work did all day [but now I know] it is easy to fill up a day.

It is not only in their time investment that stay-at-home mothers' activities seem like a job. Rachel explained that although she is not currently employed:

> I list my volunteering on my resume. Because...when I go back to work [employers] are going to ask me what I have been doing.

She continues to note that volunteering is also about transitioning to parenthood as a new stage in life.

These mothers are typical of a subgroup of stay-at-home mothers we interviewed who are actively involved in their children's schools, spending many hours volunteering. Our analyses of involved stay-at-home mothers reveals that, in contrast to the assumption that they are isolated in their homes and non-participants in the community, these women typically are doing significant amounts of unpaid work in their children's schools (Brent 2008; Burke 2001). Their activities certainly benefit their own children (see Landeros 2011 on entitled mothers), as they intend, but at least indirectly support the entire school. A subgroup of employed mothers appears much like stay-at-home mothers in their day-to-day, school-related volunteer activities.

CHAMELEON MOTHERS

Chameleon mothers are working mothers who, at least in terms of their involvement in their children's schools, appear as if they are not employed (Dillaway and Paré 2008). They volunteer in their children's schools during the day either by using flexible schedules (typically professional women) or by working schedules that allow them to be available during the day (e.g. working as flight attendants or nurses at night). Throughout interviews, there were references to having time to be actively involved in their children's schools and lives. Mindy, in describing her time spent in her children's schools, said:

> ...I have a lot of time to give...I was on the board at all three [schools], but, again, I have the time.

Mindy holds a full-time job, yet has a regular presence at her children's schools and represents herself as one of the 'fortunate' women who has the time to volunteer. She, like many of the employed mothers we met, wears time-flexibility as a uniform during the day and fits easily into the stay-at-home crowd of mothers she encounters. At a later point when discussing school-related meetings, she tells us that:

> Generally people who don't work are on the board, 'cause the meetings are in the middle of the day.

In this narrative, she appears blissfully unaware that she just reported that she is employed full-time and has been on the board at each of her children's schools.

These chameleon mothers discuss their employment with us when we ask them about it, but typically emphasize the importance of their children over their work. Unlike Dillaway and Paré (2008), we find that a significant number of the chameleon mothers hold professional or semi-professional jobs. Brenda, for example, an active partner in an accounting firm, emphasizes the greater importance of motherhood when she says that she would:

> ...rather be Esther and Brian's mom at the school, than anything else. [We are] there for the school and the kids.

As Reid Boyd (2002) argues, mothers who are employed sometimes define themselves as stay-at-home mothers because they have chosen work allowing them to prioritize 'being there' for their children (see also Garey 1995). Lane, an employed mother who appears as if she has her days free, reports that she works various hours but that her hours depend on 'what's going on' in the lives of her children. Helen, who defines herself as a stay-at-home mother, works approximately ten hours per week and deemphasizes her work and focuses her conversation on her volunteer activities at her children's school:

> I have the luxury of having time...to donate [to volunteering at the school]. Children are benefitting...that's why I [do] it.

Other working mothers add volunteering to their full-time jobs. Pam, a mother who is employed full-time but with flexibility, typically spends time each week as an officer of the parent-teacher organization. Pam reports that each week she:

> collects money, [goes] to the bank...[and completes] the [financial] reconciliation.

She further reports that she, like other mothers, took the position so she could '...be around and be involved and pay attention to what's going on.' Pam reported that most of the mothers in the parent-teacher organization are stay-at-home moms and often use the organization to have 'day to day involvement...with their children.' Nevertheless, she reported regular and frequent visits to the school her children attend and knowledge about their lives outside the home. To a casual observer, this mother looks like a stay-at-home mom in terms of her time availability.

CONCLUSION

Our data reveal flaws in the Mommy Wars rhetoric of stay-at-home versus working mother. There are, indeed, differences in the patterns of volunteering among mothers, but these differences do not simply reflect whether a mother is employed or not. Rather, we find that there is a subgroup of mothers who prioritize volunteering in their children's schools, to gather information, to offer help, or to be there for their children, and these mothers include both those who are employed and those who are not. There may be social class differences between those who volunteer and those who do not (Lareau 2003), but the distinction does not simply reflect employment status. The frequency with which employed mothers talk about their time as if they are stay-at-home mothers, using their availability as a camouflage for their employment, fosters the misunderstanding, but an accurate understanding of mothers' lives requires that we go beyond this false dichotomy.

REFERENCES

Arendell, Terry 2000 "Conceiving and Investigating Motherhood: The Decade's Scholarship." *Journal of Marriage and Family* 62(4): 1192-1207.

Brent, Brian. O. 2008 "Do Schools Really Need More Volunteers?" *Educational Policy* 14(4): 494-510.

Burke, Mary Ann 2001 "Recruiting and Using Volunteers in Meaningful Ways in Secondary Schools." *NAASP Bulletin* 85(627): 46-52.

Deen, Rebecca, and Beth Anne Shelton 2012 "Bake Sales for a Better America: The Role of School Volunteers in Civic Life." *International Journal of Interdisciplinary Social Sciences* 6(7): 25-38.

Dillaway, Heather, and Elizabeth Paré 2008 "Locating Mothers: How Cultural Debates about Stay-at-Home versus Working Mothers Define Women and Home." *Journal of Family Issues* 29(4): 437-464.

Douglas, Susan, and Meredith Michaels 2005 *The Mommy Myth: The Idealization of Motherhood and How it Has Undermined All Women.* New York: Free Press.

Gallagher, Sally, and Naomi Gerstel 2001 "Connections and Constraints: The Effects of Children on Caregiving." *Journal of Marriage and Family* 63(1): 265-275.

Garey, Anita 1995 "Constructing Motherhood on the Night Shift: 'Working Mothers' as 'Stay-at-Home Moms.'" *Qualitative Sociology* 18(4): 415-437.

Goodwin, Susan, and Kate Huppatz 2010 "The Good Mother in Theory and Research: An Overview." In *The Good Mother: Contemporary Motherhoods in Australia.* Susan Goodwin and Kate Huppatz, eds. Pp. 1-24. Sydney: Sydney University Press.

Gorman, Kristin A., and Barbara A. Fritzsche 2002 "The Good-Mother Stereotype: Stay at Home (or Wish That You Did!)." *Journal of Applied Social Psychology* 32(10): 2190-2201.

Griffith, Allison I., and Dorothy Smith 2005 *Mothering for Schooling.* New York: Routledge.

Hays, Sharon 1996 *The Cultural Contradictions of Motherhood.* New Haven: Yale University.

Johnston, Deirdre D., and Debra H. Swanson 2006 "Constructing the 'Good Mother': The Experience of Mothering Ideologies by Work Status." *Sex Roles* 54(7-8): 509-519.

Landeros, Mary 2011 "Defining the 'Good Mother' and the 'Professional Teacher': Parent-Teacher Relationships in an Affluent School District." *Gender and Education* 23(3): 247-262.

Lareau, Anettte 2003 *Unequal Childhoods: Class, Race, and Family Life.* Berkeley: University of California.

Musick, Marc A., and John Wilson. 2008 *Volunteers: A Social Profile.* Bloomington: Indiana University Press.

Reid Boyd, Elizabeth 2002 "'Being There': Mothers Who Stay at Home, Gender and Time." *Women's Studies International Forum* 25(4): 463-470.

Rotolo, Thomas, and John Wilson 2007 "The Effects of Children and Employment Status on the Volunteer Work of American Women." *Nonprofit and Voluntary Sector Quarterly* 36(3): 487-503.

14.

Eco-Momma

The Green Angel in the House

PAMELA MORGAN REDELA

INTRODUCTION

Standards and expectations for white, middle-class motherhood have been a consistent focus in feminist analysis and activism. The discussion that follows asks whether the practice of "Going Green" coupled with the phenomenon of attachment parenting is prompting an ecofeminist resurgence, a challenge to the capitalist patriarchy or simply a new (and impossible) standard in U.S. motherhood.

WHO IS ECO-MOMMA AND WHERE CAN SHE BE FOUND?

Being a middle-class mother in Coastal Southern California is interesting to say the least. This corner of the world is replete with yoga studios, doulas, support groups for home birthing and home-schooling, eco-minded specialty stores as well as "green" and organic alternatives for most products in every marketplace, including Wal-Mart (not that Eco-Momma would EVER shop there!). The cost of living is high, so most households are dual-income, but many subscribe to the traditional male breadwinner, female homemaker model. Regardless of the income generating arrangement, the ideal of "Supermom" is definitely a sociocultural norm, but with the added twist of environmental consciousness. Eco-Momma recycles like nobody's business, scoffs at those who still say "yes" to plastic bags at the grocery store, uses only chemical-free cleaning products, and if she is not yet growing her own, she gets her veggies, organic of course, from the local farmer's market.

All of these "go-green" efforts are surely laudable. Buying organically grown vegetables from a local farm supports the famous "Act Local/Think Global" meme of environmental activism while encouraging healthy eating habits and sustainable agriculture. Using plant-based cleaners keeps sulfites and other harmful chemicals out of drain water and the ocean. Parents can feel free to let their children pitch in on cleaning day without worrying when an older sibling decides that a younger sibling is dirty and needs a full body spray-down with glass cleaner. Recycling, or better yet choosing reusable containers and bags instead of disposable plastic water bottles and Ziploc bags, can make a big difference in the amount of trash each household generates. Some Eco-Mommas go as far as bringing their own containers for leftovers when eating out to avoid the dreaded Styrofoam to-go box.

While ever present in Coastal Southern California, Eco-Momma can be found in every corner of the U.S. She and other eco-minded families are not only recycling and using eco-friendly products, they are also finding creative ways to grow fresh food in the cramped spaces of apartment and townhome living. Those with even a modest plot of land are creating their own mini-ecosystems by composting for rich garden soil, collecting rain water and diverting grey water to irrigate those gardens while raising chickens for eggs and natural fertilizer. These parents (mostly moms) are also to be found in the quite prolific garden movement happening in elementary schools. Some schools are producing enough vegetables to hold farmers' markets as fundraisers and "Green Teams" are popping up in many schools. Spawned by Eco-Momma and her fellow volunteers, their energies are aimed at reducing the amount of trash generated by lunch programs and classroom parties as well as energy saving measures like the use of skylights in new construction and solar panel covered carports complete with electric vehicle parking spots.

These efforts support what ecofeminist leaders Vandana Shiva and Maria Mies define as "the subsistence perspective" to which Eco-Momma subscribes in many ways:

> Modern chemistry, household technology, and pharmacy were proclaimed as women's saviors, because they would 'emancipate' them from household drudgery. Today we realize that much environmental pollution and destruction is

> causally linked to modern household technology. Therefore, can the concept of emancipation be compatible with a concept of preserving the earth as our life base? [Mies 1993]

"Going Green" very often includes doing away with the microwave and foregoing any and all plastic products, including children's toys. Though all of these efforts are surely to be applauded and continued, a critical feminist eye into the "who?" and "where?" of all this activity is necessary. A look into the ramifications of subscribing to a competitive style of motherhood, which Eco-Momma purports to avoid, but is surely guilty of, is revealing a slippery slope on which many women are perched.

Maintaining what I call "feminist vigilance" offers a cautionary tale on the Eco-Momma phenomenon while maintaining hope that Eco-Momism and its accompanying social and cultural changes do not become a passing fad. There is a real possibility of this phenomenon becoming yet another patriarchal trap, setting women and eco-minded activists up for a failure that keeps the gender hierarchy and predatory capitalism in place.

Part of feminist vigilance is continued questioning, investigation, and self-evaluation. Are the ever-increasing standards of "good mothering" creating a new generation of Green Angels in the House or can becoming a 'green goddess', or Eco-Momma, be considered a feminist act? In this regard, Shiva and Mies' question as to whether ecofeminism can save the planet and humanity is important to consider. Women advocating from the position of mother to effect change is still not widely accepted as "real" feminism, and there is good reason to think critically in this regard. Yes, growing one's own vegetables or purchasing from a local farmer's market chips away at the demand for corporate food supply, and proudly claiming the homemaker label can be a radical slap in the face of liberal feminist ideals. The tendency to overvalue career goals and downgrade Eco-Momma's obsession with home life is a definite point of feminist vigilance. One can be an Eco-Momma and hold a job, but part of the point is that subscribing to capitalist ideals of "success" is not central to her existence; this is perhaps a page of the Eco-Momma handbook that liberal feminists may want to read.

Feminist vigilance thus pushes us to take things a step further to examine Eco-Momma's relationship with patriarchy and capitalism. Whether she holds a job outside the home or not, what does the division of household labor look like in her home? How about the gender role socialization of the children? Where does the main income that supports this lifestyle come from? If Eco-Momma's partner is working for DuPont or a transnational export-manufacturing firm, does her activism go down the drain with the chemical run-off of maquiladora worker exploitation?

A CASE IN POINT: ECO-MOMMA IN THE MEDIA

A large part of Eco-Momma's identity is her style of mothering, and most Eco-Mommas subscribe to what has become known as *attachment parenting*. This parenting style, popularized in the 1990's by Dr. William Sears, resurfaced onto the United States' national scene on May 21, 2012 when *Time* magazine ran a cover with the phrase "Are You Mom Enough?" emblazoned in red aside a picture of a hip, beautiful blonde breastfeeding her 3-year old son. To add to the shock value of the image, the child is standing on a small chair instead of being cradled in mom's lap. The article based on the cover entitled "The man who remade Motherhood" discusses the phenomenon of attachment parenting as promoted by Dr. Sears, and sparked quite a new battle in the mommy wars around not only the cover photo, but also standards and practices in contemporary U.S. mothering (Pickert 2012).

Of the controversy surrounding the image, *The Society Pages* contributor Elline Lipkin writes, "The responses, though, were mostly negative. In a TODAY.com poll about the image, more than 131,000 people weighed in; 73% saying they would have preferred not to see the image" (Lipkin 2012). Despite the fact that the content of the article focuses the benefits and challenges of attachment parenting, the general public continues to focus on the breast as pornographic and proves itself lazy and superficial in that none of the commenters seem to have done their homework regarding the woman in the photograph or the supposed "founders" of the movement. (Attachment parenting is based on the teachings of a man who was inspired by observations made of poverty stricken indigenous women in Venezuela by a childless woman; these details escape virtually everyone's "analysis" in the buzz surrounding the story, but a full discussion is outside the scope of this essay.)

The woman on the cover is Jamie Lynne Grumet. She is the author of two mommy blogs. *I am not the Babysitter*, which focuses the trials and triumphs of her transracial family, and *Mommy hates Chemicals*, which reviews chemical free beauty and cleaning products. She is also the founder of the Fayye Foundation, which "was created to aid the orphan crisis [in Ethiopia] by addressing the health, education, and vocational goals of women and mothers" (Grumet 2012). Grumet, her husband, and their biological child are white and their adopted son is Ethiopian. Though the anti-chemical blog is cheeky and laden with class privilege (as are nearly all of the mommy blogs out there, eco or not) and the foundation has noble intentions many would criticize it for subscribing to the "great white hope" meme.

As a point of feminist vigilance, it is important to contemplate the role of burgeoning Eco-Mommas like Grumet into the blogosphere and the public arena. With titles ranging from Grumet's straightforward *Mommy hates Chemicals* to others like *Peace Love Organic Mom* and *Crunchy Livin' Mama Style*, an overarching theme is the marketing of eco-friendly household goods with a few bits of quippy parenting advice thrown in. In her "I am Not the Babysitter" blog, Grumet offers very thoughtful and touching pieces on international adoption and abundantly shares social-justice minded stories and videos. She even links to a video presentation on white privilege by Time Wise. Shall the efforts of Grumet and her counterparts be taken as an ecofeminist stepping-stone into the recognition and use of white, middle class privilege for progressive social justice aims? Or are they more accurately described as egotistical competitiveness in the ongoing "mommy wars"? Could the competitive aspect be considered of the "healthy" type that fosters progress?

In support of the stepping-stone idea, Greta Gaard, in her chapter "Ecofeminism and Native American cultures: pushing the limits of cultural Imperialism?" states that when ecofeminists speak of the interconnectedness of all natural life, they can be understood to be making a political and a spiritual statement simultaneously. The only thing left is for us to realize that (Gaard 1993).

In this sense, the philosophical, emotive, "moms can save the Earth" motif that permeates 21st century Eco-Mommas' everyday mothering and parenting practices does subscribe to an ecofeminist ethic. The issue that remains is the well-known pitfalls of women's uncritical acceptance of standards placed on "good" motherhood. The bar is ever rising, and despite the fact that a great many women can handle it all, as the Jamie Lynne Grumets of the world are showing us, does not mean that they should. As pondered at the outset of these thoughts, is "buying into" the Eco-Momma identity setting women up for failure? Not only is Eco-Momma taking on the intensive mothering style of attachment parenting, she is now going to save the entire planet from environmental destruction through her use of cloth diapers and switching from tampons to the reusable menstrual cup; a daunting task to take on between making the organic squash puree for baby, maintaining a chemical free home, managing every minute and detail of her children's social and academic lives, and looking "hot" while doing it.

CONCLUSION

Rosemary Radford Ruether sums up the worldview of ecofeminism quite well in her chapter "Ecofeminism: symbolic and social connections of the oppression of women and the domination of Nature" when she writes:

> In ecofeminist culture and ethic, mutual interdependency replaces the hierarchies of domination as the model of relationship between men and women, between human groups, and between humans and other beings. All racist, sexist, classist, cultural, and anthropocentric assumptions of the superiority of whites over blacks, males over females, managers over workers, humans over animals and plants, must be discarded. In a real sense, the so-called superior pole in each relation is actually the more dependent side of the relationship (Ruether 1993).

Through this line of thought, we begin to see that the dependence on mother that Eco-Momma fosters in her family can be a transformative force. It can inspire a renewed look at the value and purpose of care work in a society that places production and consumption on a higher plane than reproduction and sustainability. It can reinvigorate innovation through a greater demand for earth-friendly products in the marketplace. It can also, and perhaps most importantly, encourage humanity to slow the pace of everyday life enough to nourish the bonds of community. If Eco-Mommas are able to maintain the momentum of the movement, keep a focused feminist vigilance, and take to heart Ruether's assertion that "there must be a conversion of men to the work of women, along with the conversion of male consciousness to the earth" (Ruether 1993), Virginia Woolf may well be able to rest in peace.

REFERENCES

Alele "Blog Comment." *Hollywood Life blogsite.* Hollywood, CA: hollywoodlife.com, May 26, 2012.

Gaard, Greta 1993 "Ecofeminism and Native American Cultures: Pushing the Limits of Cultural Imperialism?" In *Ecofeminism: Women, Animals, Nature*. Pp.309. Philadelphia: Temple University Press.

Grumet, Jamie Lynne *FAYYE Foundation*. November 20, 2012. http://www.fayyefoundation.org/about/ (accessed November 20, 2012).

Lipkin, Elline *Controversy RE: Time's "Are You Mom Enough" Cover*. May 30, 2012. http://thesocietypages.org/socimages/2012/05/30/controversy-over-times-are-you-mom-enough-cover/ (accessed November 20, 2012).

Mies, Maria, and Vandana Shiva 1993 *Ecofeminism*. London: Zed Books, 1993.

Pickert, Kate 2012 "The Man Who Remade Motherhood". *Time Magazine*, Los Angeles, May 21, 2012.

Ruether, Rosemary Radford 1993 "Ecofeminism: Symbolic and Social Connections of the Oppression of Women and the Domination of Nature." In *Ecofeminism and the Sacred* by Carol J. Adams, Pp. 21. New York: Continuum.

15.

Smart Women, Different Choices

College-Educated Women with Children Negotiating Work and Family

DIANNA SHANDY AND KARINE MOE

INTRODUCTION

Since 2004, we have been engaged in an interdisciplinary research project combining the big-picture approach of economics with the ethnographic approach of anthropology, privileging the experiences of individual women, as described in their own words. Our research stems from unexpected transformations that surfaced at the turn of the 21st century in the data regarding women's United States labor force participation and a desire to understand the story behind those numbers. Specifically, women were leaving their jobs, and this trend was most pronounced among married women with professional degrees and children under 18 years. Women with professional degrees, though not the majority, are of particular significance because they have the highest labor force participation of women across all educational groups in America. We suggest that these shifts in women's labor force participation have added a new layer to the complex and contested domain of at-home motherhood.

In this chapter, we situate our research within the broader public debate surrounding shifting trends in at-home motherhood in the United States. We describe our study, which focused on college educated women's experiences negotiating work and family. Next we update the numbers on women and work, incorporating shifts associated with the Great Recession of 2007-2009. Finally, we look beyond the numbers to discuss women's struggles with identity and the strategies they deploy in the public and private sphere to maintain self-worth. Our years of analyzing these issues have taught us that the experiences of at-home moms and employed moms are inherently intertwined. Appreciating the dynamism of women's relationship with paid employment is often absent in studies that rely on census and employment data alone. Qualitative studies representing a snapshot in time can fail to appreciate the fluid nature of a woman's changing employment status over time and can lack a sense of scale. Our mixed method approach allows us to patch together what is, in effect, a piecemeal set of data, evidence, and experiences. Approaching these issues in this way yields new insights, allowing us to harness the power of numbers and to simultaneously tell the stories behind the numbers.

Before we delve too far into a discussion of women, work, and family, it is helpful to make a few key points. First, women have always worked, just not always for pay. Thus, when we talk about women's movement into or out of the labor force, we are sensitive to the ways in which this is commentary not so much on their efforts but on the way this work is recognized or rewarded in society. Second, we are attuned to the ways in which employment rates have varied by race and class over time (Collins 1990).[1] And, finally, we appreciate that most women continue to juggle work and children because their families depend on their income. However, while this financial imperative is central to any discussion of women, work, and family, this reality shouldn't serve to silence other aspects of women's experience with work in America.

SITUATING OUR RESEARCH IN THE BROADER PUBLIC DEBATE

Around the time we became interested in this research topic, the media started to buzz regarding these same sets of issues. Journalist Lisa Belkin (2003) wrote a piece for the *New York Times Magazine* called "The Opt-Out Revolution." Women gave various reasons for resigning from their jobs, but all implied that when push came to shove, time with their families trumped career. The media jumped on the bandwagon, and a multitude of popular press articles, highlighting professional women leaving high-powered jobs, followed. These stories incited passionate debate across the country.

This initial media frenzy was followed by a spirited round of rejoinders in the form of books with titles like *Get to Work* (Hirshman 2006) and *The Feminist Mistake* (Bennetts 2007). These books warned women of the dangers (to both themselves and to society at large) of recreating a system of dependency on men. In the words of *New York Times* economic reporter Ann Crittenden describing one of these books, [the author] "tackles head-on the popular myth that a man is a financial plan."[2]

A few short years later, the economic crisis of 2007 seemed to usher in a new opportunity to reproach at-home moms who had voluntarily walked away from careers during times of economic plenty. As families looked at uncertain times ahead and recalculated budgets in light of real and anticipated losses, there was renewed interest in "re-entry" programming (See, for example, Wright 2011). A certain smugness surfaced among those who had remained in their jobs vis-à-vis their counter-parts who had left their jobs.

A striking consequence of the Great Recession has been a sharp drop in birth rates. The Great Recession may thus have an indirect effect on women's relationship with paid employment if women are less likely to have additional (or any) children, and thus may increase their commitment to the paid labor force. What remains to be seen is whether these declines represent decisions to reduce family size or rather delay childbirth until after the economy recovers. Given that the decline in birth rates weaken with mothers' age, and that older mothers showed consistent, if not rising fertility in recent years, it may be that in the long run, a decline in family size may not occur (Livingston 2011). Only time will tell what impact, if any, the Great Recession of 2007-2009 will have on how women see their relationship with paid employment.

As we move into an economic recovery, the debate seems to have gained renewed vigor. *The Washington Post* (2009) reported that new Census data "dispels the myth of the opt-out revolution" (St. George 2009). Yet, in summer 2012, academic and public commentator Anne-Marie Slaughter (2012), in the *Atlantic Magazine*, wrote a controversial and highly visible piece called, "Why Women Still Can't Have it All," detailing what she sees as the limits in being a top professional while raising children. And, on it goes.

In our work, we draw on our backgrounds as social scientists to chart a path through this maelstrom of public opinion to document how American women frame their relationship with work, the forces that shape this relationship, and what these decisions mean to these women and their families.

INTRODUCING THE STUDY

Our study is grounded in a methodological approach drawing on the strengths of both anthropology and economics. We looked at nationally representative data from governmental sources. We conducted our own online anonymous survey of nearly 900 college alumnae, who graduated between 1970 and 2006. The survey included ample open-ended questions. We figured we had hit on a topic women want to talk about when the flood of richly-detailed responses to the survey came pouring in. We also conducted 150 formal in-depth interviews and focus group interviews with women from across the country. These interviews were supplemented by roughly another 100 informal interviews. We have maintained contact with some of those we interviewed, and continue to follow, although in a less structured manner, how these issues unfold over time.

Through our years of analysis of these issues, we have adopted the view that the experiences of at-home moms and employed moms are inherently intertwined. This reality was brought home to us quite forcefully in our attempts to do research: Women refused to stay put in the categories of "at-home" or employed, as their own employment status shifted, and our research questions and methods had to attend to the dynamic nature of women's lives.

DEMOGRAPHIC SHIFTS AND STRUCTURAL CHALLENGES

To understand the experiences of at-home moms, we needed to have a grasp of the social forces that shaped their options. Elsewhere (Moe and Shandy 2009), we examine key demographic shifts in women's increased access to education that opened doors to interesting and well-paid careers. We also look at how by marrying men who were doing similar jobs, some of the college-educated women we interviewed evolved into 100-hour couples, or couples who work extremely long hours per week. We explore how by combining these long work hours with continuing responsibilities for managing the home, and increasing pressures for spending more intense time with their children, led many women to feel that they could not maintain both their careers and their families. Something had to give.

We document how certain structural characteristics of the workplace inhibit women's ability to excel in their careers while creating a home life. We focus on the concept of glass ceilings and maternal walls. Most people are well aware of the concept of a glass ceiling, meaning a form of discrimination that limits a woman's advancement at work. Fewer are familiar with the concept of a "maternal wall," which can be seen in the form of bias against women when they are pregnant or become mothers. This type of discrimination is becoming increasingly prevalent. For example, the Equal Employment Opportunity Commission (2013), the federal agency charged with enforcing anti-discrimination laws, reports that there has been a 35 percent rise in pregnancy discrimination suits during the past decade. This compares to a 13 percent rise in sex-based suits filed in the same time period (Equal Employment Opportunity Commission 2013.) Even among women who felt they had put a few cracks in the glass ceiling during the ascent of their careers, many later encountered a maternal wall, prompting them to step back from their jobs.

A lack of flexible work options forced many to choose either resigning their jobs altogether or embarking on a "mommy track," which does not allow them to devote time to family for a period of their lives and then resume upward mobility in their careers on a par with their male colleagues who are also parents.

We would be remiss if we didn't convey that some women left their careers at the top of their game. They didn't feel discriminated against or blocked in any way. They loved their work, loved the adrenaline and the competition. But there were other types of structural constraints that impeded their ability to balance work and family. An example of such a structural constraint centers around childcare. High quality and affordable childcare is hard to find, and even when found, providers often have rigid drop off and pick up hours. Many childcare centers charge parents by the minute if they are late, and will call child protective services if parents do not arrive within an hour of closing time. Of course, these rules are structured so that the childcare workers can return home to care for their own children. Nevertheless, these constraints don't necessarily mesh with workplace demands for working late or getting a last-minute travel assignment. Compelling to us was the infamous shooting that took place on an army base in Texas in 2010. Police sergeant Kimberly Munley shot the gunman, but was herself shot in the process. When asked what her first thought was following the shooting, she replied that she wanted to grab her cell phone so she could call someone to pick up her kids from childcare.

We documented a broad diversity of individual experiences — many successful, many not — of trying to combine paid work and raising children. Striking to us was how many of the bright and sophisticated women we interviewed tended to see their struggles as individualized, rather than gender-based challenges. Most jobs and workplace norms were structured originally for men who had a wife devoted full-time to managing the home life. Typically designed by and for men, few careers offer alternatives to combine work and motherhood, without invoking a significant penalty in terms of advancement and pay. For lawyers and for academics, for example those stressful years leading up to partnership or tenure coincide exactly with a woman's prime childbearing years.

Though these structural constraints are, in our estimation, a critical point to be made in understanding the realities of at-home moms, it's important to note that the issues we discuss are not black or white. Not all of the women we interviewed ever intended to combine paid work and family. Similarly, not all of the reasons that women gave for leaving or downsizing their careers were negative. Many women talked about the wonderful benefits that came to their families when they decided to downsize their careers. They noted having more time for grandparents, or to play as a family on the weekend. One mom told us, "I enjoy being able to pay attention to my kids when they need it. I'm not running at the frayed edge." Being home with children is hard work, but it can also be incredibly fulfilling. And some women seemed quite surprised by this. An important part of this story, then, is to appreciate the *affective* dimensions of parenthood and to recognize that the choice to downsize their careers led to many positives in the lives of the women we interviewed.

UPDATES TO THE BIG PICTURE

The big picture framework helps us to understand how the experiences of the women we interviewed fit into a broader context over time. Here, we outline women's labor force participation rates and discuss what this approach to understanding women and work in America overlooks.

The labor force participation rate is the percent of the working-age population (16 years and older) that is in the labor force. To be in the labor force, one must either be employed or seeking employment. The Bureau of Labor Statistics provides monthly estimates of the labor force based on surveys of about 60,000 households.

There have been some unexpected shifts in women's labor force participation over the past two decades that have grabbed economists' attention.[3] The percentage of married women who have children under eighteen and participate in the labor force fell from 72 percent in 2000 to 70.6 percent in 2011. The largest declines in labor force participation in the late 1990s were among married mothers of infants, whose participation dropped six percentage points (from 59 to 53 percent) between 1997 and 2000 (Cohany and Sok 2007). During the first decade of the 21st century, that participation level has inched back up to 56 percent. However, it was the actions of college educated women that attracted the most attention in the early 2000s. The labor force participation of college educated women peaked in 1997 at 75.5 percent, and then dropped to 73 percent in 2002. Participation rates haven't changed much since that time, though 2010 marks the lowest rate at 72.4 percent.

To put these numbers in context, we need to consider the impact of the "Great Recession," which officially ran from December 2007 until June 2009. This recession ran deeper and longer than any recent recessions.[4] Labor force participation tends to fall during recessions. Unemployed people are still considered part of the labor force, but if recessions are long and deep enough, discouraged workers may stop looking for work. These discouraged workers then drop out of the labor force, even though they still would prefer to work than not.

The recoveries from the most recent recessions (those since the 1990s) have been categorized as "jobless" recoveries, in that output rises, but it takes a long time for unemployment to fall. So although we mark the end of the recession in June 2009, we would expect to see labor force participation rates continue to fall for sometime thereafter, and that is exactly what happened. Between 2007 and 2011, the labor force participation rates of all women fell 1.2 percentage points. Economist Willem van Zandweghe (2012) reports that most of that decline can be attributed to the recession.[5] Thus, it is likely that once the economy recovers, we will see women's labor force participation rates returning to their pre-2007 levels. It is unclear whether they will ever return to their 2000 highs.

Figure 1 illustrates the decline in college-educated women's labor force participation between 1992 and 2010.

While this big picture context is important to help frame the discussion, it is important to acknowledge the limitations inherent in any analysis of labor force statistics. Though labor force participation is useful for measuring a woman's work if you are attempting to understand the American

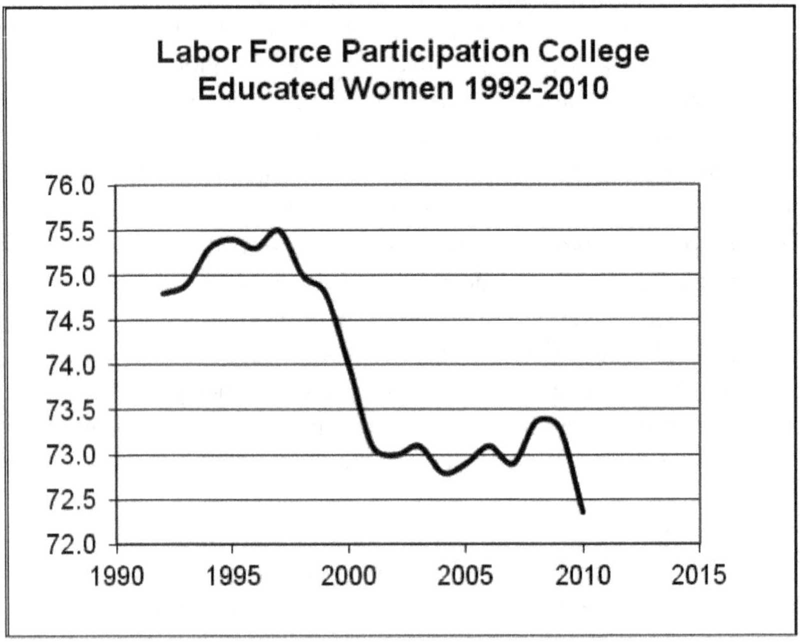

Figure 1: Labor Force Participation College Educated Women 1992 - 2010

economy in broad strokes, labor force participation rates mask the *intensity* of work. For the purposes of generating a participation rate, a woman is "in" or "out" of the labor force. This kind of analysis does not consider hours worked or full-time versus part-time status. Similarly, these big picture analyses do not reveal the ways women downsize their careers, for example, by choosing less demanding careers than the ones they were trained for, forgoing promotions, or in other ways remaining employed by sidelining aspirations for an upward ascent of their career. In this way, the big picture can fail to capture the complexity of lived experience.

A strength of the type of statistical analyses typically used by economists is that by using large enough samples, economists can move past the experiences of individuals to show trends for populations. But one of the major downsides of using these large samples in economic analyses is that they can lack nuance. Economists are often restricted to data sets that already exist, and when they do their own empirical research they often rely on quantitative data (Moe 2003). In terms of the issue at hand, economists, relying on data collected by the U.S. Census Bureau, track whether people are working, that is "in the labor force" or not working "out of the labor force." Another limitation is that economists seldom actually talk to the people they are studying. Therefore, in attempting to understand women's challenges to balance work and family, these statistics mask the myriad trade-offs mothers have made to "make it work." They also tell us little about the lives of women once they exit the labor force.

EXPLORING THESE ISSUES ON THE HOMEFRONT

Now that we have an understanding of the context in which women exited the labor force — both the cultural politics in play and the larger labor trends — we focus on how the spike in numbers of women with professional degrees exiting the work force shapes the experience of at-home motherhood. We see this happening in a number of ways.

First, very few of the college-educated women we interviewed planned for or anticipated being an at-home mom. So, for many, they found themselves in a situation they did not expect and for which they had few role models. Second, similar to what other researchers have found, we noted that given the relatively recent ascent of women into certain male-dominated fields, they had conflicted feelings about stepping off that track, even if they were deeply satisfied with the outcome of their decision (Evans and Grant 2008, Hanauer 2002, Stone 2007). Even if they were pleased with how their shift in employment circumstances benefited themselves and their families, they expressed misgivings regarding what their decision meant in societal terms.

Many of the at-home moms who left behind a career described the challenges of maintaining status in a society that dictates that so much of one's self-worth is created at work. In the words of one attorney, "If you're talking at a cocktail party you feel like a very boring person if your answer to the [what do you do question] is, 'I'm at home with my kids.'" Another mom echoed this sentiment when she said: "It's hard on my ego to be the stay-at-home mom...It's painful to see people's eyes glaze over when I say what I do." Another said, "One of the biggest challenges of being a stay-at-home parent is you have to have a really strong ego, because you essentially drop off the face of the planet as far as the rest of the world is concerned. You don't exist."

The women we interviewed resisted society's attempts to re-categorize them in some sort of diminished role when they left jobs for home. In other words, they categorized back (Malkki 1995). Here we look at the different ways women manage their identity in an attempt to negotiate this societal tendency to marginalize them for their decision to stay home.

Some women focused on the temporal nature of their decision, saying "I'm at home, for now." Others couched their decisions in terms of early retirement: "I retired when I had to go on bed rest with my first child. I was financially able to do that due to my husband's income. I wanted to work part-time at that point, but my job masters would not allow that. So I retired. I have kept myself entertained by being very involved as a community and school volunteer."

Others focused on rechanneling their efforts and energies by taking on quasi-professional positions such as on the boards of non-profits or in the schools. Another popular technique was to do intermittent project-based work. Both of these strategies serve to help women maintain skills and a professional identity, but they also illustrate how the work categories of full-time and part-time fail to capture the complexity of women's relationship to "work."

One of the most intriguing parts of our study was the importance these women placed on "running with a pack of smart women." Having social networks of women with similar circumstances provided a lifeline for many at-home moms. In our earlier work, we focused on how these social networks, perhaps, facilitated outflows of women from the labor force. It's a lot easier for an ex-veterinarian to grapple with the loss of her professional identity, if her friends the lawyers and financial analysts are doing it too. Given the shifts in the economy since we initiated our study, one has to consider the ways these same social networks form pathways for re-entry into the labor force. Who better than an at-home mom-turned-once-again-professional to recognize the untapped potential in those gaps on the resume? This is an area we did not explore systematically, but one that merits further study.

CONCLUSION

In this chapter, we have situated our research within the broader public debate surrounding shifting trends in at-home motherhood in the United States. We have focused on college-educated women's experiences of negotiating work and family through an interdisciplinary framework.

Interdisciplinary work in the social sciences may seem quite natural, as the different disciplines often study quite similar themes and phenomena. Yet, research collaborations between economists and anthropologists are rare as the research methods of these disciplines vary dramatically. Yet, each discipline can gain from the strengths brought by the other. This study combines the quantitative with the qualitative, the aggregated with the case study, taking research methodologies from both disciplines to tackle the ongoing challenges facing mothers in the U.S.

Taking the long view of women and work in America through the Great Recession of 2007-2009, we describe women's struggles with identity and the strategies they deploy in the public and private sphere to maintain self-worth when they embrace at-home motherhood. We revisit our earlier analysis to suggest that since Americans determine value based on occupation, the professionalization of motherhood in the new millennium can serve as a strategy for at-home moms to maintain status and, perhaps, as a way to invest in future, yet unseen, opportunities.

NOTES

[1]Historically, black women have worked at higher rates than white women. In 1965, when only 38 percent of white women worked in the paid labor force, almost half of black women did. Black women's participation rates did not rise as steeply as it did for white women, and in 2011 black women participated at a rate of 59 percent, only slightly higher rates than the 58 percent of their white counterparts. Black married mothers also participate at the highest rates of all married mothers. In 2010, three-fourths of Black married mothers of children under 18 years old participated in the labor force. Non-hispanic white and Asian married mothers of children under 18 had similar participation rates of about two-thirds. Hispanic mothers had the lowest rates, with a labor force participation rate of just over half (Blau, Ferber and Winkler 2006; U.S. Department of Labor 2011:16-17).

[2] Cover of Bennett's *The Feminine Mistake.*

[3]Unless otherwise noted, the data on labor force participation is taken from the United States Census Bureau (various years, and the United States Department of Labor (2011).

[4]The dating of recessions is a complicated process calculated by the National Bureau of Economic Research (NBER). Unemployment is only one of the factors that the NBER takes into account when dating recessions. The bottoming out of real GDP, or national output, typically drives the end date of a recession.

[5]Interestingly, van Zandweghe (2012) attributes only half of the male decline of 2.8 percentage points over the same time period to the recession. He argues that women may be more sensitive to business cycles. The reasoning goes as follows: women are more likely than men to develop human capital both in market and non-market activities. So when labor market conditions tank, nonmarket work can become relatively more productive for women, leading them to opt out of the labor force.

REFERENCES

Belkin, Lisa 2003 "The Opt-Out Revolution." *The New York Times Magazine,* October 26.

Bennetts, Leslie 2007 *The Feminine Mistake: Are We Giving Up Too Much.* New York: Hyperion Press.

Blau, Francine D., Marianne A. Ferber, and Anne E. Winkler 2006 *The Economics of Women, Men, and Work.* 5th Edition. Upper Saddle River, NJ: Pearson, Prentice Hall.

Cohany, Sharon, and Emy Sok. 2007 "Trends in Labor Force Participation of Married Mothers of Infants." *Monthly Labor Review* 130(2): 9-16.

Collins, Patricia Hill 1990 *Black Feminist Thought: Knowledge, Consciousness, and the Politics of Empowerment.* New York: Unwin Hyman.

Evans, Elrena, and Caroline Grant 2008 *Mama PhD: Women Write about Motherhood and the Academic Life.* Piscataway, NJ: Rutgers University Press.

Equal Employment Opportunity Commission 2013 *Charge Statistics.* http://www.eeoc.gov/eeoc/statistics/enforcement/charges.cfm. (accessed May 28, 2013).

Hanauer, Cathi, ed. 2002 *The Bitch in the House: 26 Women Tell the Truth about Sex, Solitude, Work, Motherhood, and Marriage.* New York: Perennial Books.

Hirshman, Linda R. 2006 *Get to Work: A Manifesto for Women of the World.* New York: Viking Press.

Livingston, Gretchen 2011 *In a Down Economy, Fewer Births. Social and Demographic Trends.* Pew Research Center.

Malkki, Liisa 1995 *Purity and Exile: Violence, Memory, and National Cosmology among Hutu Refugees in Tanzania.* Chicago: University of Chicago Press.

Moe, Karine S. 2003 *Women, Family, and Work: Writings on the Economics of Gender.* Malden, MA: Blackwell Publishing.

Moe, Karine, and Dianna Shandy 2009 *Glass Ceilings and 100-Hour Couples: What the Opt-Out Phenomenon Can Teach Us About Work and Family.* Athens, GA: University of Georgia Press.

St. George, Donna 2009 "Census Dispels 'Opting-Out' Notion for Stay-at-Home Moms." *Washington Post,* October 1.

Slaughter, Anne-Marie, 2012 "Why Women Still Can't Have it All." *The Atlantic Magazine,* July/August.

Stone, Pamela 2007 *Opting Out: Why Women Really Quit Careers and Head Home.* Berkeley: University of California Press.

U.S. Department of Labor 2011 *Women in the Labor Force: A Databook 2011.* Report 1034.

U.S. Census Bureau. 2013 *Statistical Abstract of the United States* http://www.census.gov/compendia/statab/ (accessed May 31, 2013).

Van Zandweghe, Willem. 2012 "Interpreting the Recent Decline in Labor Force Participation." *Economic Review* First Quarter: 5-34.

Wright, Melissa 2011 "Re-entry Into the Legal Profession After a Long Hiatus: Overcoming Difficulties With Equal Rights". *The Official Journal of Minnesota Women Lawyers* April: 8-9.

16.

"But She Has A Nanny"...With Accompanying Eye Roll

Considering Mother Work With a Live-In Caregiver

REBECCA JAREMKO BROMWICH

As a younger woman, I used to roll my eyes when my mother-in-law complained about the "nannies" her family employed when they lived in colonial Africa. It is both ironic and (some would say) just that I find myself now met with similar eye rolls about my "first world problems." Our family employs a nanny too. I write this from a place of some defensiveness, mostly because I used to be a vicious critic of people like me.

Taking mother work seriously as work, caring labor, requires a holistic consideration of the employment relationships between domestic caregivers, the families who employ them and stay-at-home mothers generally. Contemplating the increasing prevalence of paid domestic labor in North America in the context of a discussion about stay-at-home mothers is also a useful way to get beneath binary oppositions between work and home that are counterproductive to advocacy and activism that would support mothers regardless of their level of attachment to paid employment.

I am a mother of four young children. Serendipity and a period spent abroad combined to add four children in four years to our family. A period while I could not "work" full-time, because of jurisdictional barriers to my licensure, was ideal time for us to build the family we had dreamed of. I have never been fully a stay-at-home mom but there were years during which I worked from home in the evenings only or taught only about eight hours a week. During these periods, after a few months on my own, I worked collaboratively with a mother's helper or nanny. My memories of birthing and nursing four children in a four year period in a foreign country away from family support and while my husband's career demanded he be away long days, many evenings and often overnight are ambivalent. That past is something I will never regret and never wish away. It was also hard; it was not in the best interests of my children for me to try to muscle through this work on my own.

I was macho. I figured if I could handle things like law school, law practice and graduate school, I could manage four small children. I am, after all, part of a generation whose mothers were second wave feminists, who were raised to think we could "have it all." A recent article in *The Atlantic* by Anne-Marie Slaughter has raised public controversy about how the United States economy and society make "having it all" impossible for women.[1] At an earlier stage in my life than came in Slaughter's, I was faced with the same realization in a different way: I could not do it all. I had to admit my fallibility to ensure my children's best interests and my emotional health was secure. However, for me, the demands of paid work were manageable: it was the unpaid work of bearing children that I couldn't manage on my own.

Investment of my ego in the assertion that I could be superwoman was unhealthy. I did look for help from my family doctor. Despite what I was told by my physician, time has shown that I did not need anti-depressants or any other self-help intervention. I believe now I asked the wrong person for support; why did I conceive of my struggles as a medical issue? What I needed was help not with my internal coping mechanisms but with the problem: I needed someone to help me attack that pile of laundry and to change that diaper pail. *I needed three hours of sleep in a row.* I didn't need support in my self: I needed support in my work. The daily tasks of child-rearing and housekeeping had to be made possible to surmount. For how many other mothers is that also true? Without diminishing the claim that postpartum depression is physiologically real, I would bet that many new mothers have problems at least as labor-related as they are medical.

Imagine a Utopian scenario where not just pharmaceuticals but domestic helpers are made available to parents of young children regardless of the family's socio-economic status, in which there really is a "Nanny 911", on call. Consider a world where no social worker visits a young mother without diapers and a mop, who, instead of a notebook, brings rubber gloves and is ready to scrub some floors. Mother work is work. Why does it sound strange to re-imagine a world where that work is supported? Too much is said that pathologizes new mothers and too little is noticed about the magnitude of the tasks they face and the social context in which they face them. The lives of paid domestic caregivers are un-noticed to the point where the very fact of their existence is made often invisible in popular understandings of who does mother work.

Seriously considering the situation of paid caregivers in the home provides an opportunity to get beneath the binary opposition of at home mom and working mom. A home where a paid caregiver and parents share tasks of child-rearing and housekeeping traditionally associated with the mother's role is both entirely traditional and a radical space where constructions of "working" mom, "stay-at-home" mom, gender roles and whose job is what and what work means can be reconsidered.

Considering the employment context of domestic workers can unmask the constructed nature of the notion that it is "natural" and historically traditional for the biological mother of children to be their sole – or even primary – caregiver. The notion that care by a solitary, full-time, "stay-at-home" mom is *the* normal paradigm for childrearing in human history is false. In societies worldwide, a wide variety of caregiving arrangements have been and still are typical. Children are everywhere cared for by nurses, nannies, grandmothers, older children and other adults.

Homes where domestic caregivers are employed are places where the public-private sphere divide can be undermined. The private space of the employer's home is the public space of the caregiver's work and it is the public space of a managerial role for the employers. Such homes are also sites where continued colonization or neo-colonialism becomes visible. Nannies were part of colonial households through the regions colonized by European nations in the 19th and 20th centuries. Paid staff positions for childcare workers were also the norm in many households in England, Canada and the United States for many years. This working relationship has often been racialized, with women of color retained in large numbers in many contexts to care for the children of white families.

Though paid domestic labor is often considered to be a relic of historical inequality and an unsavory aspect of a Victorian, or colonial, or American Confederate history, it is in fact an area of significant growth in the late capitalist economies of both Canada and the United States in the early twenty first century. As Pierrette Hondagneu-Sotello (2001) explores in her book *Domestica: Immigrant Workers Cleaning and Caring in the Shadows of Affluence*, paid domestic labor is a major area of economic growth, and "has become the domain of disenfranchised immigrant women of color" who work often illegally, with no citizenship rights, "under the table" in that country (at xii). In Canada, the situation is similar, but slightly different, as this country has formalized "live-in caregiver" programs[2] where, in exchange for a period of two years in employment as a live-in-caregiver, women, predominantly from the Philippines, can gain a foothold on Canadian citizenship and the ability to bring their families over to share in the immigrant dream by obtaining permanent resident status.

Live-in caregivers are very often mothers themselves, sometimes separated from their children by tremendous geographical distance. The caregivers we have employed have all been working mothers, tragically and bravely leaving their own children with relatives in countries in the global south in order to provide an income stream and a chance for their children to emigrate to the first world. They ironically leave their children far away to ensure those children a better life: what could more profoundly be mother work? They are performing the most profoundly self-sacrificing act imaginable, short of dismemberment or death, in the best interests of their children. These women are incredibly vulnerable to abuse, both as illegal workers in the US and as effectively indentured workers for their first two years in Canada. Much more needs to be done to ensure they are treated justly.

Along with the work of Hondagneu-Sotello, there is an emerging – although still small – literature about the experience of domestic employment that takes seriously the ethical situation of the employer with reference to considerations about racial, gender and global inequalities. For example, Barbara Ehrenreich and Arlie Hochschild (2003) have looked at global migrations of women to fill "care deficits" in wealthy countries, whose absence from their third world countries of origin in turn leaves a "care deficit" back home. More should be written. Hondagneu-Sotello focuses on the situation of domestic caregivers themselves; Ehrenreich and Hochschild look at global economics. I would also like to see research that provides more insights about families who employ domestic workers.

Mothers who pay employees for sharing in domestic labor are not abdicating their roles as parents. Determining who does mother work is not a zero sum question. Several people often share in the task of caring for small children, and money is exchanged for some of this work. Mothers undermine our own interests when we deride or disregard those who employ paid help. Certainly the financial means to hire a nanny requires a certain level of privilege, but it is also a privilege to have living, healthy, caring extended family members and friends available to help with one's children, a spouse with time to assist, or a spouse at all.

It is problematic that Western feminism and the surge of women like me into professional roles in the paid work force appear to have been addressed less by changes to gender roles as between men and women in middle class families than it has been glossed over - *not* solved - by "outsourcing." Faced with a dearth of stay-at-home moms, many families simply import a second mother from a less developed country. This masking of problems inherent in western capitalism with solutions that rely upon third world labor and depletion of third world resources is consistent with a broader pattern evident across many productive sectors, like garment and automobile manufacture, for example. Live-in nannies from the Philippines and telemarketers from Mumbai calling on behalf of American companies are part of the same globalized economic trends that compound disadvantages faced by the developing world.

The brief-case wielding, smartphone toting, blue suit-wearing "working mom" and the lulu-lemon sporting, ponytail wearing, minivan driving, cookie baking (but not cookie eating) "stay-at-home" mom are, of course, stereotypes. They do not reflect the realities of many people. Live-in caregivers are one type of working mother. Mothers who employ caregivers are often one sort of stay-at-home mom. The assumed binary of mothers as map-able onto two categories excludes growing numbers of women, like my live-in caregiver and myself, who are also both mothers, who also have a stake in the discussion of what mothers need and in what politics mothers can and should collectively engage. We count.

Caring for children and homes is real work. It is performed by an array of people, paid and unpaid, in different configurations. Advocacy for fair labor practices for domestic workers, like nannies, should be part of advocacy for stay-at-home mothers. Advocacy for fair tax treatment of family employers' payments to nannies should be part of what is considered legitimate in supporting mother work. Work towards securing the citizenship and other human rights of women working as domestic caregivers should be a central goal of maternal feminist activism. The interests of employers of domestic caregivers and paid caregivers overlap with those of other mothers. All of our interests are served by recognizing caregiving labor as valuable, crucial, social work that ought to be counted, supported and recognized.

NOTES

[1]Slaughter, Anne-Marie, "Why Women Still Can't Have it All" *The Atlantic* (July 2012) http://www.theatlantic.com/magazine/archive/2012/07/why-women-still-can-8217-t-have-it-all/9020/

[2]Here is some information about Canada's "Live-In Caregiver Program" from Customs and Immigration Canada's website: http://www.cic.gc.ca/english/work/caregiver/index.asp

REFERENCES

Ehrenreich, Barbara, and Arlie Hochschild, eds. 2003 *Global Woman: Nannies, Maids, and Sex Workers in the New Economy 2003*. New York. Metropolitan Books.

Hondagneu-Sotello, Pierrette 2001 *Domestica: Immigrant Workers Cleaning and Caring in the Shadows of Affluence.* Berkeley. University of California Press.

Slaughter, Anne-Marie 2012 "Why Women Still Can't Have It All." *The Atlantic Monthly* July.

17.

'Quiet Desperation'

The 'Retreat' and Recuperation of the Housewife and Stay-At-Home Mother on Popular Television

ANNA MARIE BAUTISTA

Can the problem that has no name be somehow related to the domestic routine of the housewife? When a woman tries to put the problem into words, she often merely describes the daily life she leads. What is there in this recital of comfortable domestic detail that could possibly cause such a feeling of desperation? Is she trapped simply by the enormous demands of her role as modern housewife: wife, mistress, mother, nurse, consumer, cook, chauffeur, expert on interior decoration, childcare, appliance repair, furniture refinishing, nutrition, and education? We can no longer ignore that voice within women that says: "I want something more than my husband and my children and my home." (Betty Friedan, *The Feminine Mystique*, 1963, p. 29)

My name is Mary Alice Young, and before I died, my life was filled with love, laughter, friendship, and, sadly, secrets. The secrets had begun fifteen years earlier when my name was Angela Forrest, and I was living a life of quiet desperation. I'd feel it every morning as I made breakfast for my husband. And during the errands I ran in the afternoons. Even at my work

every evening. To me, each day was gray and meaningless...
(Mary Alice Young, *Desperate Housewives*, 2005)

INTRODUCTION

The 'quiet desperation' conveyed by Mary Alice Young on the television series *Desperate Housewives* apparently reiterates 'the problem that has no name' which Betty Friedan designated to 'the domestic routine of the housewife' in 1963. Indeed, the figure of the housewife and stay-at-home mother, who is largely defined by her propensity to the home and domestic space, has typically had an antagonistic relationship with the tenets of second wave feminism. Friedan's seminal ideas in *The Feminine Mystique* arguably fostered a feminist agenda that focused on challenging women's then conventional circumscription to the domestic arena. Friedan and her second wave counterparts sought to dispute the socially gendered 'scripts' which had traditionally restricted women to the domestic space of the home and to address the representative 'voice' that was calling for 'something more' than 'husband,' 'children' and 'home' (p. 29).

Since the advent of the second wave feminist movement, popular television has seemingly attempted to depict the constantly evolving and multiple roles that have emerged for women – indeed, the influence of second wave feminism has necessitated representations that do not solely confine female characters to the 'spaces' of home and domesticity that they have conventionally been associated with. From the mid 1960s onwards, notable examples of these have included representations of the 'new, liberated' woman that emerged as a direct result of second wave feminism (*That Girl* – 1966, *The Mary Tyler Moore Show* – 1970) to renowned female characters attempting to balance the dual demands of career and family (*Murphy Brown* – 1988, *Dr. Quinn, Medicine Woman* – 1993). In the more recent 'postfeminist' era, there have been a number of television programmes featuring female protagonists that are highly ambivalent about the 'choices' that are now available to them outside of the domestic space (*Ally McBeal* – 1997, *Sex and The City* – 1998, *Grey's Anatomy* – 2005, *Ugly Betty* – 2006). These shows and others do indeed offer multiple possibilities outside of domesticity to their respective female characters but these are often met with ambivalence and incongruity, signifying the diverse and myriad contradictions that define current notions of femininity and female 'space.'

In this chapter, I will assess how the figure of the housewife / stay-at-home mother has been negotiated on popular television and mediated within feminism, particularly after the domestic space has been so critiqued and reviled by Friedan and other second wave feminist writers - in the midst of the constantly evolving and multiple roles that have emerged for women in the 'postfeminist' era, there seems to be a renewed focus on domesticity, albeit in a manner that distinctly contradicts and denies the nostalgia that is commonly associated with earlier constructions of the 'happy housewife.' I will provide an overview of how 'postfeminist' theory proposes to deconstruct some of the second wave feminist rhetoric concerning domesticity, which has resulted in complex and multifarious deliberations of the housewife / stay-at-home mother figure in various popular media narratives. Diane Negra (2009) compellingly argues that 'one of postfeminism's master narratives is that of "retreatism," which operates as a powerful device for shepherding women out of the public sphere' (p. 8) With regards to this, I will evaluate current notions and portrayals of the stay-at-home mother and domesticity in relation to their traditional association with conceptions of 'female space.'

This chapter will also focus on the developments within the broadcasting institutional context of prime time television since the iconic images of the 'happy housewife' were produced in the 1950s – 60s in order to illustrate how these developments may have impacted the corresponding changes and variety in portrayals of the stay-at-home mother and notions of 'female space,' along with the postfeminist narratives that inflect representations of motherhood and women's roles. As Mona Domosh and Joni Seager (2001) claim, 'The association of home with women and femininity is so commonplace that it is often considered natural... So home, both literally and metaphorically, is intimately involved in popular definitions of contemporary womanhood' (p. 1). In a 'postfeminist' age which typically recognizes and commends women's efforts outside of the home, I will attempt to survey how this 'association of home with women and femininity' is now being manifested in a diverse and often equivocal manner on television and in the popular media, often evoking the image of the stay-at-home mother to do so.

'BACKLASH' AND THE 'FAILURE' OF FEMINISM

> 'If women really wanted to change society, they could do it. I plan to change it. I just want to get married first.' (Ally McBeal, *Ally McBeal*, 1998)

> 'It is because of feminism's success that we now call these parts of our lives into question, that we don't thoughtlessly march down the aisle, take up our mops, and suppress our ambitions. But feminism, for all its efforts, hasn't been able to banish fundamental female desires from us, either – and we simply cannot be happy if we ignore them.... It is at this intimate level that feminism has failed women...' (Danielle Crittenden, *What Our Mothers Didn't Tell Us*, 1999, p. 24)

The inclusion of fictional television character Ally McBeal on the controvertible front cover of the June 29, 1998 issue of *TIME* magazine alongside prominent feminists Susan B. Anthony, Betty Friedan and Gloria Steinem accompanied by the headline 'Is Feminism Dead?, arguably signified the ambivalence and confusion that had come to infuse representations of feminism in the media and popular culture. Indeed, the main protagonist of the eponymous hit television show *Ally McBeal* embodied this ambivalence – as a successful lawyer, Ally was representative of the new generation of ambitious, independent and capable women who had the ability to 'change society' but would prefer to 'get married first.' Ally and subsequent media incarnations celebrated their professional achievements and financial independence but also bemoaned the cost of this 'success,' on their (more personal goals of marriage and motherhood), ultimately echoing journalist Danielle Crittenden's (1999) contentious claim that 'feminism (had) failed women' (p. 24).

Twelve years after Crittenden's negative assessment of the impact of feminism, it would appear that the media is still indeterminate about its ramifications. Representations of successful single women since *Ally* (notably *Sex and The City* – 1998, *Grey's Anatomy* – 2005, *Ugly Betty* – 2006, amongst others) have largely been defined by their irresoluteness to the numerous 'choices' that are now available to women outside of the domestic space, reiterating Diane Negra's (1992) observation that, 'the popular culture landscape has seldom been dominated as it is today by fantasies and fears about women's "life choices" (p. 2). As depicted on *Ally*, popular media representations are still intent on portraying the woes of 'hordes of thirtysomethings speaking worriedly about such things as biological clocks, career vs. motherhood, the cost of day care, infertility clinics, and the sudden shortage of available men' (Crittenden 1999, p. 188) The media's continued preoccupation with the anxiety inherent in women's vast options outside of 'husband, children and home' would suggest that the present response to *TIME*'s question posed in 1999, would be that if not 'dead,' feminism is at best, expiring.

On the contrary, 'postfeminism' is arguably regarded as a counter to this 'expiry date' – in opposition to a second wave feminism that has been 'associated with a number of female crises and predicaments, as Crittenden describes above, from work-induced stress and loneliness to insanity and psychosis', postfeminism can be 'read as a healthy rewriting of feminism, a sign that the women's movement is continuously in process, transforming and changing itself' (Genz and Brabon 2009, p. 11-2). Ann Brooks (1997) has also positively characterized postfeminism as 'feminism's "coming of age", its maturity into a confident body of theory and politics, representing pluralism and difference' (p. 1). Similarly, Negra (2009) accentuates postfeminism's simultaneous continuation of and shift away from second wave feminism by postulating that, 'This widely-applied and highly contradictory term performs as if it is commonsensical and presents itself as pleasingly moderated in contrast to a "shrill" feminism. Crucially, postfeminism often functions as a means of registering and superficially resolving the persistence of "choice" dilemmas for American women' (p. 2). These "choice dilemmas" have often been embodied in the typically contradictory and diverse media and cultural representations of domesticity, the housewife and motherhood.

As Stacy Gillis and Joanne Hollows (2009) note in their introduction to *Feminism, Domesticity and Popular Culture*, 'the figure most closely associated with the domestic – the housewife – often operates as the feminist's 'other' (p. 1). Along with Friedan's *The Feminine Mystique*, Ann Oakley's *Housewife* (1974) is another cogent second wave diatribe against the 'naturalized' relationship between women and domesticity. Oakley (in) famously thanked her 'own family for the experience of (her) own oppression as a housewife' (p. x), underscoring the second wave's staunch disputing of the correlation between women and the domestic arena. Following this trajectory, several writers explored the tensions between feminism and the 'oppressed' figure of the housewife, with most privileging the 'public space' that the housewife had traditionally been denied access to over the 'private' domestic space that she is commonly delimited to. Rita Felski (2000) charged the space of the home with 'familiarity, dullness, stasis,' (p. 86) while Elspeth Probyn aligned the domestic with 'narrowmindedness' (in Hollows 2006, p. 100). Germaine Greer contentiously ascertained that ' the life of a full-time housewife (was) one of absolute servitude' (in Genz, 2009, p. 51) while Judy Giles (2004) alleged that 'leaving home' was a necessary condition for the feminist experience, (p. 141-2), also recapitulating Oakley's (1974) deduction of the housewife as the symbol of 'antifeminism.' In these analyses, 'the housewife statically remains in her old-fashioned, homely prison, unable to take part in the gender developments and transformations of a rapidly changing world' (Genz 2009, p. 51).

The second wave feminist consensus would appear to be that domesticity should be 'left behind' (Giles, 2004) in favour of Friedan's notion of 'a real identity' formed through the pursuit of 'higher education, achieving a rewarding career and performing a meaningful role in the public sphere' (Gillis and Hollows, 2009, p. 7). Indeed, the 'cult of the housewife' that Friedan (1963) and others had resoundingly attacked was arguably obsolete by the late 1990s, when Crittenden (1999) contended that 'feminism had failed women' and Ally McBeal had articulated her desire 'to get married first' before embarking upon her aspirations to 'change society.' This questioning of 'feminism's success' is indicative of the 'backlash' discourse identified by Susan Faludi (1992) – her book conspicuously detailed a range of media texts in the 1980s and 1990s that seemingly rendered the 'sad plight of millions of unhappy and unsatisfied women' as a result of the feminist movement:

> Professional women are suffering 'burnout' and succumbing to an 'infertility epidemic.' Single women are grieving from a 'man shortage'... Childless women are 'depressed and confused' and their ranks are swelling... Unwed women are 'hysterical' and crumbling under a 'profound crisis of confidence'... High powered career women are stricken with unprecedented outbreaks of 'stress-induced disorders...' (p. 1-2)

According to the backlash discourse, women have suffered on account of feminist ideals, resulting in the myriad of female crises constituted above. It is within this backlash thesis that 'conventional versions of femininity and domesticity' have been 'rearticulated' (Genz and Brabon 2009, p. 54), including that of the figure of the housewife and stay-at-home mother.

WOMEN'S 'PLACE' ON TV

> Television's reliance on constructing numbers of viewers as commodities involves reproducing female images that accommodate prevailing (and dominant) conceptions of 'woman,'

> particularly as these satisfy certain economic needs. (E. Ann Kaplan, 'Feminist Criticism and Television' in *Channels of Discourse*, 1992, p. 223)

Prevailing (and dominant) conceptions of 'woman' have continued to impact television representations of women, including those of the housewife and stay-at-home mother. The economic imperatives underlying the developments in television programming and consumption have also had profound effects on the subsequent content and images produced. As with most media texts and products, television's main function is that of a commodity, with popular prime time programming created with a particular audience market in mind. The specificity of this audience has diverged as a result of the marked shifts from 'broadcasting' to 'narrowcasting,' but as Kaplan points out, 'television's reliance on constructing numbers of viewers as commodities' has remained. Thus, television continues to have a valued interest in (re)producing images that sell, and this has arguably influenced the shifting constructions of women, motherhood and concepts of women's 'place.'

Amanda Lotz (2007) categorized the modifications within the television broadcasting context in terms of three broad stages, commonly identified as the 'network era' (1952 – mid 1980s), the 'multichannel transition' (mid 1980s – mid 2000s) and the 'post network era' (mid 2000s – present). The 'network era' is typically characterized by the dominance of three principal networks, namely NBC, CBS and ABC whose preeminence remains synonymous with US television culture (Boddy 1993, Haralovich 1992, Lipsitz 1992, Lotz 2007, Spigel 1992). The 'network era's' credence on these three broadcast networks was defined by content and programming targeted towards a mass audience, formulaic structures within genres and representations and limited options in terms of viewing and scheduling.

Thus, the scope of female portrayals was significantly narrower during the early days of television and the primary stages of the 'network era.' Television was a symbolic element of the period of post war prosperity after World War II and contributed much to the ideal of suburban comfort and prosperity in delineating the 'American Dream.' As Lynn C. Spangler (2003) documents, 'As the popularity of television grew, so did American families and the idyllic myth of the housewife' (p. 25). Thus, it is unsurprising that television roles for women during this period were largely restricted to the domestic setting, clearly positioning them as wives and mothers. This would also correspond with the rise of advertising and consumerism in the years of postwar prosperity, with the 'happy housewife' a keen objective for advertisers in the marketing of household products that were deemed essential to the maintenance of a blissful home and family. Notable contributors to the 'idyllic myth of the housewife' were Harriet Nelson in *The Adventures of Ozzie and Harriet* (ABC, 1952 – 1966), Margaret Anderson (Jane Wyatt) in *Father Knows Best* (CBS / NBC, 1955 – 1960), June Cleaver (Barbara Billingsley) in *Leave It To Beaver* (CBS / ABC – 1957 – 1963), Donna Stone (Donna Reed) in *The Donna Reed Show* (ABC, 1959 – 1966) and Laura Petrie (Mary Tyler Moore) in *The Dick Van Dyke Show* (CBS, 1961 – 1966). Despite marginal differences in each of these iconic 'housewife' portrayals, they all reflect the distinct cultural expectation towards women in the immediate postwar era to 'specialize in meeting expressive needs and routine tasks within the family' (Benson 1968, p. 16), and are rarely, if ever, depicted outside the space of the home.

Indeed, these series appeared to glorify the position of the housewife and stay-at-home mother – in particular, Margaret Anderson and Donna Stone have been observed to 'operate explicitly as paragons of housewifery' (Leibman 1995, p. 195) in their cheerful, unquestioning and effortless management of the household and domestic duties. This could be regarded as serving as a reminder of the significance and value of the wife/mother role, particularly in the postwar era when the numbers of women entering the workforce were increasing. Leibman goes on to describe 'the dominant, capable, and charismatic women of *Father Knows Best* and *The Donna Reed Show*' who 'continually and in quite explicit terms remind the viewer that the most successful housewife is one who does her duty sweetly and unheroically' (p. 200 – 1). Both Margaret and Donna are never untidy, harried or impatient in their undertakings of family and household matters and despite very tentative forays into the public space outside the home (Margaret enrolls in university courses in one episode to the chagrin and disdain of her family) and innocuous musings on their circumscription to the private, domestic arena (Donna sincerely questions the merits of the term 'housewife' on one occasion), both are presented as entirely accepting and content with their domestic role, reinforcing the postwar directive that 'women are happiest when engaged in domestic duty' (Leibman 1995, p. 188).

One of the most iconic and beloved television housewives and mothers of the period, Lucy Ricardo (Lucille Ball) in *I Love Lucy* (CBS, 1951 – 1957) is commonly singled out for her repeated and comic attempts to escape the position of housewife and the domestic space allotted to her. Each episode of the immensely popular series would focus on Lucy's hapless efforts to thwart the wishes and demands of her bandleader husband Ricky (Ball's real life husband Desi Arnaz) and to enter into the public space outside the home (she makes several attempts to become a part of Ricky's nightclub act throughout the series, as well as attempting various other forms of employment, most memorably and humorously with friend and sidekick Ethel Mertz (Vivian Vance) in a candy factory). As Spangler (2003) remarks, Lucy is clearly 'not content to be just a housewife and mother' (p. 32), but by the close of each episode, she agreeably acquiesces to Ricky's will and is securely restored her housewife role. However, several critics have commented that Lucy is a critical housewife figure in her suggestion of resistance to the domestic role. Lori Landay (1998) describes her as 'a model of female ambition that is relentless in its craving for freedom, participation and equality' (p. 193). This presence of 'female ambition' in a 1950s television housewife is noteworthy and important, although it is contained within Ball's brilliant slapstick comedy and 'despite Lucy's unrest at being "just a housewife," the recurring lesson is that, ultimately, that is what makes her most happy and she cannot successfully have both a career and a family life' (Spangler 2003, p. 34).

The 1960s and 1970s witnessed a marked decrease in television representations of the stay-at-home mother, possibly due to the influence of second wave feminism and the expanding social awareness of new and varied roles for women outside of the domestic space. The impact of Betty Friedan's book was one of the prime instigators in the women's rights movement and women's own incentive to explore their options apart from that of wife/mother. The recognition of these options eventually moved into various aspects of popular culture, including television which was intent on targeting the market potential of independent working women. This phase of the 'network era' saw the emergence of the 'New Woman' who was mainly characterized by her unmarried status and career ambitions, which set her in direct contrast to the 'happy housewife' image. Prominent incarnations of the 'New Woman' included Ann Marie (Marlo Thomas) in *That Girl* (ABC, 1961 – 1967), Mary Richards (Mary Tyler Moore) in *The Mary Tyler Moore Show* (CBS, 1970 – 1977), and Laverne DeFazio (Penny Marshall) and Shirley Feeney (Cindy Williams) in *Laverne and Shirley* (ABC, 1976 – 1983). In spite of their single status and positioning outside of the private space of the home, the narratives revolving around these characters and others focused on their personal and romantic experiences, thereby still situating them in the traditional 'feminine' realms of romance and relationships. However, the extraordinary success and popularity of these shows demonstrated the audience interest in female representations outside of domesticity, as well as the marketability and potential of single and independent female characters, a trend that has proliferated into the current era.

The wife/mother characters that were presented on television during this period largely conformed to expected notions of the stay-at-home mother figure. Carol Brady (Florence Henderson) in *The Brady Bunch* (ABC, 1969 – 1974), Edith Bunker (Jean Stapleton) in *All In The Family* (CBS, 1971 – 1979) and Marion Cunningham (Marion Ross) in *Happy Days* (ABC, 1974 – 1984) were all versions of the smiling and unassuming wife/mother, satisfied with her role in the domestic space. *All In The Family* was noteworthy in its inclusion of social issues that had not previously been featured in primetime television sitcoms, such as breast cancer and rape, indicating the influence of feminism and the raised consciousness of women's issues. Perhaps the most memorable housewife of this era was not just merely a housewife at all – Samantha Stephens (Elizabeth Montgomery) in *Bewitched* (ABC, 1964 – 1972) literally charmed audiences with her portrayal of a witch / suburban wife and mother, happily ensconced within the domestic environment. It is equivocal that Samantha willingly chooses a life of domesticity to care for her hapless husband Darrin (Dick York, replaced by Dick Sargent after 1969) and their children, despite the numerous and considerable options due to her infinite powers of witchcraft, suggesting that even with the multitude of options open to them (even magic!), women are most content and suited to the realm of domesticity.

The television industry underwent substantial developments during the 1980s, ushering in the 'multichannel transition' and the end of the 'network era.' The 'multichannel transition' is widely identified with the growth of cable television programming that began to rival the dominance of the broadcast networks, as well as significant technological advancements that impacted television consumption and viewing practices, such as remote control devices and VCRs (Lotz 2007, Walker and Bellamy, Jr 1993). Two of the three networks were sold to major corporations (ABC to Capital Communications Inc. and NBC to General Electric – CBS would be acquired by The Westinghouse Electrical Corporation in the mid 1990s). Amidst these administrative conversions, new broadcast networks emerged as viable competitors to the previous network dominance, notably FOX in 1986. The Lifetime cable network became the first network to explicitly target female viewers upon its launch in 1984. These elements of choice created an unprecedented climate of greater viewer control, leading to the shift towards 'narrowcasting' as the increased variety in programming encouraged audience fragmentation and polarization. These changes would have a considerable impact on television representations, offering much more heterogeneity and possibilities in programming, content, narratives and characterization, including those concerning women and their increasingly fractured negotiations of female 'space.'

The inclination towards representing independent and successful women resoundingly continued with viewers captivated by the antics of the ensemble in *Designing Women* (CBS, 1986 – 1983), Murphy Brown (Candice Bergen) in *Murphy Brown* (CBS, 1988 – 1998), as well as the female lawyers and career women on *LA Law* (NBC, 1986 – 1994) and *Thirtysomething* (ABC, 1987 – 1991) respectively, amongst others. *LA Law* and *Thirtysomething* were representative of the accession of the hour long ensemble dramatic series in the 1980s, a genre which continues to dominate primetime television programming. *Cagney and Lacey* (CBS, 1981 – 1988), focusing on the experiences and relationship between two female police officers (Sharon Gless and Tyne Daly) is consistently hailed as a landmark series for female representation and was believed to shape 'cultural definitions of women' (D'Acci 1992 in Spigel and Mann, p. 169) on television in its relentless representation of women's issues ranging from sexual harassment, rape, abortion to breast cancer. These series and others could be seen as representative of television's 'quest' in the 1980s for the 'working women's market' (D'Acci 1992 in Spigel and Mann 2003, p. 169), resulting in images of women occupying the 'public' space outside of the home becoming more commonplace and familiar. However, certain ideologies concerning women's 'place' continued to linger despite the frequency of these representations in that the career success of these female characters' is often tempered by the relative lack of in their personal lives – Murphy Brown, in particular, is 'depicted as a woman who had paid a price for her success in terms of the barrenness of her personal life and her lack of traditionally feminine attributes' (Dow 2005 in Wasko 2005, p. 386), clearly corresponding to the 'backlash' tendencies of the popular media discussed in the previous chapter.

Representations of the wife/mother who was primarily defined by her domestic and household duties became even more scarce during the 'multichannel transition.' Mothers on television were often working mothers – notable examples include Elyse Keaton (Meredith Baxter Birney) in *Family Ties* (NBC, 1982 – 1989), Clair Huxtable (Phylicia Rashad) in *The Cosby Show* (NBC, 1984 – 1992) and Maggie Seaver (Joanna Kerns) in *Growing Pains* (ABC, 1985 – 1992). All are successful career women (Elyse Keaton is an architect, Clair Huxtable is a lawyer and Maggie Seaver is a journalist), yet they are most often presented in the domestic setting in their roles as wife and mother. This echoes Douglas' (2003) assertion that 'although women may be shown to work outside the home, they continue to perform the duties of the homemaker so that their status is ambiguous' (p. 108). This 'ambiguity' would seemingly allow for television's commercial imperative of representing the reality of working women, yet simultaneously uphold traditional ideals concerning gendered 'space.'

Perhaps the most contentious wife/mother television figure of the era was Roseanne Connor (Roseanne Barr) in *Roseanne* (ABC, 1988 – 1997). Always scrutinized in sharp contrast to the other successful, attractive and dignified television mothers of the time, Roseanne is observed for her crude and brash demeanor, as well as her physical appearance which did not conform to the svelte and cultivated images of conventional television heroines. In her ironic and self-proclaimed interpretation of the term 'domestic goddess,' Roseanne is often cited as the prime example of Kathleen Rowe's (1995) concept of the 'unruly woman' who is intent on demolishing the 'tropes of femininity' that produce conceptions of the 'ideal' wife and mother. The Connor family's working class background, unkempt household, caustic family interactions and Roseanne's biting sarcasm confirm Spangler's (2003) remark, in citing television critic David Bianculli that the series is not 'concerned with proper behavior, language and role models' (p. 169). Yet the series and its titular character received critical praise for its representation of the gritty realities of working class life and was fundamental to illustrating the actual difficulties of conforming to the paradigm of the 'happy housewife' myth, especially in particular social and class contexts.

The 'multichannel transition' has seamlessly segued into the 'post-network' era that Lotz (2007) distinguishes as 'the erosion of (network) control over how and when viewers watch particular programs' (p. 15). By the mid 1990s, network dominance had consistently been dissolved by multiple industry mergers, as well as continuous competition from new broadcast networks (namely UPN and the WB in 1995) and the rapid expansion of cable television. The 1990s witnessed the ascendancy of HBO, which has been heralded as a principal innovator in its programming and representations, including those of women. Two more cable channels explicitly targeting female viewers were launched (Women's Entertainment in 1997 and Oxygen in 2000) and along with the previously established Lifetime, increased in prominence with their popular rosters of daytime talk shows, reality series and syndicated programming.

Amidst these progressive and diverse conditions, the multiplicity of female representations on television flourished. The 1990s saw an increase in dramatic series which 'explore(d) a new multiplicity of stories about women and their lives' (Lotz 2006, p. 6). Indeed, the era is conspicuous for its 'representation of competent professional women in ensemble dramas such as *ER* (NBC, 1994 – 2009), *The X-Files* (FOX, 1993 – 2002) and *The Practice* (ABC, 1997 – 2004)' (Dow in Wasko 2005: 389), indicating television's continuing adherence to portraying women outside of the domestic space. The most prolific of these characters would arguably be Ally McBeal (Calista Flockhart) in *Ally McBeal* (FOX 1997 – 2002) whose contended association with postfeminism was mentioned in the previous chapter. The polemical Ally divided feminists between those who praised her rendering of a capable and successful lawyer thriving in the public space and those who deplored her 'obsession with finding a relationship' (Dow in Wasko 2005: 389). Indeed, the series would reiterate the 'New Woman' prototypes of the 1960s / 1970s in that a woman's navigation of the public space would ultimately centre on the 'feminine' realms of love, relationships and 'personal' issues typically related to the 'private' sphere of sociality and emotions.

Ally is frequently credited as the forerunner to the women of *Sex And The City* (HBO 1998 – 2004), the series that is commonly lauded as the preeminent postfeminist television text. The four female protagonists inhabit the public space ('The City') in a manner never previously witnessed on network television, not only in their professional attainments (all are established career women at the start of the series), but more notably in their romantic and sexual exploits. Indeed, the explicit sexual encounters and frank conversations about sex that the characters routinely engage in would not have found an avenue on broadcast television, just one of the ways HBO has distinguished itself from its broadcast network competition. Carrie Bradshaw (Sarah Jessica Parker) and her counterparts were clearly not restricted to the 'private sphere' of 'home and family life' (Hollows and Gillis 2009, p. 4) – in their typical and habitual occupation of the public sphere, they enthralled and provoked viewers with their audacity towards the gendered nature of the 'public/private' divide and the characteristics commonly associated with them. In the pilot episode, Carrie asserts that having 'sex like a man' equated 'own(ing) the city,' suggesting that the 'specific values and functions' affiliated with women and the 'private sphere' (Hollows and Gillis 2009, p. 4) have shifted in accordance with the shifting qualities between the public and the private.

As series depicting women's endeavors in the public sphere dominated during the early years of the 'post-network' era, representations of women within the private space of the home, particularly the housewife, became relatively scarce, but working and single mother characters were commonly featured in various series, notably Grace Kelly (Brett Butler) in *Grace Under Fire* (ABC, 1993 – 1998), Lily Manning (Sela Ward) in *Once And Again* (ABC, 1999 – 2002), Amy Gray (Amy Brenneman) in *Judging Amy* (CBS, 1999 – 2005), and Lorelai Gilmore (Lauren Graham) in *Gilmore Girls* (WB, 2000 – 2007).

In recent years, popular television appears to be reverting their female characters back to the domestic space – in the midst of the constantly evolving and multiple roles that have emerged for women in the 'postfeminist' era, there seems to be a renewed focus on domesticity, albeit in a manner that distinctly contradicts and denies the nostalgia that is commonly associated with earlier constructions of the 'happy housewife.' Indeed, the popular media has recently been saturated with images of the housewife and stay-at-home mother – notable examples range from the ubiquitous *Desperate Housewives* of the hit ABC television drama to the glamorous and provocative escapades of the *Real Housewives* on the titillating Bravo reality series. Although domesticity is seemingly enjoying a revival of sorts within popular culture, its presentation definitively varies from its earlier idealization in the post-war era.

DOMESTICITY MUTATED: RECUPERATING THE STAY-AT-HOME MOTHER

> Domesticity did not die; it mutated. (Joan Williams, *Unbending Gender: Why Family and Work Conflict*, 2000, p. 3)

> This stay-at-home parent thing? The full-time thing? Harder than I thought. (Julia Graham, *Parenthood*, 2012)

The 'mutated' form of domesticity that Williams (2000) describes is present in the diversified ways that stay-at-home mothers are currently being represented on popular television. The considerable number of programmes that feature a stay-at-home mother signifies that 'domesticity (has) not die(d),' in spite of women's tangible entry into the workplace and public sphere. Indeed, gendered distinctions and ideals of domesticity persist in demarcating female identities and representations. In Williams (2000) goes on to proclaim that, 'Domesticity remains the entrenched, almost unquestioned, American norm and practice' due to the continued naturalization of traditional gender roles which ensure that 'men "naturally" belong in the (work) market because they are competitive and aggressive' while 'women belong in the home because of their "natural" focus on relationships, children, and an ethic of care' (p. 1). Such sustaining beliefs continue to frame the rhetoric of 'independence' and 'choice' that women are now prescribed with due to the 'gains' of feminism which have enabled women unprecedented access into the public sphere. It is within this context that this 'mutated' configuration of domesticity that currently imbues cultural notions and representations of feminine identity continues to confuse and interrogate 'the stay-at-home parent thing' that *Parenthood*'s Julia Graham and others are navigating on popular television.

Julia's decision to leave her rewarding career as a lawyer in order to focus on her family is reminiscent of the 'New Traditionalist' discourses, which 'articulates a vision of the home as women's sanctuary from the stresses of their working lives' (Genz and Brabon 2009, p. 52). This parallels notions of Negra's (2009) 'retreatism' and Faludi's (1992) 'backlash' in its similar tendencies to 'resituate women in the home' as a response to their perceived 'anxieties about changing family forms and roles' and 'disillusionment with the workplace' (Leslie, in McDowell and Sharp 1997, p. 308). Leslie (1997) asserts that the 'new traditionalist woman' is a response 'to the increasing presence of women in public space' and a means in which to 'reaffirm the blurring distinctions between public and private and to reinforce the association of woman with the home' (p. 305) and domesticity, thereby further contributing to the spatial confusion that appears to characterize women's roles. Other noteworthy television characters that have 'retreated' from the 'public' space and 'returned' to the home to concentrate on the roles of domesticity and motherhood include Lynette Scavo (*Desperate Housewives*), Reagan Brinkley (*Up All Night*) and Charlotte York-Goldenblatt (*Sex And The City*).

It is critical to note that these character's decisions to 'retreat' back to the home at all is highly dependent on their class and economic status. Indeed, 'retreatism' can often operate as a site of fantasy for women who do not have the luxury of choice and for whom working outside of the home is a necessity. This recalls how 'retreatism' is apparent in Joanne Hollows' (2006) assessment of "an increasing fascination with the domestic as a forbidden pleasure" (p. 107) within postfeminism, echoing Lily J. Goren's (2009) claims that 'part of contemporary feminists' aim is to reject the notion that women must meet masculine standards or norms to be seen as equal,' allowing for 'diverse expressions of femininity and a revaluing of women's traditional knowledge and experience,' (p. 6) such as those pertaining to domesticity and the space of the home. In contrast to the 'prison' that Oakley (1974) ascribed to domesticity, 'retreatism' is discernible in various popular representations on film and television which '(prioritize) "housewife chic," the spectacle of an affluent wedding, the allure of luxury commodities, and achievement of a sumptuous domesticity, the disappointments of the world of paid work, and the rewards of motherhood...' (Negra, 2009, p. 8). This 'sumptuous domesticity' of which 'luxury commodities' are a key feature is arguably most clearly embodied by the ubiquitous *Real Housewives* (of Orange County, New York, Atlanta, New Jersey, Beverly Hills and Miami) who are largely construed by their ostentatious lifestyles, rather than any propensity towards domesticity and motherhood itself.

'Mutated' domesticity is also exhibited in the number of subversive housewife figures that have featured prominently in popular television dramas in recent years. *Big Love* (HBO, 2006 – 11) is noteworthy for its uncommon representations of domesticity – this drama features three domestic characters who not only share the same household, but the same husband as well. The show depicts the experience of a fundamentalist Mormon family who practice the principle of polygamy – although the show centers on the perspective of the main protagonist Bill Henrickson and his struggles to reconcile his religious convictions with the paradigms of the society he works in, the travails of his three 'sister wives' Barb, Nicki and Margene feature profoundly in the narratives of this very discrepant and controversial construction of the domestic space.

The United States of Tara (Showtime, 2009 – 11) seemingly offers a rather confounding and inimical commentary on the housewife and the domestic arena. The eponymous Tara is a suburban housewife suffering from 'Disassociative Identity Disorder,' (DID) - the multiple personalities that inhabit her persona range from a caricature of the 1950s 'happy housewife' to a vampy teenager to a hypermasculine (male) Vietnam War veteran named Buck. Similar to the constructions in the other two shows, Tara's family is also maladjusted and dysfunctional, with the added dimension of a mother/wife who literally embodies the variety and confusion that currently informs the figure of the housewife/mother and her conventionally prescribed domestic role.

AMC's *Mad Men* (2007 -) has perhaps offered the most recent incarnation of the underside to Friedan's 'happy housewife' image. Betty Draper, a former model and (now ex) wife to the series protagonist Don Draper is expansively delineated by her mental instability which is apparently resultant from her restriction to the domestic space, with minimal support from her advertising executive husband who is invariably occupied with business (both personal and professional) outside of the home. Betty's psychological state manifests itself physically in the first season of the series, in the numbness she develops in her hands, impacting her driving skills, as well as her ability to apply lipstick. As Melanie Waters (2011) articulates, Betty's 'performance as the perfect wife and mother – is often represented as uncanny, functioning as a mask for her aggression and the dangers that she (potentially) poses to domestic stability' (p. 66).

These representations clearly designate the ways in which the private, domestic space has seemingly transformed from a site typically associated with safety, sentimentality and nostalgia (Massey 1994) to a rather more unstable and precarious terrain. The 'rearticulation' of domesticity that is currently found on popular television has largely taken place underneath a 'postfeminist' lens – as noted by Genz and Brabon (2009) postfeminism can be 'read as a healthy rewriting of feminism' (p. 11) and an attempt to 'fix' some of the obstructions that feminism has encountered, notably that of the housewife/mother and her proclivity to the domestic space. As Genz (2009) suggests in her essay 'I Am Not a Housewife, but...,' 'postfeminism's changeable life indicates a move away from binaries, including the dualistic patterns of (male) power and (female) victimization on which much feminist thought and politics are built' (in Gillis and Hollows, 2009, p. 53). Postfeminism's focus on diversification, plurality and the deconstruction of such 'binaries' has had a significant impact on the reassessment of the relationship between the housewife, stay-at-home motherhood and feminism. However, the 'doctrine of feminine domesticity' (Oakley 1974, p. 49) is still extensive – in it's 'mutated' construction, this 'doctrine' continues to saturate and reflect the 'quiet desperation' inherent in television's complex and enigmatic representations of feminine identity and conceptions of 'women's place.'

REFERENCES

Brooks, A. 1997 *Postfeminisms: Feminism, Cultural Theory and Cultural Form*. London, New York: Routledge.

Crittenden, D. 1999 *What Our Mothers Didn't Tell Us: Why Happiness*

Eludes The Modern Woman. New York: Simon and Schuster.

Domosh, M., and J. Seager 2001 *Putting Women in Place: Feminist Geographers Make Sense of the World.* New York: Guilford Press.

Douglas, W. 2003 *Television Families: Is Something Wrong In Suburbia?* Mahwah, NJ: Lawrence Erlbaum Associates.

Dow, B.J. 1996 *Prime Time Feminism: Television, Media Culture and the Women's Movement since 1970*. Philadelphia: University of Pennsylvania Press.

Faludi, S. 1991 *Backlash: The Undeclared War Against American Women.* New York: Crown Publishers.

Felski, R. 2000 *Doing Time: Feminist Theory and Postmodern Culture.* New York: New York University Press.

Friedan, B. 1963 *The Feminine Mystique*. London: Penguin.

Genz, S., and B. A. Brabon 2009 *Postfeminism: Cultural Texts and Theories*. Edinburgh: Edinburgh University Press.

Gillis, S., and J. Hollows, eds. 2009 *Feminism, Domesticity and Popular Culture*. New York: Routledge.

Goren, L. J., ed. 2009 *You've Come A Long Way Baby: Women, Politics and Popular Culture.* Lexington, KY: University Press of Kentucky.

Hollows, J., and R. Moseley, eds. 2006 *Feminism In Popular Culture*. Oxford, England; New York: Berg.

Leibman, N. C. 1995 *Living Room Lectures: The Fifties Family In Film and Television.* Austin: University of Texas Press.

Lotz, A. D. 2006 *Redesigning Women: Television After The Network Era.* Urbana and Chicago: University of Illinois Press.

Lotz, A. D. 2007 *The Television Will Be Revolutionized.* New York: New York University Press.

Massey, D. B. 1994 *Space, Place and Gender.* Cambridge: Polity.

McDowell, L., and J.P. Sharp, eds. 2006 *Space, Gender, Knowledge: Feminist Readings.* London: Arnold.

McDowell, L. 1999 *Gender, Identity and Place: Understanding Feminist Geographies.* Minneapolis: University of Minnesota Press.

Negra, D. 2009 *What A Girl Wants?: Fantasizing the Reclamation of Self in Postfeminism*. New York: Routledge.

Oakley, A. 1976 *Housewife*. London: Pelican Books.

Spangler, L. C. 2003 *Television Women From Lucy To Friends: Fifty Years*

Of Sitcoms and Feminism. Westport, CN: Praeger.

Spigel, L., and D. Mann, eds. 2003 *Private Screenings: Television and the Female Consumer.* Minneapolis: University of Minnesota Press.

Wasko, J., ed. 2005 *A Companion To Television.* Malden, MA: Blackwell Publishing.

Waters, M., ed. 2011 *Women On Screen: Feminism and Femininity in Visual Culture*. Basingstoke, NY: Palgrave Macmillan.

Williams, J. 2000 *Unbending Gender: Why Family and Work Conflict and What To Do About It.* Oxford: Oxford University Press.

18.

Making it Work

CATHERINE FOURNIER

My four-year-old stood at the living room window, watching intently. The big yellow school bus came around the corner. Yelling, 'Ti!Ti!' he ran for the door. His sixteen-year-old sister stepped down from the bus just as he reached her and launched himself into her arms. Tina came into the house, with Robert clinging happily to her neck. I heard her murmur into his hair, 'Thanks, buddy, I've needed that all day.'

Thirty-four years ago, I had it all figured out. Our 16-month-old daughter was enrolled in subsidized daycare on the University campus; classes were due to start within the week. In just a few more years, I'd have a degree in History, and then I'd get a job with the federal government and settle down to start my career. My husband had a degree in Biology; there were good government research positions available for him as well. We were on our way to double-income, two-kid working parent success.

Then one day I arrived at daycare, an hour early. I scanned the bustling chaos of the toddler room for Tina. Not at the tables, not at the painting centre, not in the playhouse, where was she? I finally found her standing in a corner with her blanket, sucking her thumb, looking sad and lost. And I suddenly had an uncomfortable thought. 'My daughter needs a full-time mommy more than I need a degree.'

I picked her up and hugged her hard. Then we went home. In the midst of the clatter of dishwashing, I gathered up my thoughts and courage. 'Peter, I'm not going back to school or work. I'm going to stay home and take care of Tina. So you're going to have to make the money.' To my surprise, Peter said, 'Okay. I guess that makes sense.'

It's a little embarrassing now to admit how naïvely optimistic we were. We were both students, living on summer jobs and student grants, renting a basement apartment in his parent's house. Peter hadn't been able to find full-time work, only short-term lab contracts. In fact, the only work he'd been able to find the summer Tina was born was fieldwork a thousand kilometres away. He rode an all-terrain vehicle for an hour once a week to call home. Try as hard as I might, I cried every time.

Still, he did have work and we did have a place to live. We thought we could maybe save money by cooking cheaper meals, making our own clothes and buying from second hand stores. We agreed to give it a try. He'd find work outside the home and I'd work at home, 'earning' by saving money.

Only a month after we made this agreement Peter came home from work and told me that his contract had been cancelled. I told him I was pregnant again. It seemed a disaster, but what could we do? We laugh about it now. Andrew was born the next spring.

We needed more room than a basement apartment, so with the help of a small inheritance (about a third of the price of a small home at the time) we bought a fixer-upper in a neighbourhood on the way up. We taught ourselves to paint, install tile and lay flooring, and sold it 18 months later for nearly 25 percent more than we'd paid. We repeated that pattern five times over the next eight years (always in the same school district to minimize the effect on our children) and ended up with enough equity to build a six-bedroom house on half an acre about an hour's drive out of the city.

Those were busy years. We had four more children, another girl and three more boys, partly because we thought siblings were good for each other and partly because we didn't worry, we knew we could make it work. At the time, people told us we were stupid and crazy. Now they tell me how lucky I am.

They were lonely years too, in a way. Nearly everyone else I knew was at school or in the work force. To combat the loneliness, I joined a parent-preschool organization, was elected to its board, and helped create three playgroups in my area, some of the first in our city. Later I volunteered at my children's schools, and at our local parish. When the children joined Air Cadets, I volunteered there too, eventually becoming a Captain in the Canadian Reserve.[1]

We moved to the country for a number of reasons, the simplest of which was that housing prices were much lower out of town and we needed growing room. The more complicated reason is that two of our children turned out to have bi-polar disorder. Even though they weren't diagnosed until ages 16 and 25, as children they needed a lot of attention and management. A house in the country gave them room to run and yell, away from the many unsupervised temptations of city life.

I acted as the general contractor for the building of our house, interviewing and overseeing tradespeople, scheduling inspections and buying materials. This wasn't as daunting as it sounds. I scoured the local library for books about construction and surreptitiously asked the more helpful and sympathetic contractors lots of questions. They were happy to help, often pointing out issues I hadn't considered, and offering advice. We did a lot of work ourselves as well: the plumbing, tiling, painting, floor finishing, and exterior finishing. This last task went very slowly since we're both afraid of heights! The older children learned to cook while we were building. I'd yell instructions from wherever I was working and they'd yell back questions.

I found lots of ways to save. Since I had learned to sew at school and from my mother, I sewed a lot of our clothing. Some of my first efforts were dresses for our daughters made from cut-down women's clothing from the Salvation Army store[2] and snowsuits for the boys from old jeans and quilt batting. A personalized quilt for each child celebrated the transition from crib to grown-up bed. I asked my family for a knitting machine one Christmas, and knitted sweaters for the family and as gifts. (The children have all outgrown theirs; I'm still wearing one of mine.) Again, the library was a great resource of information about sewing, knitting and design.

I planted a huge vegetable garden, spent hours with the children at pick-your-own berry farms in the spring and summer and bought apples by the bushel in the fall. I made maple syrup from the maple trees on our property. A chance conversation with a local farmer revealed that my great-grandmother's family had made maple syrup from the same trees more than a hundred years before! We build a tree fort for the children, and went on canoe trips in the summer, exploring Algonquin Park in rented canoes.

Tina once told me that she never realized we were 'poor' until she went to high school. Technically, we *were* poor. For most of this time, while the children were young, we had not quite enough income to make ends meet, yet too much income to qualify for any social safety nets. Even when Peter made a good salary, we lost a significant portion to income taxes. His net income was well below the Statistics Canada defined poverty level for a family of our size. I'm not sure what that means though; we had a house, two cars, enough food, everything we needed and a little bit more.

I won't deny it was difficult. Our economy assumes double incomes and sets prices accordingly. My husband and I went without many small comforts, like an occasional bottle of wine and larger luxuries like dinner out or vacations. I often considered trying to find a job. Yet without a degree my employment prospects were limited. Could I possibly earn enough to make working worthwhile? Should I go back to school? Could we afford to go without the savings my work at home earned for us? Every time we considered these questions, we concluded the answer was no. My work at home was worthwhile and the children had the full-time mommy we both believed they needed.

Shortly after Robert was born, my stay-at-home work evolved in an unexpected direction: freelance writing. Peter nagged me into it; he saw a talent I didn't know I had. I sold thirty-seven articles before my first rejection! I wrote a monthly column for a national newspaper, volunteered as the assistant editor of a small Catholic magazine, then worked on several federal government publications. We launched a Catholic family website (www.domestic-church.com); I wrote an article a day for two years to populate it and later used the material as content in – to date –seven Catholic family tradition resource books. We travelled around North America speaking at conferences and parishes about Catholic family traditions. The money I earned was very welcome too; it paid for braces and ski equipment, bicycles and fashion jeans, non-essentials that nonetheless were needed.

When Peter was laid off from Nortel twelve years ago, I joined him in technical writing on contract for the high tech. firms in our area. About five years ago, I began working full-time for an international fiber optics manufacturer; my first office job. My first career as a stay-at-home mother prepared me for my second career as a technical writer. I learned administration and leadership skills from Air Cadets, materials management through building our house, organization from volunteer work, management skills through raising six strong-willed children, and confidence through public speaking. I now support the three of us while my husband and our son Matthew launch a software company.

It might sound like we planned it all to work out this way, one evening thirty-four years ago. We really didn't. All we knew then was that we wanted to follow our instincts about mothering, give our daughter a full-time mommy, and find the ways to make it possible. This story is only the briefest outline of what I and we did, of what work, what planning and what decisions helped us get us to where we are today. I've left out buying our first computer in 1984 to give the kids a head start in the computer age, why buying older second-hand cars made more financial sense than buying new, installing a wood stove for cheaper heat and protection against power outages, and all the funny stories that go along with six children and a dog in the country. I've left out the criticism from family, friends, neighbours and strangers on the street, as well as the economic discrimination against single income families and – even more! – against large families.

But I hope I've made one thing clear. If your mothering instincts call you to stay home with your children, it's not impossible. It's a choice that should be considered and explored. It's hard, and it's hard work, but it's not impossible.

Peter and I sat together on the bench, trying not to squint in the bright sunlight. 'What do you think our chances are?' he asked. 'That we get this done in less than 20 minutes?' I replied, 'I'll be surprised.' The rest of the family gathered around us, bride and groom, daughters and sons, daughters-in-law and son-in-law, and grandchildren. Unlike other years, no one started a tickling contest, or wandered off for more pie, or closed their eyes or started singing the Philosopher's song. 'Not the way we thought our lives would go, is it?' Peter said, as the photographer aimed the camera. Click.

NOTES

[1] The Air, Army and Sea Cadets is a national program, jointly funded by the Canadian government and local service groups, for youth interested in participating in a variety of fun, challenging and rewarding activities while learning about the sea, army and air activities of the Canadian Forces. Most importantly for us, it's free!

[2] The Salvation Army Stores sell donated clothing, furniture and household goods to fund its many adult rehabilitation programs.

19.

The Day After, and the Day After That

Reflections on Keeping Your Options Open

KATHRYN CLARKE

D and I stood in the foyer of the hospital like two startled chickens. The bundle I was clutching resembled a boiled lolly, swaddled tightly as it was in a white wrap with lime green stripes. We bumped into A, a colleague of mine who was waiting for her husband to emerge from day surgery. I handed her the bundle, then took a photograph. A's lipstick pink shirt as a background to the lime-striped lolly made for a carnival-like image, and I felt as though I'd been on the merry-go-round for a lap too long.

What to do next? Leave the building and walk to the car? Tackle the innumerable serpentine straps of the baby capsule? Drive home? It all seemed utterly impossible, yet that was exactly how things transpired … as they do for countless first-time parents who have shared the same rudderless, unprecedented anxiety that comes with those first moments of depriving their new baby of all competent adult company.

Irrevocably breech, T arrived by Caesarean section at 37 weeks precisely. We had three days' notice. I went into the office the day before her delivery, to get a few things done. It was the end-of-year break, so I saw only one colleague; someone I barely knew. At the end of a brief chat, he asked what I was up to for the rest of the week. "Oh, I'm having my baby tomorrow," I said casually. It felt like the oddest sentence I had ever uttered. And as to what I would be doing after that, I had precious little idea.

D and I were 45 years old. T was the product of IVF, a desperately wanted baby who had been some six years in the making. The draining, all-consuming, emotional journey to parenthood focused us almost exclusively on what seemed like the end-point: holding a healthy baby in our arms. We are intelligent-enough women, so in hindsight, it probably should have occurred to us once in a while that – should we ever be fortunate enough to reach that point – there would be a day after, and a day after that.

Having left family and friends on the other side of the country some 11 years before, we were largely absent for the infancy of the clutch of nieces and nephews produced by our younger siblings. D had reared countless small animals during her childhood … but we were relatively clueless. We had at least, however, discussed and agreed upon our working arrangements: I would take maternity leave for 12 months, while D continued to work full-time.

I became, therefore, a limited-term stay-at-home parent. The limit on the term is significant: I had a job to return to if I wished, more or less on my terms thanks to a workplace with generous maternity leave and return-to-work provisions. (Thereby keeping my options open – but more on that anon.) There is a difference between 'stay-at-home parent' and 'administrative officer on extended maternity leave'. Having always described myself as the latter, on recent reflection I have redefined myself as 'parent who works part-time'. My daughter is my number one priority; my terminology – and perhaps my perception of myself – has taken some time to catch up.

Why *parent* as my title rather than *mother*? I muse, prising open a can of wriggling semantics. The gender-neutrality of *parent* appeals. I have seen both men and women 'mothering' a child. At a more personal level, if I claim the title mother, then what is D? The 'other' mother. This feels vaguely disrespectful. *Two mothers* smacks of redundancy, two parents sounds like a team. So what does it mean, 'to mother'? No room in this piece for that minefield, saints be praised. But be assured (and possibly confused): any shyness about the term 'mother' only underscores my respect for the title.

Prior to becoming one myself, my view of the stay-at-home parent was neutral. D and I had each had a full-time mother, a privilege which, in the 60s and 70s, seemed largely unremarkable. (A full-time father would have widened more eyes.) As a young adult, perhaps I thought of full-time mothers as lacking in ambition or drive; perhaps I saw them as a little dowdy. I certainly saw them as 'other' – I couldn't imagine myself as a mother at all, let alone as one that took on the role full-time. In the circles I frequented, I didn't actually *know* any stay-at-home parents.

For 18 months, though, my time extended with unpaid leave, I sampled the experience of the stay-at-home parent. I had been warned about the boredom, the monotony, the desperate need for 'adult' conversation, and the loss of identity or purpose previously derived from one's paid employment that might beset the person who rocked the baby full-time.

Happily, such demons did not plague me; not, however, thanks to any great mental effort on my own part. In my early adulthood, I over-identified with my work. In my mid-30s, I entered the lower ranks of senior management, and soon discovered a powerful indifference to a management career. After a decade of conforming to the prevailing macho culture of long hours and living and breathing my job, my appetite for it had quite vanished.

With boredom, I have had little acquaintance. Yes, there's a certain monotony in changing dirty nappies and cleaning up yet another bowlful of mush flung in multiple directions by a small person with minimal coordination and maximum capacity for experimentation. But it was all new to me. I was not bored. And so enthralled was I with the new addition to our family that I found her every move interesting.

I was not without adult conversation. I had an entertaining partner to chat to every evening, and I visited friends from time to time; I even joined a mothers' group. (My persistent reference to this as a 'parents' group' was eventually defeated by convention; admittedly it *was* bereft of father members.) I tend towards the dozing clam side of the introversion/extraversion scale, and clams like me don't yearn for company.

Lest I should give the impression that I was therefore a *successful* stay-at-home parent, allow me to disclose: I experienced no major problems, other than a total lack of suitability for keeping the home fires burning. The term 'domestic goddess' has never been bandied about in my general direction, and my experience would have been disastrously different without the extraordinary capacity to take up the slack that was demonstrated by my loyal and long-suffering partner. While working full-time, D continued (and continues) to do most of the domestic tasks in our home, including the shopping and the cooking. There, I have shattered my reputation into tiny shards. (D will sweep them up, bless her.)

For my part, I breast-fed (and that went well, so we're still going). I played with the baby (easy). I changed most of the nappies (no drama – I've dealt with a variety of mammalian droppings over time, and frankly, poop is poop). But back to the confessional: ironing? Heck, what are a few wrinkles between friends! And housework? D and I are hoarders, with several rooms made inaccessible by 'stuff' that needs to be sorted. Our dogs and cats live indoors. It was never easy to clean a house like that, and – here's a surprise – *the addition of a baby didn't make it any easier.* Oh yes, we were going to get rid of the stuff before T arrived. It did not happen. In any case, we've become hygiene theorists, embracing our dirty dwelling as an investment in our daughter's immune system. (For the record, I really believe that, which is not to say I wouldn't like the house to be just a *little* more orderly.)

For me, the downside of staying at home with a baby concerned being out of my depth. At work, I knew what to do (or if not, I knew how to fudge it). But my formal education happened during the keep-your-options-open era, and as a result, I'm unable to commit to any particular method of doing anything. I'm extraordinarily good at seeing things from a range of points of view, and extraordinarily bad at deciding how to proceed for myself. One shelf of our many bookcases bulges with dog-training tomes, presided over by two very poorly-trained terriers. The shelf beneath sags under the weight of knitting manuals, yet a completed woollen item has never left my needles. And so on and so forth.

'Definitive' baby-wrangling manuals, therefore, were a seriously bad idea. The profusion of mutually exclusive instructions from assorted authors with apparently sound credentials sent me into agonies of indecision – it soon became clear that by the time I determined how best to deal with cradle cap, T would have crocheted her own beanie to disguise the affliction. I wanted to prepare myself for Things That Might Happen, but frankly, *nothing* can prepare *anyone* for the first time the whole household contracts gastro simultaneously. (Who would even have thought such horror possible?!) At work I had enough knowledge to make an informed decision based on experience; at home with a baby, I was a just-in-time parent flying by the seat of my pants. Eternally grateful for the remarkable resilience of babies, I simply had to learn to navigate a path of my own.

So to recap, in spite of my total lack of suitability for the role, being a stay-at-home parent caused me little angst: I had previously ceased to define myself through paid employment; I'm not prone to boredom; monotony was outweighed by my fascination with my daughter; I'm comfortable with limited social interaction; and I had comprehensive, live-in domestic support. Oh, I'm well aware of how fortunate I was. In retrospect, I did little more than baby-wrangling; I hardly deserved the honourable title of 'stay-at-home parent'. Timidly I proffer a mitigating factor: T was not fond of sleeping, and day-time sleeping in particular wasn't at all to her taste. But many a stay-at-home parent has wrangled a far more complicated baby than T, while managing the cooking, the housework, several other children and the local historical society. I take my hat off to those parents. (And single parents? *They are superheroes.*)

It all came to an end too soon. At 17 months, T started in day care two days per week, and a month later, I returned to work. When T was two-and-a-half, we increased her to three days of day care, so I could 'get stuff done' at home.

The angst I faced in deciding to put T in day care was more ferocious than I anticipated. Both D and I continue to grapple with the fact that our three-year-old spends three days per week with other people. We chose day care for pragmatic reasons: although we could manage without, life is certainly easier *with* my part-time income, and at my age, should I give up my job altogether, finding another down the track will only become harder. (*Keeping our options open.*) But also, day care offers T something which, with no family close at hand, and no friends with young families, we are rather short on: other children to play with.

T attends an excellent – and above all, *caring* – day care centre, walking distance from my office. After a shy start, she blossomed. And we have to admit that at least ninety per cent of the time, she loves it. My manager is compassionate, understanding and flexible. Without these conditions, we wouldn't do it.

So my title, to remain so indefinitely, is now Parent Who Works Part-time. In a rare moment of decisiveness, we have agreed that in years to come, T will not return to an empty house after school. And in three months' time, T will revert to two days of care so that we can spend more time together before the onset of kindergarten and school. At two days, the balance is better for our family, and we all relish the relative calm of those weekday mornings when only *one* person is scrambling to get to work on time. In having such options open to us, we know that we are fortunate indeed.

The day after, and the day after that came and went, and many days have followed since. Ahead of me and D lie years of torturous decision-making, as we face the fact that some options can't be kept open forever. Are we earth mothers or tech-savvy urban mummies? (We bake all our own bread and have smart phones, so I think we're aiming at a hybrid.) Should T have a country upbringing with freedom to run, or a city one with an iPad and designer sneakers? (For now, we offer chooks in a large-ish suburban yard and reliable internet access.) Home-schooling or a Steiner education or the local primary? (Hmm, getting harder.) Do we let her join the circus before the age of 16? (Help!)

Meanwhile, we can't help but marvel – and not without a tinge of sadness – at how quickly our tiny, squirming newborn has morphed into a lively little girl, with friends, dreams, moods, character traits and very long pigtails. While we struggle on, T is learning to make decisions for herself. And to support her in *that* is the best decision we can make.

Section IV: When the War is Over: Re-imagining Stay-at-Home Mothering

20.

How Alternative Mothering is Transforming American Stay-at-Home Motherhood

HALLIE PALLADINO

INTRODUCTION

There is a lot of ambivalence in American culture about mothers who stay home with their children.[1] They are sometimes romanticized, sometimes chastised, often marginalized. Stay-at-home mothers represent a small minority subject to the endless mommy wars that cause many to feel they must constantly justify their decision to be at home.[2] It is then, perhaps, understandable that an increasing number of stay-at-home mothers feel drawn to alternative styles of mothering, not only because of the prospect of joining a community in which their choices will be supported, but also because it gives them an opportunity to oppose a culture in which their work is largely devalued.

Although there have long been mothers who parent outside the mainstream in the United States, it is only recently that many of the approaches to parenting promoted by alternative mothers have become part of a broader national discussion about how children should be raised. Many of the alternative ideas that are gaining traction with this current generation of stay-at-home mothers can be traced to the 1960s and 70s, coinciding with the natural birth movement and the renewed interest in breastfeeding and natural living that accompanied it. Today, alternative mothering has expanded to include a diverse array of parenting practices that reject well-established cultural conventions or beliefs about childrearing.

What do stay-at-home mothers gain when they participate in alternative styles of mothering? Beyond the numerous ways in which these mothers believe they are benefitting their children, I argue that alternative mothering gives stay-at-home mothers a number of personal and social advantages that conventional mothering does not. First, because alternative parenting styles challenge social conventions, they give stay-at-home mothers an avenue through which to resist a culture in which their contributions are often diminished. Second, because alternative practices hold a larger political, moral or social significance for the mothers who choose them, alternative mothering gives stay-at-home mothers a way to connect their political beliefs and personal values with their everyday lives, helping them better integrate their public sense of identity with the largely private work of childrearing and homemaking. Third, participating in alternative movements provides opportunities for women to connect with other likeminded mothers over their shared interests or commitment to a particular practice or philosophy, combating isolation and creating community.

Alternative mothers at home are transforming American stay-at-home motherhood, not only through their persistent rejection of dominant cultural norms of childrearing, but also by their refusal to allow the work of mothering to be contained at home through their activism in areas related to mothering. The reverberations of this push can be felt across the culture.

CHALLENGING CONVENTIONS

Alternative mothering offers stay-at-home mothers concrete ways to address their concerns about contemporary culture through the rejection of aspects of that culture that they find to be destructive to children and family life. Alternative mothers ask: which conventional parenting practices aren't working? They wonder if a different kind of mothering could turn out healthier and more well adjusted children.

This leads many mothers to investigate attachment parenting and natural mothering, two styles of parenting that are closely related, although not identical. Attachment parenting (AP) is based on the writings of William and Martha Sears and consists of a codified system of maternal conduct that includes birth bonding, on demand breastfeeding, baby-wearing, sleeping with or near baby and a fierce rejection of "baby training" methods especially sleep training (Sears 2003:4-9). Natural mothering, as Chris Bobel defines it in her 2002 book, *The Paradox of Natural Mothering*, "merges two lifestyle practices—Voluntary Simplicity and Attachment Parenting—while taking inspiration from Cultural Feminism" (48).[3] She adds that natural mothering often includes the practices of home birth, eating unprocessed foods, alternative medicine, and in many cases homeschooling.

Beyond these two widely recognizable parenting styles, there are alternative practices to be found in nearly every area of childrearing, some of which are borrowed from natural mothering or attachment parenting, and others inspired by books and their related blogs, as in the case of *Radical Homemaking*, *Free Range Kids*, *Unconditional Parenting* and the Hip Mama movement (inspired by Ariel Gore's book series, zines (limited circulation magazines)) and related publications.[4]

None of the cultural conventions of childrearing commonly taken for granted by American parents are held sacred by alternative mothers. Co-sleeping mothers reject cribs and nurseries, advocates of baby-wearing swap out slings for strollers and proponents of baby-led weaning dispense with pureed baby food.[5] The mothers of "free range kids" reject the helicopter-parenting phenomenon, boldly letting their children walk to school alone. Homeschoolers reject the need for institutionalized education. Un-schoolers take this further still, rejecting any kind of set curriculum. Cloth diapering has made a comeback with a huge variety and selection of user-friendly options. Diaper-free mothers go a step further and use elimination communication to potty train their infants. Radical homemakers grow much of their own food and make almost everything in their home from scratch.

All of this means that alternative mothers at home are often taking on a significant amount of additional labor in the area of childcare and homemaking. So what compels alternative mothers to make a tough job even tougher? One possible explanation offered by Sharon Hays is that "the more intensive the techniques of appropriate child rearing become, the more mothers can claim that their job is a demanding and complex enterprise requiring high levels of knowledge and skill" (1996:159). In this way, natural mothering, AP and many similar variations of alternative mothering, may be choice affirming for a certain subset of stay-at-home mothers who want to fully immerse themselves in the project of mothering.

When stay-at-home mothers choose unconventional modes of childrearing, their choices enable them to differentiate themselves from the dominant culture. In this way, they embrace the often-stigmatized declaration, "I'm a stay-at-home mother," refusing to add the identity-diminishing word "just" and without rushing to qualify with, "but I also..." or "I used to...". Instead of allowing stale pre-conceptions of stay-at-home motherhood define their identity, these mothers are redefining stay-at-home motherhood on their own terms.

CREATING COMMUNITY

Stay-at-home mothering, especially when a mother lives far away from extended family, as many American women do, has the potential to be an isolating experience. When a mother leaves the workplace she might find herself alone with her baby during business hours and feel too exhausted to socialize with working friends by the time the evening rolls around. This transition often requires a woman to rebuild her social life as she tries to befriend other mothers who are available to socialize on weekdays and with children present, a daunting prospect on top of the work of caring for an infant. In this way, joining a community of alternative mothers has definite social advantages. Mothers in these types of communities, whether formally organized (such as a homeschool co-op or a meet-up group), or informal (such a neighborhood playgroup) will go to great lengths to be welcoming and accepting of newcomers, giving new mothers a chance to bond over the challenges of motherhood, forge friendships and build community. Sharon Hays observed that mothers tend to seek advice, whether it is from childrearing manuals, friends or family members, to be reassured that they are on the right track. They "are seeking affirmation that the ideology of appropriate child rearing is a *shared* one" (Hays 1996:75). Because alternative mothers often face criticism from friends and family who are perplexed by, or even actively disapprove of, their parenting style, it can be very affirming for mothers who are drawn to alternative practices to make connections with other mothers who are able to provide this type of reassurance. Homeschooling co-ops are a perfect example of how alternative mothers at home are able to make connections based on their attraction to alternative choices and use those connections to support each other and build community.[6]

Before my son was born I spent two and a half years teaching literature and writing to homeschoolers in the Chicago area. During this time I taught students from close to a hundred families in five different homeschool co-ops, each organized almost entirely by stay-at-home mothers. As is characteristic of the homeschool community, both progressive liberals and conservative Christians were heavily represented.[7] But in spite of political and religious differences, the homeschooling mothers I encountered shared a common concern that conventional education has the potential to impede children's intellectual, creative and spiritual development. This was something they were determined to avoid, often sacrificing much to do so, often having stepped away from careers, creative pursuits and personal projects in order to homeschool. But, as many were also quick to point out, they also felt they had much to gain from this choice including access to a tightly knit community of mothers who offer each other both emotional support and concrete help with the work of childrearing.

In addition to observing the social advantages that alternative mothering communities such as these can offer, since becoming a mother I have also experienced this personally on a number of occasions. On my last day of teaching, the mothers in one of the Christian homeschool groups surprised me with a baby shower. Although I was in many ways an outsider in their group, being neither a homeschooling parent nor a Christian, this generous group of women always made me feel incredibly accepted. On this occasion, they went even further as they welcomed me as a soon to be mother. They baked cookies and cakes, decorated elaborately and filled the trunk of my car with baby clothes, blankets, books, and toys. I was also given practical advice about labor and breastfeeding and offered prayers for my child's safe delivery.

A few months later, I had a similar experience of community among an entirely different demographic of alternative mothers when I joined a meet-up group of over two hundred and fifty women called The Chicago Hip Mama Collective (CHMC). As their name indicates they are self-proclaimed, "admirers of Ariel Gore and the Hip Mama zine...striving to be a safe-haven for queer mamas, single mamas, and mamas who feel marginalized by society."[8] Shortly after joining the CHMC, I posted on their message board that I was having trouble nursing my easily distracted three-month old anywhere but at home in a completely quiet room. As soon as he got hungry, I would have to drop everything and rush home to avoid a meltdown. A mother who I had never met came to my rescue. Upon reading my post, she immediately loaded up her toddler and biked five miles to my house to loan me a special kind of sling for nursing.

Mothers making alternative choices can be found across the political spectrum and hold a wide range of personal views, but what they have in common is a belief in the importance of mothers reaching out to each other. By choosing alternative forms of mothering, stay-at-home mothers can gain access to a variety of strongly established networks of likeminded mothers, social environments that welcome infants and children and the chance to establish groups and organizations of their own.

INTEGRATING PUBLIC AND PRIVATE IDENTITY

Regardless of their reasons for staying home, when women do become stay-at-home mothers, especially when it involves leaving a career track job, they may feel like they are out of step with a culture that largely defines adults by the kind of work they do. Stay-at-home mothers may struggle to integrate aspects of their public identity with the often invisible work of childcare and homemaking that can consume the majority of their time and energy. When new mothers withdraw from working in the public sphere they might feel cut off from their pre-motherhood identities. Alternative mothering can enable stay-at-home mothers to create connections between their political beliefs and personal value systems through mothering related advocacy and activism. Some key issues that are important to alternative mothers include: improving maternity care including expanded access to midwifery and home-birth, advocating on behalf of breastfeeding mothers including nurse-ins, letter writing campaigns, milk donation, or La Leche League participation, improving or developing alternatives to public education, and environmental protection including supporting sustainable agriculture.

Advocacy and activism can help mothers integrate the personal with the political on three levels: the individual level, the community level and at a national or international level. At the individual level, mothers can make choices at home that are in alignment with their political, social or environmental concerns. One common example of this is cloth diapering, a highly accessible way that alternative mothers can live their personal values through individual daily choices. Mothers who make this choice feel they are safeguarding their children from any potentially harmful chemicals in disposable diapers, protecting the environment and combating consumerism by refusing to purchase a throwaway product.[9] At the community level, mothers can engage in public actions stemming from their personal choices. The practice of mother-to-mother breast milk donation is an example of how alternative mothers can extend their commitment to a private choice (in this case, nursing) into a public act by coming together to create informal milk-sharing networks to provide milk for mothers in need. Through the use of social media this process has become even easier and more efficient. Groups such as Eats on Feets connect mothers who have breast milk to donate with parents in need of milk.[10] For dedicated nursing mothers who view the widespread use of artificial baby milk as a public health crisis (a social issue) that is driving up the cost of health care (a political issue), this is a direct way that they can get involved in becoming part of the solution. It is activism that dovetails with their lived experience of mothering. Finally, at the national or international level, alternative mothers often contribute to, volunteer for or even found their own not-for-profit advocacy groups devoted to mothering issues. Examples include the Campaign for a Commercial Free Childhood, a parent driven not-for-profit that targets companies who market junk food and violent movies to small children and Baby Friendly USA, the official not-for-profit dedicated to implementing the World Health Organization and UNICEF's Baby Friendly Hospital Initiative.[11] Attachment parenting also has its own not-for-profit, Attachment Parenting International, which serves as the public relations arm of the movement and whose lofty mission according to their website, is to "educate and support all parents in raising secure, joyful and empathic children in order to strengthen families and create a more compassionate world."[12]

By engaging in value-laden private daily actions as well as public ones, and through supporting related organizations, stay-at-home mothers who spend the bulk of their time doing childcare can leverage their alternative mothering choices to strengthen the connection between their private and public identities, maintaining a more integrated sense of self.

CHANGING ATTITUDES AND CUSTOMS ACROSS THE CULTURE

As an increasing number of American women embrace alternative styles of mothering there has been a shift in the public perception of what constitutes, to echo Hays's term, socially appropriate mothering choices. For instance, a June 2012 article in the *New York Times* style section asked, "Are midwives becoming trendy, like juice cleanses and Tom's shoes? It seems that way, at least among certain well-dressed pockets of New York society, where midwifery is no longer seen as a weird, fringe practice favored by crunchy types, but as an enlightened, more natural choice for the famous and fashionable." This observation could be easily extended to include many other parenting practices popular with today's alternative mothers; choices that used to be considered as on the fringe are rapidly becoming de-stigmatized.

The popularization of the natural mothering movement illustrates this trajectory. Since the publication of Bobel's book in 2002, natural mothering has continued to expand. There has been an explosion of natural mothering related blogs authored by those who are seriously engaged with the movement. But more significantly, the some of the core values of natural mothering are catching on with more conventional mothers, both working and at home, who in turn find ways to incorporate aspects of them into their own parenting styles.[13]

These trends have implications for social change, not just within the alternative parenting community but also for American parenting in general. It's true that most mothers, stay-at-home or otherwise, probably aren't going to throw themselves into radical homemaking and start making their own soap, but maybe a sleep deprived working mother will feel emboldened to reconnect with her baby by co-sleeping at night, or an expectant mother alarmed by c-section rates at her local hospital might have an easier time finding a qualified midwife to deliver her baby at home. The stay-at-home mothers today who are pioneering new styles of parenting are forcing a national discussion about which American childrearing conventions are worth preserving and which ones ought to be reconsidered.

NOTES

[1]The question of what constitutes true choice when it comes to a mother's decision to stay home is complicated by factors too numerous to mention here including the availability of quality affordable childcare.

[2]According to the U.S. Census Bureau there were 5 million stay-at-home mothers in 2011, down from 5.3 million in 2008. Accessed Mar 18, 2013.

[3]Many scholars in this area have observed that although there are obvious conflicts between feminism and alternative parenting styles, many of which seem to hinge on a return to traditional gender roles. Some feminist mothers are nevertheless drawn to many of the values and ideas contained in these parenting philosophies. Bobel found that many mothers in her study reconciled this issue by embracing the essentialist attitudes of cultural feminism. Personally, I also face this conflict as a feminist and a stay-at-home mother whose mothering is heavily influenced by both AP and NM. I agree with Petra Büskens who answers the essentialist argument thusly, "I believe infants do require a long period of intensive, embodied nurture. The problem is not the fact of this requirement but rather that meeting this need has come

to rest exclusively, and in isolation, on the shoulders of biological mothers."(81) As for how to remedy this issue, I share the hope of May Friedman who believes, "it is possible for attachment parenting to become less patriarchal if we focus on the withdrawal of attachment parenting choices from attachment parenting theory."(140)

[4]Though not every popular book or blog about parenting is going to inspire a movement, I have mentioned the ones above in particular because so many mothers across social media platforms self-identify with these particular styles of parenting beyond just reading the books. It is not uncommon to see mothers on alternative parenting message boards refer to themselves as AP, UP, Free Range, or Hip Mamas, etc.

[5]Baby Led Weaning, by Gill Rapley and Tracey Murkett, is a book that gave a name to the increasingly popular practice of avoiding pureed baby foods, especially ones that are commercially produced. Proponents suggest that the self-regulation involved when babies feed themselves easy to chew finger foods might contribute to healthier eating habits and lower instances of obesity later in life.

[6]Homeschooling is a rapidly growing alternative parenting movement. There are an estimated one and a half and two million school aged children in the United States currently being homeschooled. The National Center for Education Statistics reported 1.5 million students (or about 3% of US school aged children) were being homeschooled in 2007 up from 850,000 in 1999. A 2010 study published by a homeschool advocacy group, The National Home Education Research Institute, claims that number has since risen to two million.

[7]Two of the groups were specifically Christian, one was for gifted children (as identified by their parents) and the other two were open to any nearby families.

[8]Full group description can be found here: <http://www.meetup.com/chicagomamacollective/> accessed Jan. 31, 2013.

[9]An often cited 1999 study, authored by Rosalind Anderson and Julius Anderson, found that certain brands of diapers cause asthma in mice. They also found that disposable diapers contained endocrine disrupters and neurological and respiratory toxins, some of which have been linked to cancer.

[10]For more information see: <http://www.eatsonfeets.org/about> (accessed Jan. 31, 2013.)

[11]More information can be found at: http://babyfriendlyusa.org

[12]API's full mission statement can be found on their website: http://www.attachmentparenting.org/about/about.php>

[13]Bobel is careful to remind her readers that although many alternative mothers live simply, alternative parenting is something made possible by a certain amount of social privilege, especially having the advantage of an employed partner (171-172). This means that perhaps there are many more mothers who would like incorporate alternative mothering practices into their childrearing but are unable to do so because they don't have the luxury of making that choice.

REFERENCES

Anderson, Rosalind, and Julius Anderson 1999 "Acute Respiratory Effects of Diaper Emissions." *Archive of Environmental Health* 54(5): 353-8.

Bobel, Chris 2002 *The Paradox of Natural Mothering*. Philadelphia: Temple University Press.

Büskens, Petra 2004 "Impossibility of 'Natural Parenting' for Modern Mothers." In *Mother Matters: Motherhood as Discourse and Practice*. Andrea O'Reilly, ed. Pp. 75-86. Toronto: Association for Research on Mothering.

Friedman, May 2008 "Everything You Need to Know About Your Baby: Feminism and Attachment Parenting." In *Mother Knows Best: Talking Back to The "Experts."* Jessica Nathanson and Laura Camille Tuley, eds. Pp. 135-141. Toronto: Demeter Press.

Hays, Shannon 2010 *Radical Homemakers: Reclaiming Domesticity from a Consumer Culture*. Richmondville: Left to Write Press.

Hays, Sharon 1996 *The Cultural Contradictions of Motherhood*. New Haven: Yale University Press.

Kohn, Alfie 2005 *Unconditional Parenting: Moving From Rewards and Punishments to Love and Reason*. New York: Atria.

National Center for Education Statistics 2008 *1.5 Million Homeschooled Students in the United States in 2007*. U.S. Department of Education.

Pergament, Danielle 2012 "The Midwife as Status Symbol." *New York Times,* June 15. http://www.nytimes.com/2012/06/17/fashion/the-midwife-becomes-a-status-symbol- for-the hip, accessed Jan 28, 2013.

Sears, William, and Martha Sears 2003 *The Baby Book: Everything You Need to Know About Your Child from Birth to Age Two*. New York: Little Brown.

Skenazy, Lenore 2009 *Free Range Kids: How to Raise Safe, Self-Reliant*

Children (Without Going Nuts). San Francisco: Jossey-Bass.

Stadlen, Naomi 2007 *What Mothers Do: Especially When it Looks Like Nothing*. New York: Penguin.

Rapley, Gill, and Tracey Murkett 2008 *Baby Led Weaning: The Essential Guide to Introducing Solid Foods - And Helping Your Baby to Grow Up a Happy and Confident Eater*. New York: Vermilion.

21.

It's Time to Move Beyond the "Mommy Wars"

SOLVEIG BROWN

I started a Ph.D. program in anthropology shortly after my first child was born, and I effectively withdrew from the program after my second child was born. I spent a lot of time with other mothers, and noticed that our daily conversations, which on the surface seemed about everyday events, actually related to deeper cultural issues that we were all dealing with in our own way. I kept wishing that anthropologists would write more about mothers in American culture, until it occurred to me that I had found a perfect dissertation topic. When my youngest child started school, I returned to graduate school. During 2007 and 2008, I conducted in-depth ethnographic interviews with forty mothers, and collected extensive survey data from eighty mothers residing in the Minneapolis-St. Paul Metropolitan area. The majority of participants were white, college educated women, with household incomes above the national norm. The women ranged in age from twenty-two to fifty-three, with an average age of thirty-six; and their children ranged in age from four months to nineteen years, with a mean age of four. I used grounded theory methodology to code and analyze the data.

American media stories often portray working mothers and stay-at-home mothers as rival groups of women, sensationalizing topics such as the "Mommy Wars." I found that in spite of our cultural environment, which fans the flames of discord between groups of women, most women support the choices other women make with regard to working or staying home with children. I suggest that media reports ignore the diversity within these groups of women, overlook the common ground between them, and obscure the broader social, emotional, and structural factors that individual mothers (and fathers) routinely navigate in their efforts to reconcile the conflict between market work and family work.

Most married women expecting their first child will be asked, "Are you going to keep working after the baby is born?" This routine question shows the deeply engrained cultural belief that after a child is born or adopted, a woman will make a "choice" to work full-time, part-time, or stay home full-time with her child. Our underlying cultural assumption is that women are responsible for managing the conflict between market work and family work, and her "choice" is whether she wants to stay home with children, or find someone else to care for her children while she works.

We talk about the end-result of a woman's particular choice, which officially makes her a stay-at-home mother or a working mother, but we rarely talk about the rationale behind the choice a mother makes. A few of the women in my study always knew they wanted to stay home with children, but for most women, choosing to stay home is a complex decision, often constrained, or influenced, by external circumstances. For example, some women made an agonizing decision to leave a job that was deeply rewarding to stay home with children, whereas other women felt either sad about losing a job, or relieved about quitting an unfulfilling job. Some women leave the work force because their job, or their spouse's job, has a demanding schedule that is not conducive to family life. Some couples agree that having one parent stay home with children is a good thing; whereas, others fight when one parent thinks someone should stay home, and the other believes both partners should work. Some women stay home because they have a spouse or partner who makes enough to money to support the family comfortably. Others struggle financially to stay at home. Some mothers stay home because they fear putting their child in daycare; other women stay home (especially after a second child is born) because they cannot afford to pay for daycare. Additionally, cultural, community, and familial expectations for combining market work and mothering—which differ depending on one's race, class, religion, region, sexual preference, marital status, and socioeconomic status—influence women's choices about staying home or working after a child is born.

It is also difficult to characterize a typical mother because the women in my study had diverse experiences. Some women stayed home with children for several years; others were at home for a much shorter time. Some mothers have strong support networks within their community, whereas others feel lonely and isolated. Some women's transition to staying home is relatively easy; others find it difficult. Some mothers do the bulk of household and childcare duties, whereas others have a more equitable division of labor. Some women thought about being a mother in idealized terms and were surprised that it was not necessarily a good fit for them. Other mothers adapted as they anticipated.

The mothers I interviewed identified both positive and negative aspects to focusing primarily on family work. On the positive side, several mothers felt that they did not miss anything, and appreciated not having to leave home in the morning. Erika described being home as similar to having her own business. *Yes, you're working twenty-four hours a day, but you're the one that's calling the shots.* Haley enjoys watching her daughter grow. However, she comments, *sometimes it gets to the point where you can't do it anymore [laughter] like when we're reading the same book for the third time in a row. I should be doing it because reading is good, but I really don't want to read this book again'* [laughter]. Haley complains about being a mom, but concludes that overall, *the good definitely outnumbers the bad experiences.*

Many mothers who had both worked and stayed home felt that a stay-at-home mother's work is challenging and often goes unrecognized in the broader society. During the 2012 presidential election, democratic pundit Hilary Rosen's comments that Ann Romney "never actually worked a day in her life" dominated news cycles for several days. Ann Romney tweeted, "I made a choice to stay home and raise five boys. Believe me, it was hard work." The following day, President Obama stated, "There is no tougher job than being a mom." Rosen's comments reflect the stereotype our culture has of mothers: mothering does not really count as work.

Over the last two decades, the "Mommy Wars" metaphor has emerged to describe an assumed conflict between mothers in the United States. Most of the mothers I interviewed did not experience the "Mommy Wars." Emily said, *I don't know if I just have blinders on and choose not to see it. I read about it, and I think, shame on both of these sides for attacking each other, but I haven't personally seen it or felt it.* Many mothers expressed respect for the choices others make. Rachel adamantly exclaimed, *whatever people choose is their own business.* Valerie noticed that among the people she interacts with, everyone is careful to be "politically correct" about the topic. Many women thought the people they knew personally respected their choice, but still felt judgment from people they did not know, in part because they feel that people generally undervalue stay-at-home mothers.

In some cases, negative representations of stay-at-home mothers in the media influenced individual women's perceptions of what others in their own community may think about them. For example, Abby, a stay-at-home mother commented, *if I'm at a party where there's a lot of working moms, I think they probably think, 'oh why don't you just go and get a job.'* She paused for a minute and observed, *I don't even know why I'd have that thought. It must be from the media.* Abby's comments suggest that she assumes that working mothers are likely to hold negative stereotypes about stay-at-home moms represented in the broader culture. Her comments also show that media stories about the rivalry between mothers have influenced Abby's beliefs about what working mothers she does not know might be thinking about her.

Haley saw a *Today* show focus group of mothers and commented, *I don't know anybody who would say those things, at least I would hope not. Why put each other down? It's hard enough as it is.* Haley has many friends with children who are working outside the home, and they all try to support each other. Haley feels that most of her friends who work feel pressure that they should be staying home; whereas, Haley feels pressure to work because she thinks people do not see staying home with children as a job. Erika believes there is *a big misunderstanding between each camp as to how much time the other one has. I think it must be easier to get exercise if you work because you could go to the gym before work, or just go for a walk at your lunchtime. I have this pre-conceived notion, that I'm sure is completely wrong, that it would be so much easier to carve out time for yourself if you worked.*

The reference to time (or lack of time), which came up so often throughout my interviews, reflects the fact that time has become an important commodity in American culture. When I asked mothers what is the hardest thing about being a mother, one of the most common responses was *not having enough hours in the day to get things done.* Anthropologists have shown that in most societies it is a mother's job to provide her child with scarce resources. For millions of mothers in the world, their scarce resource is food. For present-day U.S. mothers, their scarce resource is time. I observed that every mother was mindful that her time is an important resource to give her child, and mothers strive to balance spending time with their children and other commitments. Working mothers tend to bristle at the question "How do you do it all?" because many feel that the underlying implication is that they are not spending enough time with their children. Stay-at-home mothers feel annoyed if someone asks, "What do you do with all of your time?" The implication is that they have the luxury of extra time because they are not productive members of society.

Our national conversations rarely move beyond a superficial discussion of "choice," or the "Mommy Wars," to talk about the complex issues women face in managing the conflict between family work and market work. We talk about choosing to work or stay home with children as if this choice occurs in a vacuum, rarely discussing the factors that constrain a woman's choice to work or stay home with children. In so doing, we absolve the government and employers of any responsibility to implement policies supporting all parents, such as longer job-protected leave options, longer paternity leaves, and affordable or subsidized daycare. The continued portrayal of the "Mommy Wars," has created negative stereotypes for all mothers, leaving many women feeling defensive and judged about their work status. At the personal level, most women have moved beyond the "Mommy Wars." It is time for our national conversations about mothers to do the same.

22.

Seeing Themselves

Stay-at-Home Mothers Reject Stigma

HESTER VAIR

INTRODUCTION

The public discourse about stay-at-home motherhood is rarely neutral. It is common to hear rhetoric that uses stay-at-home mothers as symbols in a clash between two, ostensibly opposing, value sets. Stay-at-home mothers are either vilified for their attachment to oppressive roles for women, or valorized for their rejection of the selfish pursuit of individual success. In all of this there is a shared assumption that stay-at-home mothers are more invested in the traditional view that mothers are naturally oriented towards child rearing and should forgo careers to take care of children. What do stay-at-home mothers make of the exaggerated images of themselves as doormats or angels?

In Canada stay-at-home motherhood is declining. In 1976, 39.1% of mothers were employed, and in 2009 the number was 72.9% (Ferro 2010). Family policy in Canada assumes that women work; however, that has not led to policies that facilitate childcare. Family policies tend to be that the care of children is a private family responsibility, not a social responsibility (Boyd 1997). Public discourse and policy neither pressure women to stay home, nor suggest that there should be any broad social sharing of the burden of childcare. The message to mothers from this does not have the level of vitriol that sometimes seems to seep from the mommy wars in the United States, but neither is it supportive of working mothers. Canadian mothers struggle to establish supportive policies for working mothers in an environment permeated with a familial ideology.

The rhetoric of the mommy war sets up a dichotomy of right and wrong ways to mother; any discussion of working and staying home becomes transformed into ertaz ethical stances (Podnieks 2012). The stay-at-home mother is the ideal mother who has chosen to sacrifice her own ambitions for their children. With this as the ideal of motherhood, the working mother is characterized as ambitious and selfish. In this war of rhetoric there is now a counter-position that presents working mothers as capable managers of the complex balance between work and family, who contribute both financially and emotionally to their families. In this counter-discourse the working mother is seen as a better mother because she is a model to her children of achievement and full involvement in society, whereas stay-at-home mothers are depicted as conservative and unambitious, and often as less capable and less hard-working than working mothers.

Both positions now claim a normative status. Stay-at-home motherhood remains the traditional ideal and is defended by those with an axe to grind about appropriate roles for women. Outside this group, working motherhood is now the standard because almost all other mothers are in the workforce. Although the pro-family voice is not numerically significant, the power of old ideologies of motherhood is great enough that working motherhood must still be defended; this defense has helped to generate the view that stay-at-home mothers are backward in their thinking, self-indulgent, lacking in skills, and unable to make a real contribution to society.

In a study of stay-at-home mothers on the East coast of Canada I found that stay-at-home mothers are aware of this description of themselves and vehemently reject it. Twenty-five mothers were interviewed for a qualitative study; the mothers were well-educated, middle class women. None saw child rearing as a woman's natural task and all had ambitions in the sphere of paid-work. Their views on motherhood are contrary to the common perception of stay-at-home mothers: they do not laud the sanctity of the mother-child relationship. Rather, their orientation towards mothering is practical and they see the work as extraordinarily difficult, intellectually stimulating, highly challenging, and necessary work. The stay-at-home mothers were acutely aware of how they are seen by others as engaging in activities that are unskilled, involve little challenge, and make little contribution to society. In the conflict between how they are seen and how they see themselves, the mothers experience what is essentially the imposition of a derogatory master status. This chapter explores the mothers' understanding of how they are seen, and how they respond.

ATTITUDES TO PAID-WORK

Contrary to the stereotype, the stay-at-home mothers in this study saw themselves as ambitious and competent women who valued achievement in the sphere of paid work. They saw achievement in paid-work as a natural part of what they had worked for and as part of their entitlement to be part of a more gender-equitable world. As young women, these women were excited by the possibilities open to them; they expected to work hard and to establish a career. In Colleen's words:

> Before I had children my work was everything. And I was satisfied with that; that was great. It was fine to go in on weekends, and every evening going to a meeting.

These mothers did not think they were forsaking the work world when they chose to stay home, and they still saw themselves as highly competent, energized individuals. They see themselves as a new generation of women, not housewives with motherhood as destiny, but as women with a place in the world that they are struggling to balance with motherhood. Although they are at home with their children at present, they remain oriented towards work in a conventional sense, as measured by occupational status, a professional mien, and by a good salary. This causes some difficulty as they try to manage the dichotomous split between work and home. For example, Joan expresses discomfort that her expensive education and training is wasted:

> I find that it is really difficult for women, especially if you have been brought up to feel that education is important, and you have spent all these years studying and working and then all of a sudden, that's it!

Neither does their approach to motherhood fit traditional assumptions; they value work of care, but do not valorize motherhood as part of women's natural disposition. These women do not hold a traditional ideology of motherhood that assumes an exclusive mutual need between mother and child (Oakley 1989). This group of stay-at-home mothers was frequently vehement in their assertion that children certainly need care, but not necessarily mother-care. Michelle says:

> I get sick and tired listening to people saying that things would be better if women did not want to work so much. Why does it have to be women? I do believe that two working parents is more difficult, and I think one person should stay home.

Kathy refutes the notion of a special bond between mother and child that constitutes her as the appropriate caregiver:

> Don't kid yourself. I know that I have a special relationship with my child, but I'm not going to say it can't be duplicated with anybody. If I die tomorrow, he would be fine.

Jill puts this more bluntly:

> I don't think he needs a mother, or any of that crap. I would be pleased if my husband stayed home instead.

They do not see the activities of motherhood as part of the exclusive, loving, natural relationship of mother and child; their view is that this is difficult, challenging, work. The mundane work of motherhood, the physical caretaking tasks and basic protection from harm, is the most obvious part of motherhood work. These tasks are often seen as separate from mothers' responsibility for guiding children through the world, simultaneously directing them to learning opportunities, and protecting them from challenges yet beyond them. These responsibilities vary with class and with the times, but all are acknowledged as cognitively sophisticated (Everingham, 1994, Ruddick 1989). Currently, a middle-class mother in Canada faces an exacting standard: her child must be given the skills to compete in a future marketplace for scarce jobs and flourish in a culture that values individual achievement in all endeavors; the child must be a good citizen, moral, and able to think about complex issues; and must also be happy and well adjusted. For the stay-at-home mothers these responsibilities are integrated with the mundane work; they are hands-on tasks which are informed by sophisticated thinking and decision-making, careful planning, and an extensive skill set which puts this into practice at the quotidian level. Lisa explains:

> To be a good mother you need to have a wise plan, a wider view than I got to get this kid to its next school day. You have to be looking, even before you have children. What kind of 19 year old do I want to have? I think that colors everything that you do.

Surely at no other time in history has the standard been so high. The mothers in this study are occasionally critical of this standard, but when they are it is with a passing comment, not a challenge to its legitimacy; most accept it unthinkingly. They accept, as do working mothers, the ideology of intensive mothering, which requires devotion to their children and the provision of every opportunity (Hays 1996). However, the stay-at-home mothers take direct responsibility for the shaping of the child. The essence of mothering for this group of mothers was their pro-active stance. They don't just respond to the child's environment, they attempt to create it. They don't just guide the child through the situations that emerge; they try to shape the situations before their child encounters them. To put this into an occupational context, this requires that they be front-line workers, teachers of an array of skills (some of which they learn in order to teach them), program planners, developers, and evaluators, child psychologists, conflict resolution specialists, and spiritual guides all at once. These stay-at-home mothers put all of their skills into the work of motherhood and they find the work stretches them well beyond their expectations. The traditional shibboleth of womanly fulfillment through the nurturing of her children has little place in their view of motherhood. The focus is, as Michelle points out, on the task:

> I don't have room for a whole lot of mistakes when it comes to mothering. You make plenty of them. But when you make them, it hits you hard.

EXPERIENCING THE STEREOTYPE OF STAY-AT-HOME MOTHERS

The stay-at-home mothers are aware that through the lens of the mommy wars they are seen very differently. They report that the full diversity of who they are disappears from view, overwhelmed by the ideal of the full-time stay-at-home mother. Mary says:

> It is hard; People show real surprise that I ever did anything other than be a mum.

It works the other way as well, of course, with equally unwelcome results. Angela is uncomfortably aware of being cast as a poster girl for motherhood:

> People will look at me out in public with my three kids and they will smile, and be sweet to me. 'There she is! There's mom!' I want to crawl under a rock because I feel so conspicuous.

The mothers report that assumptions about full-time motherhood dominate all their interactions; the assumption that, without paid-work, they have profoundly limited lives is a constant feature of their conversations. Angela explains:

> When you work people understand who you are and what you are doing. They have a bit of an understanding of who you are, they orient towards you a little differently. Men particularly have difficulty orienting to me because they think I must be boring.

Paid work establishes us as someone of value to society; whereas, domestic labor is seen as menial, requiring no special training or skills, and as a personal activity that is of trivial interest outside the home. The stay-at-home mothers are frequently reminded that to stay home is to spend one's days in activity that is self-indulgent and socially wasteful. Stephanie recounts her experience:

> I know that what I do is hard, and that I am busy all day, but when people ask me: 'are you working yet? Are you going to find a job?' They are focusing on that I am not doing anything productive. 'Are you going to find a job?' That is what they are saying, because I don't mean anything unless I have a job.

Many people assume that little domestic labor is even necessary. In Gayle's words:

> Some people think that being at home is boring. A lot of people ask me 'Are you working?', and I say, 'No, I'm at home'. They say, 'what do you do?' I just think 'Oh, my God'.

Anna helps us to understand that the problem is about the verb to do:

> There are so many expectations from others. When people ask you, "what do you do?" I say, 'well, I'm a mother.' You know they think: 'Yes, but what do you do?' Well, that's what I do.

There is no answer to the 'what do you do?' question because it is asked from inside a discourse where motherhood is not work; it is an identity, or a disposition, but not an activity. The stay-at-home mothers are trapped by the discursive dichotomy between 'real' work, which is paid, and care-work, which only has value as an expression of love. To stay at home is to choose love and family over paid-work. To see this choice in the realm of work, as a way of managing care-work by doing more of it oneself, is not possible in this discourse because the private nature of domestic labor means it is superficial and unimportant. Michelle's remarks illustrate the gap between this discourse and her view of work and care:

> What annoys me is when someone says, 'Oh, to stay home just does not challenge me enough'. I think, 'You know what? Maybe you weren't doing it right then.'

The mothers find they are seen as conservative, perhaps even misguided, because this discourse understands their choice to stay home as rejecting the opportunity to contribute to society by using their education and skills in the labor market. They are thought to be living a life of luxury, privileged by their husband's income, and thus able to escape from the hard work that faces women who have to work for a living as well as raise their children. Of course, there is much to be done in maintaining a house and raising children, all the more without two incomes available to purchase commercial substitutes; but this work seems to be even more invisible than it was a generation ago when aphorisms about the invisibility of women's work were common fare decorating fridge magnets. A mother symbolizes nurture and love, not activity, and certainly not creative, challenging work. With the work that they do hidden beneath the ideal of the loving mother, the stay-at-home mothers are seen as leisured, if not lazy, and with this comes contempt.

THE STIGMA OF STAY-AT-HOME MOTHERHOOD

Stay-at-home mothers experience the imposition of a persistent stereotype. There is an impermeable quality to it that makes it difficult to assert any other identity; it becomes a master status, a stigma, which broadly defines how they are seen in the world (Goffman 1963). Their diverse characteristics are suddenly invisible to others, apparently erased by their stay-at-home mother status. With the stigma of stay-at-home mother status these mothers have lost their ability to present themselves as important and valuable in society. In Jennie's words:

> Motherhood has no value in the world. I wonder if subconsciously that is why I volunteer. It is very difficult to answer. Because motherhood is very fulfilling and challenging. But it definitely does not have a place in the world.

This loss of status in the world hits this group hard because of the contrast with their early expectations. They began from a position where they were fully clothed in a status achieved though educational attainment and often subsequent professional success, and it is as if they are stripped naked overnight when they become stay-at-home mothers. All that remains is the borrowed status of their husbands and the ascribed status of motherhood; neither of these speaks of their individual identity, their competence, their values, or their contribution to the world.

They are reflective about their situation and do not accept the definition of their status that they experience around them; nevertheless we can hear an element of bravado, of whistling in the dark, in what they say. Stephanie comments:

> I know that I am much lower in status than I was. I know my career is in the pits, I know that it is horrid, but I don't care. I made the choice to do this, and I knew full well that it was going to be pretty bad, status-wise, but that is not what life should be all about.

The experience of seeing a muted self-image in the mirror of society is a difficult one, distressing despite their assertion that they are content with their choice. Karen acknowledges that, although she made a conscious choice to do what she does, she feels the perceptions of others.

> With work you have that paycheck attached to it, and with that a sense of self-sustenance. From being paid for what you do comes the feeling that you are self sufficient and independent. At home, unfortunately, the hardest job in the world, has so little value on it. Whether you believe it or not you still feel it. You feel the lack of self-sufficiency and independence.

This erasure from the world can be a source of bitterness and anger. It was often a source of resentment against others who devalue their contributions and it emerged frequently in the interviews with stories about the common remark: 'Oh, you are so lucky to be able to stay home'. This comment presents their choice as a luxury, part of the odious stigma they cannot escape, rather than as a hard choice with attendant costs to finances, career, and autonomy; it downplays the contribution to society that is made by the work done at home, and as we hear in the following voices from Stephanie and Mary, it is bitterly resented:

> That comment 'you're so lucky', that just makes me angry. It is so stupid to say it. Such a God dammed ... Because they could be in these shoes same as I am. But they have chosen to do something different because their values are different from mine. I think, 'Don't tell me I am the pampered person and that I don't make the effort to go out and work'.

> I hear: 'Oh I really wish I could stay home, we just can't afford it'. I just let that one go, because we can't afford it either. I always think, 'well, you know, we make our choices'.

We can hear the frustration and anger in these voices, but notice that their anger is silent, mute. They report what they *think*. Why do they not say instead of think? Because they understand that the stigma is a boundary that excludes their perceptions and experiences from the conversation. The 'you're so lucky' remark is grounded in the normative understanding that paid work is the way we all contribute and sustain ourselves, unless we are 'lucky' (wealthy), whereas motherhood is not work; it is an indulgence.

One mother told an illuminating story which is an exception to this pattern of silence and gives us a broader sense of how the stigma is experienced. The story reveals both her anger and her pleasure in rejecting the people who deride what she does, and at the same time, it reveals her impotence to change their perceptions. Gwen was invited to be interviewed for part-time teaching at university, and in the course of that interview the interviewers discovered that her expertise was a very good fit for a full-time job they were having trouble filling, so they tried to convince her to apply for it. She found it surprising and insulting that, despite the fact that she had been invited for the interview and that they were trying to convince her to work for them, there was little attempt to conceal their disdain for her years at home.

> Their attitude was 'What have you been doing?' Right away the attitude from them was you've wasted the past eleven years of your life'. So I just got up. I said, "I'm sorry". I said, 'I'm not interested'. I didn't need to listen to that. 'You called me. You need me'.

To her interviewers, her choice to be a stay-at-home mother is an incomprehensible anomaly in the context of her admirable qualifications for the job. Motherhood is presumed to be an experience completely outside of the skills for which they would hire her. From their perspective, the choice to stay home is so outside of the admirable qualities that make her, in one sense, just like them that, it required explaining.

This story was unusual; in most of the stories the stay-at-home mothers did not express the frustration they felt. Their silence is not simply because they are intimated; they have a sophisticated understanding of how they constituted as outsiders and, although they know that their non-response tends to confirm others' view of them as limited, it is the only response possible. It is impossible to present the value they place on their work and on themselves forward in social interactions. Their current lives make it difficult to present themselves in ways that they know would be valued, to pass, to use Goffman's terms.

I was struck by one mother's story of an experience where she simply could not see herself in the image reflected back from society; it is a wonderful illustration of the stay-at-home mothers' resistance to the label. The feedback loop between ourselves and society generally ensures our personal conformity to normative views; we are, after all, shaped by our interactions with others. However, this does not always fit those who face a stigma, because they may resist labeling, as many stay-at-home mothers do. This mother did a self-esteem test in a university course she was taking, and was disturbed to find that her score marked her as having very low self-esteem, in sharp contrast to her sense of her self. She recounted that she answered honestly, but, after thinking it over, she decided that the questions were wrong: they asked about her abilities and her confidence in situations where she, as a stay-at-home mother, knew she would not be taken seriously. She said she was bound to fail, because the test only asked about her worth in terms of how others saw her. She remarked that she was no fool, and was perfectly aware that people would respond with incredulity to claims she would make of importance, competence, and skill in her activities as a stay-at-home mother. She pointed out that the work of motherhood was challenging; she used all the skills she used in her education and at her workplace, and had learned a great deal through motherhood; however, she would only receive respect for these skills when she put them to work in an activity valued by the world. This mother commented that the test did not allow her to make the distinction between how she knew she was perceived in the world, and what her own sense of her strengths was; the test did not test self-esteem, it tested her understanding of how she was esteemed by the world.

This example is illustrative of the perceptions of other stay-at-home mothers as well. They have little confidence in social situations, not because they have little confidence in themselves, but because they felt, as another mother put it, 'like the abstract painter at the convention of philistine accountants, who knew he was perceived as doing art that any six-year old could do'.

These stay-at-home mothers understand how they are seen, and what it is about them that triggers this view. They have, as Carol Gilligan says, 'another voice', but they are aware that it is a voice that cannot be heard (Gilligan 1982). Their expressions of discomfort and resentment are not surprising; what is surprising is that they do not dwell on the individuals from who they experience dismissal. Their analysis is social, not personal. In this they reveal that they are not the conservative pro-family angels/doormats of the mommy wars. On the contrary, they are critical and thoughtful about ideologies of motherhood. Karen's remarks are representative of their emphasis on the social context:

> Is there really an expectation that when you have a child you should drop everything that you have worked for and everything you have accomplished, just because you have a child. Sometimes I lash out at my husband, but I think my resentment is focused towards our culture. Why is there is never any expectation that maybe my husband should stay at home a day a week? The frustration and anger that I have is towards social expectations of women.

Gwen suggests that in a different society, it might be possible to value this work enough to pay for it:

> I've had no money. I've had to depend financially on my husband and if there's any resentment it's that. Its not resentment

> towards my husband, its towards society. If I lived in different society perhaps I would have some money for the work I do.

Forced to be self-reflective, the stay-at-home mothers develop a sophisticated understanding of the social context of their experience. Although few mothers described themselves as feminists (all were 'sympathetic' to feminist issues) their analysis of their situation was such that sometimes it was as though I was interviewing students in a women's studies class. Tammy points out, that the world around them does not value what they do: 'We don't have dignity and purpose in the world because the world does not recognize it'. Monica echoes Tammy's sentiments, and links this to the rhetoric about motherhood:

> Society does not put kids first, they don't value mothers. Although in the same breath they exult them.

Stephanie points out the contrast between the 'wonderful thing' that she is doing, and its 'real value':

> Staying home has been the most exciting and fulfilling and passionate thing, but there is no respect or appreciation from the outside. People say, 'oh, what a wonderful thing', but real value? Zero. It is nothing. It is really nothing. It is not something of value in the world.

Mary takes this one step further with her observation that the talk about motherhood is a way of covering its devaluation' it is a way of not-acknowledging:

> People will say to me, 'Oh, that is the most important job you will ever have', but they never say it is challenging, or difficult, or demanding; it is just a blanket sweep. As though they are saying, 'Oh, I don't want to go there, [making brushing motions] let's just find a place to sweep this'.

Feminists have made the argument that the rhetoric around motherhood is a sham, and provides a cover for the social devaluation of their work, and it is significant that we hear this analysis echoed by a group of women presented in the mommy wars as the antithesis of feminism.

The stay-at-home mothers' reflection on their situation is a strategy to cope with the position they find themselves in, not, largely, the result of a feminist perspective on women's subordination. Using a social lens to view their situation allows them to understand the way the stigma is constructed, and thus it helps them to resist the label; nevertheless, the strategy is also the start of a critical understanding of the institution of motherhood.

How is this knowledge used? Is there a worm in the rose? Do the stay-at-home mothers' stigma provide them with a standpoint to challenge the social value of care work? This is an enticing idea; however, the possibility is thwarted by the individualistic way that the mothers frame solutions. Their understanding that care work is socially devalued generates an alternate way to view themselves; they are able to see themselves as outsiders who are unjustly characterized and they create an alternative identity as strong self-motivated, authentic women who are going their own way. Thus, despite the clarity with which they see the social structural constraints that shape their lives, they see their lack of status in the world as a problem that they have to solve.

REFERENCES

Boyd, Susan B. ed. 1997 *Challenging The Public Private Divide: Feminism, Law, and Public Policy*. Toronto: University of Toronto Press.

Everingham, Christine 1994 *Motherhood and Modernity: An Investigation into the Rational Dimension of Mothering*. Buckingham: Open University Press.

Ferro, Vincent 2010 "Paid Work". *Women in Canada: A Gender Based Statistical Report. Statistics Canada Catalogue* No. 89 503 X. 6th edition. Ottawa: Ontario. http://www.statcan.gc.ca/pub/89 503 x/2010001/article/11387 eng.pdf

Gilligan, Carol 1982 *In a Different Voice: Psychological Theory and Women's Development.* Cambridge, MA: Harvard University Press.

Goffman, Erving 1963 *Stigma: Notes on the Management of Spoiled Identity*. Englewood Cliffs NJ: Prentice Hall.

Hays, Sharon 1996 *The Cultural Contradictions of Motherhood.* New Haven, CT: Yale University Press.

Oakley, Ann 1979 *Becoming A Mother*. London: Martin Robertson.

Podnieks, Elizabeth. ed. 2012 *Mediating Moms: Mothers in Popular Culture*. Montreal McGill-Queens University Press.

Ruddick, Sara 1984 *Maternal Thinking: Toward a Politics of Peace*. New York: Ballatine Books.

23.

Motherhood as an Act of Personal and Social Co-creation

TARA ULBRICH

Motherhood is a biological opportunity afforded to women that offers up a profound connection to human purpose. In the personal evolution of identity the 'work' of pregnancy, birthing, nurturing and educating is deeply challenging. As a mother a woman is entrusted with forming and nurturing the human expression of what will come after her. She resides creatively in each moment, bearing witness to an unfolding human being; yet, she is intimately involved in this co-creation; in which each act and spoken word affects the future. Women have been told to fear losing themselves in motherhood but what if the complete opposite is true? It is possible to find oneself?

Making meaning is a psychological journey and yet the undertaking of raising children is profoundly influenced by culture and society. Within the role of mother, as defined by each woman, exists the potential to be both empowered but also disconnected, from personal and social strength. The opportunity can flower into a creative expression of the resilience of humanity though it can also be co-opted by the dominant cultural discourse at the expense of both women and children.

In this paper I share my own lessons as I birthed and raised my four children. Motherhood became my quest for personal, spiritual and social fulfillment but it required a process of actively engaging with the social norms of my culture and redefining them at key nexus points. I expose five key cultural myths that threatened my personal unfolding. These myths represent ideas that had to be tackled front on to reclaim my strength and generate a personal ideology and motherhood practice.

I entered motherhood in my mid twenties with two university degrees and several years of family centered social work practice. Pregnant, I had high expectations of my partner, my society and myself. I thought I would be supported to birth and care for this new life I carried within by a modern medical system. Cultural myth one: *the care provided by modern medical institutions is necessarily best for babies and mothers.*

From the moment of conception every cell in my body felt inexorably altered, leaving me reconsidering my self-concept. This visceral, psychic experience exacerbated as my belly grew. The patriarchal medicalisation of what was happening to me failed to take my whole spiritual experience into account. I was treated disrespectfully by doctors, as if I was ill; as an uninformed patient who needed treatment. It was with much relief I turned towards traditional midwifery care for support. I began to read more widely and talk with women who possessed birthing wisdom, my first encounters with radical homemakers. My midwife provided woman centered care which empowered me to walk boldly across the threshold of woman to mother.

Cultural myth two: *mothers and fathers can interchange their roles; mothering is the same as fathering, that is parenting is a unisex overarching term for infant care.* As my body struggled with the enormous physical changes I was undergoing, and I began to perceive the new identity I was creating for myself, I came to realize that my experience of child bearing was profoundly different from my partner's. I imagined that my partner and I would share in the daily care of this little baby. I was soon shown otherwise. My employment contract was suddenly not renewed in the face of maternity leave and I began spending time with mothers who had chosen to stay home with their babies.

When my son was born I realized that though our one body was now two, we were intertwined in a physical connection that was not the same as his connection to his father. My son breastfed but it was more than this. My body felt a biochemistry beyond that precious self-regulating, milky nurturing. I felt responsible for using this maternal intensity to make something bigger than the two of us and its source lay in this profound *womb-knowing* of one another.

The experience was similar with my other three children who were all born at home where I was supported by the care of my midwife. Though I saw my children each as separate individuals, we were deeply involved in a process of co-creating perceptions, beliefs and experiences. Language acquisition was a continuous wonder as we sang, played, told stories, dressed up, lit candles and walked in gardens. And there was this richness in the web of connections between siblings and parents, all making for vibrant family creating.

The power of mothering work and acknowledging its importance helped me to face the third cultural myth: *childcare can do it better.* I was soon asking myself, and being asked, about returning to 'work'. Even with my fourth child I was still challenging this thinking, as if what I was doing with my children was not meaningful labor, or even more frighteningly, the suggestion that a rotation of paid carers, especially institutionalized care, could better nurture my child's unique unfolding. With four children under six years old and a community of likeminded families, a home life rich in creativity and nourishment, a mother excited and interested in the possibilities around her and a partner who supported the dynamic family he was part of creating... money can't buy that and childcare can't even imagine it.

I made a choice to remain at home and continue to be with my ever-changing children. And then we decided to go deeper. We moved from the gentle, leafy suburbs of a capital city to a small regional town in Northern Tasmania. We arrived with four children aged four weeks, two, four and six years old. We had a vision to be more connected to the family hearth and the natural environment. My partner was able to return to study and, ultimately, part-time work. We sent our children to a small local school but we were sitting uneasily with the fourth cultural myth: *schooling best supports learning, creativity and personal growth.*

We had already nurtured our children to walk, talk, use a toilet, eat with a fork, play, co-operate, and be compassionate and passionate. Why stop now and outsource the 'work' of this new life stage? But it takes strength of conviction to follow through in the face of a global movement. Now education is a commodity, something that one buys, and the more you pay the better you get. This dominant belief system says that life is about competition and the sooner you get in the race the faster you'll get to the top. Learn to read and do your tables earlier and quicker, learn to pass exams better than everyone else and you win. But win what? We began to meet with families who stood in their power as home educators and we read widely on the subject.

In truth, deciding to home educate followed on naturally from the earlier decisions to claim home as the centre, the hearth, the place of conception, birth and raising a family. As a mother I responded to the very important physiological and psychological messages, the intensity of the relationships with my child and children and a growing sense of responsibility to generate a new story for my children, the future of our society and for myself. I chose not to let other people or institutions instill consumerist, materialistic values in my children. And I wanted to explore a new way of living alongside their questioning minds. Everything was up for renegotiation and it was a powerful feeling.

To this end we removed ourselves from mainstream culture physically and ideologically. Though we read widely, made use of the Internet and viewed international films, we didn't have a television in the home, choosing real life adventures above virtual ones. We walked in the wild places of this island and sought out people who share their passions. We travelled. Our home remained open to overseas visitors who wish to explore their own cultural myths and truths. As a family we continued to evolve a curriculum of life.

This picture of mothering did not just happen; it was imagined and re-imagined many times over. Home was defined as a vital space of freedom and play, imagining and reflecting, of safety and security. Mothering, therefore, became the practice of creating and maintaining this space. Fundamental to such a design was a conscious decision to reject cultural myth five: *buying things improves your quality of life and your personal happiness.* I chose to make my mothering journey an exploration of creating for myself that which I was invited to purchase. We didn't buy childcare or schooling and in addition we also chose to make our simple daily bread and the cloth on our backs, to plant the seeds in our soil and to, to help make shelter over our heads.

We all experimented with whatever we identified as an area of interest. Conversations, borrowing books from the library, mentoring and then experimenting became a well-practiced methodology. We focused on tending relationships with each other, the wider world, the natural world and ourselves. We read literature, joined local theatre, played musical instruments, wrote poems and made journals. We became our own small community and learned that homemaking through relationships is meaningful work indeed.

Now, as my children move to a more community-centered life, a home core remains. They seek out education experiences beyond the hearth;

work, learning and participation in organized social activities. They have special friends and close relationships with each other. They're engaged with living life as fully as they are able. I am happy to continue to bear witness to their unfolding from a place of heartfelt curiosity. I am grateful for my early mothering experiences; they equipped me with the personal authority to honor my unique role as their mother. I birthed in my power, and drew upon that wellspring to ensure that each life stage for my children and myself was supported in a cradle of intimate, human compassion. For this I thank my midwife, the mothers who went before me and the writers who offered their stories and ideologies. A mother once said to me that no matter what your idea is someone has written a book about it. Find your quest, but also find inspiration in our collective conscious.

Now all humanity is grappling with ideas requiring rapid social change. A key location in this conceptualization is the home. Individual stories, like mine, are finding platforms in social media and the social movement of people creates conversations previously unimagined. Women, as mothers, can find their feet on such a domestic platform, a base from which radical new ways of living can be tested. The time has come to reclaim the beauty of mothering by unshackling the endeavor from consumption and reconnecting to its inherent creativity. Mothers, as homemakers, can design their own personal and social futures.

REFERENCES

Balaskas, J 1989 *New Active Birth: A Concise Guide to Natural Childbirth.* London: HarperCollins Publishers.

Copperthwaite, William S. 2007 *A Handmade Life: In Search of Simplicity.* White River Junction, VT: Chelsea Green Publishing Company.

Gaskin, Ina May 2002 *Spiritual Midwifery.* Summertown, TN: Book Publishing Company.

Gatto, John Taylor 2002 *Dumbing Us Down: The Hidden Curriculum of Compulsory Schooling.* New Society Publishers.

Grille, Robin 2005 *Parenting for a Peaceful World.* Alexandria, Sydney: Longueville Media.

Hayes, Shannon 2010 *Radical Homemakers: Reclaiming Domesticity from a Consumer Culture.* Richmondville, NY: Left to Write Press.

Holt, John, and Patrick Farengal 2003 *Teach Your Own: The John Holt Book of Homeschooling.* Cambridge, MA: Perseus.

Kumar, Satish 2008 *Spiritual Compass: Three Qualities of Life*. Sydney: Finch Publishing.

Salter, Joan 2011 *The Incarnating Child, Holistic Parenting and Child Health Series*. Gloucestershire: Hawthorn Press.

Schmidt-Brabant, Manfred 1996 *The Spiritual Tasks of the Homemaker*. London: Temple Lodge Publishing.

24.

The Free Gift

How U.S. Stay-at-Home Mothers Sustain Themselves in a Culture of Nonreciprocity

ANA VILLALOBOS

> "It's all giving, all day, every day." "I'm just fried." "Isolated." "It's out of balance and I need to refuel, to receive, but there's *no time.*"

In the mid-1900s, French feminist Simone de Beauvoir wrote: "[W]hat gives mother love its difficulty and its grandeur is the fact that it implies no reciprocity... [S]he expects no return for what she gives, it is for her to justify it herself" (1952:513). Over sixty years later and an ocean away, stay-at-home mothers in the United States continue to experience themselves as almost always giving without recompense.

Although the "free gift" reigns as the U.S. cultural ideal for mothering, it presents a great challenge to those giving it, and also presents a theoretical challenge. Almost all grand theorists of society, such as Emile Durkheim, Max Weber, Karl Marx, Mary Douglas, and Pierre Bourdieu, describe human behavior as motivated by the drive for *something*, be that integration with the broader society; status and power; creative, self-driven productivity; maintenance of the current social order along with one's position in it; or social distinction. Such social goods are, according to these theories, why non-oppressed people do what they do. So how do women who choose to stay home with their children manage to maintain round-the-clock giving in a cultural context where staying home isolates them from society, curtails their self-driven productivity, and diminishes their status, power, and ability to socially distinguish themselves?

Some research has suggested American women do not, in fact, have a choice. For underprivileged women, their earnings are so minimal, work hours so unpredictable, and childcare so expensive, that the costs of wage work are simply not sustainable (Damaske 2011, Edin & Kefalas 2005). For privileged women, professional work frequently demands such long work hours and there exist so few opportunities for proportionately compensated part-time work, that many women are forced out of the workplace entirely if they seek even moderate balance between work and family (Stone 2007). By whatever route U.S. mothers end up at home, it remains a puzzle how they maintain their giving with so few social rewards.

To understand what women need and seek in order to sustain giving in this cultural context, it is necessary to delve into women's own experiences and subjectivities. Therefore, I use women's narratives as my data source and conducted semi-structured, face-to-face in-depth interviews with twenty stay-at-home mothers from two regions in the western United States to examine what resources they draw on to make stay-at-home mothering work. Interviews occurred almost exclusively in the respondents' homes with children or babies present, and the mothers' statements were coded for themes around what made their experience of stay-home mothering either subjectively easier or more difficult.

Analytically, this work falls into the interpretive sociological tradition of such scholars as Arlie Hochschild (1983, 1989, 2012) and Annette Lareau (2003) who use in-depth analysis of cases to uncover meanings and conceptual understandings. The strength of such a methodology is in theory-building. However, the small sample size does not lend itself to testing its own theoretical contributions, which would be a welcome next step with a larger sample.

Respondents were recruited both through snowball sampling in a middleclass neighborhood in suburban Washington state and from birth classes in California prior to the birth of the women's babies. Both forms of recruitment elicited a sample of primarily middleclass white women, most of whom worked prior to having a child. Thus, the observations provided here apply to that segment of the population.

CULTURAL CONTEXT: THE U.S. IDEOLOGY OF INDEPENDENCE AND NON-OBLIGED SELVES

In my analysis, I interrogate the notion of the "free gift" among stay-at-home mothers in U.S. culture, with its strong ideology of independence. I find that mothers do need something to sustain themselves in giving, and in absence of the traditional reciprocity of labor, material goods, or care, what this tends to be is some form of *visibility*.

Anthropologist Marcel Mauss (1950) classically conceptualized the "gift" and the relationship-deepening that occurs in many cultures with obligatory reciprocity. Mauss observed that in indigenous societies, giving is often a form of power placing the recipient in debt to the giver and commanding honor and respect from both the recipient and those who witness the giving. The obligation to return the gift also creates a moral bond between the giver and receiver, leading to social solidarity. Mauss' conceptualization seems to help resolve the stay-at-home mother puzzle in light of this moral bond and the Durkheimian urge for social solidarity. However, the solidarity Mauss discusses is premised on a culture of obligatory reciprocity whereas stay-at-home mothering in the United States is culturally situated at the far opposite end of the spectrum. In fact, the American ideology of independence frequently draws on market dependence as a way to avoid interpersonal dependency (Dizard & Gadlin 1990, Hochschild 2012).[1] Whereas in the Middle Ages, European parents "spent only as much time, energy, and money on children as children promised to give in return" (Hays 1994:23), the ideology of independence problematizes mutual obligation, such as children being required to give back to their parents in kind. Thus today's U.S. parenting goal is to raise children to be free and independent agents who neither need further assistance from the family nor owe it any reciprocation (Dizard & Gadlin 1990:156). Indeed, since the demise of family-based productivity, American children have been, as Viviana Zelizer (1985) describes them, "economically worthless." This worthlessness extends to adult children as well. Since the 1970s when middleclass women entered the paid workforce in droves and eldercare shifted from the family to market-based institutions, most U.S. parents believe they should take care of themselves in their old age rather than impose on their adult children for a turnabout of care (Hochschild 2012:199). Children, therefore, are expected to contribute neither economically nor with hands-on care either in their youths or adulthoods. This "lack of return on one's investment" makes women's ability to sustain full-time caregiving somewhat mysterious and stands in stark contrast both to the mutually obliged traditional societies Mauss describes and to most contemporary European, Asian, and African societies where some form of obligation to parents typically continues throughout the lifespan.

Is there, then, no "give back" in U.S. stay-at-home mothering? Exchange theorists would have difficulty with this apparent lack of reciprocity. Such theorists "explain the existence and endurance of social groups such as the family by their appeal to the self-interest of individual members… Of course, membership in social groups may also necessitate compromise and even costs to the individual member. [Yet] if the costs of group membership exceed the rewards… then membership in the group is no longer a rational choice" (Klein & White 1996:60). Is full-time parenting in the U.S. context, then, an exercise in irrationality? Or is exchange theory's view of social cohesion based on individual self-interest missing the subjective, interpersonal, micro-level wherein a parent may so identify with a child that loving that child is actually an act of caring for an extension of one's self? Alternately, and less philosophically, are these parents simply receiving their sustenance from a source we have yet to uncover? Like Genevieve Vaughan who views "gift giving (and therefore mothering) as economic, a mode of distribution of goods and services to needs" (2007:7) and Arlie Hochschild who articulates the exchange value of emotions (1983, 1989), I examine the *emotional economy* to see how women emotionally sustain themselves in the face of near-constant giving, especially in a work-identified culture that undervalues caregiving.

I begin by establishing that staying home is problematically difficult for many American women, then look at the emotional resources some manage to draw upon to sustain themselves for this apparently one-way giving in a culture where there is no expected financial or caregiving return from children.

THE HARDEST GIFT

For many American women, full-time caregiving is "the hardest thing I have ever done." The primary difficulties they point to are the inability to focus on things other than the children, and the relentlessness of children's needs. These two mothers each describe the difficulty of their own simple hygiene:

> Stacie: If I [go] in the bathroom, they're both there with me. Um, you know, if I sit down, for just a minute, just to re-

> lax—they're on top of me; they're on my lap... *[T]hat's* what's draining. Like, you know, [*hushed*] 'Can I have just, just five minutes here?'
>
> Pamela: If I try to take a shower, Liza will go into the bathroom and she'll claw at the shower door, 'Mommy!' You know it's just, it's horrible. So [*laughing and gesturing to her hair*] I haven't showered yet today!

Laura believes even *trying* to have "me time" in the presence of children is a mistake because it sets up unrealistic expectations. When asked if she is ever able to recharge her battery in the presence of her children, she replies:

> No... My kids are too little... A couple times, I've tried to read, like if they're playing or something. I think, 'I'm going to go read my book!' It's usually a disaster because then I end up really wanting to read and I'm excited about it, then something happens and I have to stop and it's horrible 'cause I've just started. So I've found that's almost more frustrating than it's worth. It's better just to wait 'til they're asleep.

By contrast, adamancy about one's goals in the presence of children, either goals for accomplishment or for a moment of repose, can lead to anger. Miranda—a self-described "task-oriented" mother—struggles with her needs to accomplish things:

> The point when I'm the absolute worst mom, is when I, I have something that I need to do. I, ah, I can have zero patience with them. When I focus on them, we do okay, but... I've really lost it with them... when I'm trying to do something: I need to write a letter, I need to do something at the computer, and I'm just trying to sit and concentrate—I just need ten minutes. And they won't give me ten minutes.

This gravitational pull of young children toward a mother trying to focus on something else, is captured beautifully by Adrienne Rich (1998:312):

> [A]s soon as [my son] felt me gliding into a world which did not include him, he would come to pull at my hand, ask for help, punch at the typewriter keys. And I would feel his wants at such a moment as fraudulent, as an attempt moreover to

> defraud me of living even for fifteen minutes as myself. My anger would rise; I would feel the futility of any attempt to salvage myself, and also the inequality between us: my needs always balanced against those of a child, and always losing.

CHILD RECOGNITION

One way some women resolve the conflict of needs is by limiting their focus to the process with children rather than to visible goals. They forego a product-orientation. For example Jennifer believes "type-A" people, whether male or female, should be out in the workplace, not raising children. In fact, she describes a girlfriend's difficulty with stay-at-home parenting precisely because her type-A task-orientation creates a different set of skills and expectations than those needed for full-time caregiving:

> She'd always been a career woman—she worked at Digital in an executive position—and she ended up at home, in this weather, with four children, at like age 37. So she had a little bit of, you know, it was *difficult*. And so she went back to work, she got a nanny 'cause... she's a real driven kind of person and she has really high expectations and she wants to accomplish things every day. And I think a lot of, you know, raising children, you don't accomplish anything for like years... [I]t was just classic: we were both buying plants last week, and... I had all these little tiny plants with no flowers, you know, that won't flower for like two years, perennials, and she had these HUGE plants, in full flower, and I said, 'Look at the difference!' and it was so funny because it was so, I mean it was so clear to me... hers would all be done in a month and they'll probably die in her yard, and mine will be blooming two years from now, but that's just, I think that's why I'm happy doing kids.

Jennifer believes that the drive to accomplish which fuels women's success in the workplace runs counter to the need for patience necessary for full-time parenting. When women do focus their energies on the process with children, they often describe rewards there, such as these three mothers, below:

> Constance: If I'm having a bad day, they'll just come and give me nice hugs. You know, you, um, you're always just wonderful in your kids' eyes and that comes in handy on some days.

> Laura: Even when they cry, I just love it, I'm just like, 'Oh you sweet thing!' 'cause they're just so open and they just, they feel bad and they're gunna show you every minute of it…I know I'll look back on this time and I'll weep with joy. So, that keeps me going 'cause I do know that, that this is the best time.

> Pamela: [My daughter] tells me every day, 'I love you, Mommy, I love you,' and…she loves bedtime stories, and she wants me to carry her and hold her, and…to me, there is nothing so precious in the world as having that.

It makes intuitive sense that a child saying loving words or affirming the relationship would make a parent feel good. Yet "feeling good" and what "keeps a woman going" are not necessarily the same. When we run a marathon, we need water, calories, electrolytes, and oxygen. The fuel must match the losses. So on the surface, it seems incongruous that words, hugs, or emotional support, which seem to reside in the expressive world, could sustain the practical, material activity of everyday caring. Kathy makes sense of this when she points out, "It is a physical occupation…but it's emotionally draining. It is just [*pause*] *incredibly* draining. You know, they have needs…they get upset about every little thing, or, everything is a big deal to them. There is nothing that's simple or easy."

Despite the physical nature of mothering young children, what is depleted most is one's emotional stores. Thus many women seem to require sustenance on the emotional level: either from witnessing and participating in the "emotional preciousness" of children (Zelizer 1985) or from their children *recognizing and affirming* them.[2]

SELF RECOGNITION

In addition to this expressive visibility with children themselves, American stay-at-home mothers deal with the subsuming of their self-directed interests in the presence of children by mobilizing at least one of the following resources to support them: (1) time alone, (2) creatively or intellectually challenging productivity, or (3) appreciation from peers. I will illustrate each of these briefly, then discuss how again *visibility* is the underlying issue and the critical form of reciprocation in modern U.S. caregiving.

First, these women "refuel" by spending time alone. As Rich declares, "I could love so much better…after even a quarter-hour of selfishness, of peace, of detachment from my children. A few minutes…beyond our tightly circumscribed life together" (1998:312). Likewise, Laura says she "would die without my down time." When asked what down time does for her, she replies:

> I'm turned off. Nobody needs me…I only have to worry about myself. That's why I don't want to do any work [after the kids go to bed], 'cause if I'm doing work, I'm really doing it for everybody else still, and so it, even though it's so much more pleasant to clean the bathroom or something all by myself, I can't use that time to do that. I have to have it for me.

This tending to a "me" is a repeated refrain in interviews with American women who manage to sustain stay-at-home mothering. However, solo "me time" begs the question of what one is actually seeking. I argue that the most valued prize is recognition from one's own *self* that one is a person with needs. By contrast, those women who express the most difficulties with stay-at-home mothering often struggle with a loss of "me."

> AV: What are your needs?
> Trudy: *My* needs?
> AV: Mm hm.
> Trudy: [*incredulous tone of voice*] *My* needs?…I haven't been successful yet at finding out what really rejuvenates me…I'm searching that out now…I know that God loves me so I'm like turning to God and then I'm also…[trying] to remember what it was like as a kid, and what I really love, and—because I'm totally neglecting myself, and um, and what I love to do. And…[that] sometimes leads to resentment because you're resenting that you don't have *yourself* anymore. And it's not [the children's] fault—it was my fault, I gave it freely—but then I would blame them because I don't have me anymore.

For most mothers, this "me" they long for cannot be expressed exclusively in the presence of children, and they seek time alone. Interviewees mention with resounding frequency their children's bedtimes and naps as sanctuaries in time in which to refuel themselves. These moments of quiet solitude present the rare opportunity to focus on something other than parenting. As it is not always easy to shift gears toward self-recognition, this sometimes requires a ritual of some sort. Meredith uses a special chair upstairs which symbolizes calm personhood for her:

> I can sometimes be crawling inside my skin, you know, as you play that tenth game of monopoly or whatever...and I definitely, I can feel my blood pressure just drop as I sit down in my chair... This house is the first time I've had, like, one certain area that I like to read, and I keep my little candle and my books—I mean, it's almost like a little haven.

This sanctuary of self-visibility acknowledges her worth beyond what she can give others or accomplish.

CREATIVE PRODUCTIVITY AND PEER RECOGNITION

In addition to recognition from oneself and from one's children, a third way U.S. stay-at-home mothers need to sustain themselves is through productivity and giving still more through creative endeavors with a visible product. This, like the transition to downtime, may require a mental shift. Pamela says:

> This is going to sound really funny to you maybe, but I have this sort of ritual before I write or before I start planning to do some work-related things; I need to have the kitchen countertop cleaned. [*laughs*] It's kind of my mental preparation... [to] "adultify."

Like Pamela, Laura's response to motherhood's lack of immediate visible product is to be productive elsewhere in her life:

> I need to feel successful. I mean, I'm definitely an over-achiever, so it's kind of hard being a stay-at-home mom, especially since I don't like to be the over-achieving type of stay-at-home mom who needs to see, you know, that their kids are

> doing perfect... I don't want to be that way, so it's kind of hard to feel like I'm really an achiever.

Thus, Laura is caught in a dilemma. She wants to be successful, but the only avenue she sees available to "over-achieve" in mothering is to be a "Super Mom," a mode of parenting that does not correspond to her values. Her resolution of this dilemma is to be a community organizer on the side. For example, she sits on the board of her children's preschool (she introduced the idea of a parent board in the first place). She also saw a need for better fund-raising and for a parent volunteer structure at the preschool, and implemented both. But Laura's desire to organize did not stop there. She also created a "Mom's group" which, according to other neighborhood mothers I spoke with, changed their own lives and the nature of community life in their neighborhood. This creation was partly to fulfill Laura's productive and organizational needs, and partly because she herself wanted to be part of such a group:

> Right after I had [my third child], I decided I had to have adult contact, so [organizing the group] was a complete repercussion of having a baby. And everyone's like, "How could you have done this when you had a baby?" and that's like the reason I did it! I had no contact with adults; I was so isolated. So I decided to form a neighborhood group of moms... that's just blossomed into this huge thing. Everyone's like, it's hugely important to them, 'cause everyone's in the same boat.

In addition to organizing the gatherings, she does such things as producing a neighborhood parent directory including contact information and children's birthdays. "Everyone's like, 'Wow!' and that makes me feel good 'cause I'm very capable of handling this and it's turned into this huge thing for so many people."

In her case, people saying "wow" about what she has created is a form of community recognition, acknowledging her wherewithal, skills, and generosity. Similarly to the dynamics in the societies Mauss (1950) describes, Laura's giving produces honor within her community.

The other form of peer recognition women seek regards their mothering itself. With other mothers, the tendency is not merely to seek affirmation of their competence as mothers, but also empathy for and connection with others in the struggles of motherhood: that is, the visibility of their suffering. It is not uncommon for women primarily caring for children to "confess" to researchers. For example, Rachel, one of sociologist Mary Blair-Loy's (2003:13) respondents, describes caring for her three- and four-year-old daughters: "I've never hated a job as much as I hate this... I was not prepared for... this sleep deprivation, constant demands, boredom, lack of stimulation."

Likewise, Trudy has a need to "confess" and says she would like to be able to share more of her problems with people. When asked if sharing is usually helpful, she replies:

> [*emphatically*] Yes! YES! Being validated, just being not alone in your pain is the most valuable thing in the world... Just, even the way you're nodding your head [*referring to interviewer*], you feel like, "Oh my God, somebody understands," or, "I'm not alone. I won't die with this pain by myself." That's–if I could just do that to [my husband], and just like say, "OAH!" and just bitch and then he'd go, "Oooh, you had such a bad day," I would be *fine*. It's out, it's over, it's great. [pause] I think Catholics have a good thing just confessing all the time.

Katrina, mother of three young children including a "high needs" son, shares that she's "never felt such raw rage and not known what to do with it before in my whole life... I mean, the real anger you can feel towards them, it's kind of scary sometimes... [Y]ou're lying if you don't know what that feels like." For her, it is incredibly helpful to connect with others so she can recognize the normalcy of her difficult feelings and experiences:

> I have a friend who has a child that's high needs, and... the feelings that are elicited are the same, and we talk about them. And that makes me feel like—she's older than I am, she's mature, I see her as a well together person—so for her to have those same feelings kind of makes it, me feel like I'm not some freakazoid that has these crazy feelings... I'm finding there's more and more of us out there... and when you talk together it helps.

Meredith, who has a Master's degree and used to work in Human Resources, moved to the Pacific Northwest just after having her second child. It was in the dead of winter and she felt isolated, not "knowing a soul," and her husband had just started a new long-hours job.

> I don't think I was really...conscious of how hard it was until it was near the end of it. You know, I was kind of muddling through and then I just started realizing I've got to get *my* life together. And so that's when I started looking...and found a mom's group. And it was like this whole door opened.

In an atomized world where stay-at-home mothers are often alone with their children, difficulties from simple frustrations to all-out rage can be trapped within the family walls and can easily turn into a source of self-doubt. This is frequently relieved when mothers connect to other mothers for whom the same situations or feelings have occurred. Connecting with other mothers during the baby days was important to Meredith precisely because those women were "in the same situation as me, and that was a tremendous relief to be able to, being a new mom, to be able to share stories..."

In such a group, difficulties that were once a source of shame and isolation suddenly become a source of connection as the women realize their experiences are shared. In a world that does not see them, they are seen. And this helps them "get on with it."

APPRECIATION

Visibility to oneself is acknowledgement of one's needs, visibility to one's children comes from expressive words and physical affection, and visibility to one's community is recognition of one's productive capacities or recognition of the magnitude of one's struggles in the plight of mothering. A fourth and very crucial form of visibility that partnered stay-at-home mothers seem to need is from the other parent of their children. What women especially seek from their partners is *appreciation* for the work they do as mothers, what Hochschild (1989) calls an "economy of gratitude."

Particularly for women accustomed to being valued for their work in paid careers, transitioning to the unpaid and often isolated work of parenting can be difficult. Given the current societal undervaluing of care work (England & Folbre 1999), the social value once placed on care must be expressed in concentrated form by certain individuals in women's lives. Therefore, for example, a husband's appreciation may not merely represent the appreciation of one man, but may stand in for a whole society, and as such, be utterly indispensable. One stay-at-home mother says, "Appreciation is everything." Another says, "I've always needed that kind of pat on the back." Still another adds, "I don't think taking care of little kids is hard. But it's all in the appreciation."

Katrina points out, "Your kids are not going to go up to you and say, 'Mom, you did a great job today,'" and most women agree with Jennifer that "a mother does not get appreciation from her children." Laura, in fact, says with conviction, "I don't expect anything from my children... I don't think their job is to do anything for me. This is a gift thing."

Even though Pamela's toddler, Stephanie, thinks she is "just the greatest," that does not substitute for recognition from adults.

> Pamela: I don't know if it's the way I was raised or what, but I need feedback. And, you get a different kind—Stephanie tells me every day, ten times a day, she loves me, and that is wonderful, wonderful feedback, but it's very different from someone giving you kind of professional feedback, and I need it—I guess I'm insecure—but I just really love getting feedback, professional kinds of feedback. And so I think that's part of my motivation.
> AV: And by "feedback," do you mean people telling you you're doing a good job or—
> Pamela: Yeah, yeah. I wish I didn't depend on it as much as I do... but it's something I've always strived for.

It can be difficult for stay-at-home mothers if their care work is taken for granted. In a paid job, even if it includes no evaluations, no promotions, and no professional feedback, at least there is always a paycheck to say one's work is worth something. But at home, there is no pay to affirm one's worth, so without verbal reinforcement to balance the ledger, it may be particularly easy to feel taken for granted. Meredith captures this:

> Because I'm staying at home there's a lot of probably assumed, um, things that are assumed that... are just part of that job... and [my husband will] admit it, too. You know, there are times that, um, it would be nice if he came in, 'Oh, the house looks nice.'

Her work being "assumed" can translate into a perceived lack of appreciation.

Jennifer, while considering herself a feminist, believes the feminist movement has exacerbated the tendency to take mothers' work for granted.

> AV: [If] you didn't have your husband telling you that he appreciated you, how would that be?
> Jennifer: I think that's probably the norm for most women that stay-at-home because…instead of us being appreciated for what we do…the feminist movement kind of got us tweaked around so it's like we're responsible for [mothering] plus bringing in money.

Jennifer believes that now, women are simply expected to do both breadwinning and caregiving and their contributions in both realms are assumed rather than appreciated. In order for husbands to avoid this assumption and not take their stay-at-home wives for granted, some understanding of the wife's job seems to be necessary. Kathy says:

> Until you've done it, you just…cannot appreciate what is involved and how hard work it is…I used to be, 'What do stay-at-home moms *do*?'…Well, they work *hard*!…I think about nannies, you know, that's a lot of hard work, but you know what? They're not also trying to get the house clean and work in the yard and run the errands and do the grocery shopping, you know, they're not doing all of that…

Echoing this, Laura states:

> The husband doesn't usually understand—I mean, Michael has flat out said, 'I don't have any idea what you do.' There's that funny e-mail that goes around: Dad comes home and everything's an absolute mess, food everywhere, an absolute wreck, and the dad's like, 'What happened today?!' And she goes, 'You know all that stuff that I do all day that you don't know what I do?…Well, today I didn't do it!' It's just so funny!

Laura does believe her husband gains deeper appreciation for her each time he stays with the girls himself:

> It's hard for the husband to understand what you do…The couple times he's stayed with the girls, you know, a couple times I've gone away for the weekend—which a lot of guys wouldn't be able to do—I get back and he's like, 'Oh my GOD! You are *amazing*!' And of course I love that and I want

> him to tell me more, everything he did and how amazing I am. I'm very much, I need praise. I need everyone to know that I'm wonderful.

Similarly, when Pamela spent a week in L.A., though her husband left the girls at a friend's house for ten hours each day, Pamela felt he gained a greater understanding of what she does. "It's only because he's been through it [that] he can connect now."

For Jennifer, who almost never goes on trips away from the children, her husband's support in their day to day lives has been extremely important to her:

> [My husband] has just always thought that I had a really hard job, and just really, really appreciated and valued me. And, I mean, I could say to him, 'I've had the worst day of my life,' and a lot of husbands would say, 'What are you talking about? You know, you're home all day with these kids, you can go to the park.' I mean, we were in California, it was sunny, we had a beautiful backyard with a pool, you know, everything that I could want, I had all the money that I needed to spend, and what was I complaining about? But he would never, ever say that. He would take the kids and he would put them in the tub and he'd tell me to go sit down and read a book and was just always really, really supportive.

Jennifer believes this degree of partner support and valuing of her work is critical, particularly for getting her through difficult days and the routineness of child-raising:

> There's a kind of monotony, when you're doing the same thing every day... [and] I probably wouldn't have had six kids if my husband didn't appreciate me 'cause I would have—I think then the monotony of it probably [would] turn into drudgery, so then you would lose your joy.

Appreciation is more than simply a nice gesture that elevates a mother's mood. Appreciation can determine number of children or distinguish drudgery from joy. It is the necessary glue holding the precariously undervalued work of mothering together. As Laura summarizes:

> If Michael is working long hours and I can barely handle it all, if I know he realizes what I'm doing and appreciates me for doing it, I can keep going. I can do almost anything no matter how hard, just so long as I know I'm appreciated for it. And if I'm not, the whole thing just falls apart.

CONCLUSION

In a society where women generally lose both status and financial rewards for engaging in fulltime mothering and where children are not expected to repay their parents in kind for the care and financial provisions given them, it may seem mysterious how U.S. stay-at-home mothers sustain themselves for this task. Yet women draw on four sources to sustain seemingly one-way giving. The first is to meet their emotional needs through the relationships with their children themselves, particularly through children's expressive love and esteem for their mothers. Second, the women take breaks from the children, giving themselves time for self-acknowledgment and attending to their own needs. Taking breaks, however, is not enough and only has its full rejuvenating effect if the women are also valued by others. Thus, a third way women sustain themselves is through the value incurred by creating a visible product, inextricably tied to cultural importance placed on productivity versus relationships. Organizing events, creating artwork, or improving institutional forms are all activities our society recognizes as productive and therefore appreciates. In partaking in such activities, these women may be seeking not only the enjoyment of creative work, but also emotional validation for who they are through doing something commonly recognized as producing worth. And finally, these mothers sustain themselves through the empathy and appreciation of others. Because the energy drain of childrearing is emotional, what women need to sustain themselves is primarily emotional support. This comes from their friends and spouses, and forms a sort of care chain (Hochschild 2000) where individuals outside the mother-child relationship give recognition, empathy, and value to mothers, and mothers energetically transfer that into the daily labor of childrearing. This chain may not be directly reciprocal between mother and child, but it is far from the modern ideal of the "free gift," and more closely resembles Mauss' traditional model of interdependence and mutual obligation.

In fact, in none of these four strategies of rejuvenation can we say the modern world of seemingly autonomous individuals has freed itself of the moral, obligatory interconnections of traditional culture. Even among mothers who themselves value autonomy and independence, we still see them endeavoring to sustain their giving through connections with others, primarily through some form of being *visible*. In addition to being recognized by their children, women create their own networks of empathy and cultures of appreciation consisting of their partner and a handful of friends. From these tiny, truncated societies, they strive to receive, in concentrated form, a whole traditional society's worth of recognition and value.

NOTES

[1]Note that "U.S. culture" is an amalgamation of numerous cultures. However as those in privileged positions tend to be the rule-makers, the most powerfully articulated social guidelines for parenting in this country are those espoused by middleclass whites. This does not mean all races, classes and ethnicities of women follow these guidelines, but they are at least aware of them and recognize that these expectations are those by which their parenting may be judged in the broader society (Hays 1994).
[2]See de Marneffe (2004) for a rich discussion of other benefits to mothers from their direct engagement with children.

REFERENCES

Blair-Loy, Mary 2003 *Competing Devotions.* Cambridge: Harvard University Press.

Damaske, Sarah 2011 *For the Family? How Class and Gender Shape Women's Work.* New York: Oxford University Press.

de Marneffe, Daphne 2004 *Maternal Desire: On Children, Love, and the Inner Life.* New York: Little Brown.

Dizard, Jan E., and Howard Gadlin 1990 *The Minimal Family.* Amherst: University of Massachusetts Press.

Edin, Kathryn, and Maria Kefalas 2005 *Promises I Can Keep: Why Poor Women Put Motherhood Before Marriage.* Berkley: University of California Press.

England, Paula, and Nancy Folbre 1999 "The Cost of Caring." *Annals of the American Academy of Political and Social Science* 561: 39-51.

Hays, Sharon 1996 *The Cultural Contradictions of Motherhood.* New Haven: Yale University Press.

Hochschild, Arlie Russell 2012 *The Outsourced Self: Intimate Life in Market Times.* New York: Metropolitan Books. 2000 "Importing Motherhood: The Global Nanny Chain." *American Prospect,* January 3. 1983 *The Managed Heart: The Commercialization of Human Feeling.* Berkeley: University of California Press.

Hochschild, Arlie Russell, with Anne Machung 1989 *The Second Shift: Working Parents and the Revolution at Home.* New York: Viking Penguin.

Klein, David M., and James M. White 1996 *Family Theories: An Introduction.* Thousand Oaks: Sage Publications.

Mauss, Marcel 1950 *The Gift: The Form and Reason for Exchange in Archaic Societies.* W.D. Halls, trans. New York: W. W. Norton & Company.

Rich, Adrienne Rich 1998 "Anger and Tenderness." In *Shifting the Center: Understanding Contemporary Families.* Susan J. Fergusson, ed. Pp. 310-321. Mountain View, CA: Mayfield.

Stone, Pamela 2007 *Opting Out? Why Women Really Quit Careers and Head Home.* Berkeley: University of California Press.

Vaughan, Genevieve 2007 *Women and the Gift Economy.* Toronto: Inanna Publications & Education.

Zelizer, Viviana 1985 *Pricing the Priceless Child.* New York: Basic Books.

25.

Conclusion

Caring Choices

ELIZABETH REID BOYD AND GAYLE LETHERBY

In *A Vindication of the Rights of Woman* (1985/1792) Mary Wollstonecraft asked whether any rational man would choose the domestic sphere. Her use of the word rational was, of course, deliberate and specific. It is the rational, productive individual/citizen/worker who can make rational, economic choices. It is this representative who has been used to overlook or discount in fundamental ways the experience of many women, and indeed, many men.

Maternal ethicist Virginia Held contends that in using rational choice theory we can treat any entity as an individual. But "the issue is this: how should we react, and think about, various social realities? [Rational choice theory] may capture some of the realities ... of the marketplace but misses the realities of mothering (1993: 196)." For Held the social and contextual relationship between mother and child are partly constitutive of what they are. She suggests that more of the world should be understood in these terms. It is not just the relationship between mother and child that is relational and connected. All relationships are such, whether at home or at work.

The choice to stay at home cannot be separated from other childcare choices. For many of the women represented in this volume, the decision to stay at home was shaped personally and politically, emotionally and economically, rationally and relationally. Some women wanted to 'be there'. Some women would have preferred to be working. Some were at home due to familial expectations and pressures. Some considered they had a choice, some felt they had none. Women in paid employment, in the public sphere, working for a diversity of reasons, may find their mirror image in stay-at-home mothers in the private sphere, rather their opposite. In reflection, so can stay-at-home mothers.

But whatever decision she makes, viewing each individual mother as making her own childcare choice means she is left alone – holding the baby - and taking her own childcare chance. Such a dichotomous pairing creates an impossible choice: all or nothing, wrong or right. Yet as this volume reveals, mothers are not alone in their childcare choices. All over the world, mothers are making decisions, sometimes easily, sometimes in hardship, to provide care for their children. To isolate them as lone decision makers, to be applauded or blamed, is to obscure outstretched arms that might hold and embrace them.

Backed into a corner, many a mother is forced defend her choice (here a snarling tiger-mother, there a tight-lipped martyr) causing further separation, distress and conflict. When women are trapped in their personal conflicts, divided within themselves, they are also separated from other women and mothers, as well as from men and fathers. Thus childcare remains a woman's issue (still holding that baby). It also separates mothers from society and the community at large. All too easily, skirmishes break out as to how to share the common coin between individual women in divided camps.

It is necessary to recognize and appreciate differences between women, as well as differences between men. But as this volume reveals, it is perhaps more important to recognize what we share. A fully human re-visioned ethics of care is beyond duality and opposing choices, it goes beyond personal, national or moral traditions. Such an ethics will re-frame care – moving beyond limited options of so called gender appropriate childcare choices. New childcare choices will emerge when the caring needs of women, men and children are envisaged, beyond male and female, beyond public and private, beyond working and stay-at-home mothers. 21st century childcare choices will emerge from a new conversation. This global conversation has now begun.

REFERENCES

Held, Virginia 1993 *Feminist Morality: Transforming Culture, Society and Politics.* Chicago: University of Chicago Press.

Wollstonecraft, Mary 1985[1792] *A Vindication of the Rights of Woman.*

Harmondsworth: Penguin.

26. Contributors' Biographies

Anna Marie Bautista is Lecturer in Media, Communications and Cultural Studies at the School of Professional and Continuing Education at the University of Hong Kong (HKU SPACE). Her teaching and research interests include various aspects of film and popular culture studies, particularly in representations of gender.

Ann A. Berry is an associate professor and Extension Family and Consumer Economics Specialist at The University of Tennessee. She received her Ph.D. in Human Resource Education and Workforce Development from Louisiana State University. Her current Extension educational programs and research include personal finance, housing, healthcare, and economic well-being. She is an American citizen.

Geraldine Brady is a Senior Research Fellow at Coventry University. Her research contributes to providing insight into the lives of often-marginalised groups, through qualitative and creative research methods. Geraldine's research interests include: the barriers to social inclusion faced by young parents, young people's views and experiences of sex, sexual decision-making and teenage pregnancy and reflections on the politics of research.

Rebecca Jaremko Bromwich and her husband have four wonderful children and a dog. She is a lawyer and part-time professor of law currently pursuing her PhD at Carleton University in Ottawa, Ontario, Canada while teaching at the University of Ottawa Faculty of Law. Rebecca is a Canadian citizen.

Geraldine Brown is a Research Fellow at Coventry University. Her research interests include: public policy and practice, community engagement and action, and 'race' and ethnicity. A key focus of her work is exploring the mechanisms and processes that may contribute to groups identified within public policy being excluded or marginalized, in order to consider the effectiveness of institutional responses.

Solveig Brown, Ph.D. is an anthropologist who has spent several years researching mothers in American culture. She lives in Minneapolis, Minnesota.

Paula J. Caplan, Ph.D., Associate at Harvard University's DuBois Institute, is an American and Canadian clinical and research psychologist, former Full Professor at Ontario Institute for Studies in Education, author of eleven including *Don't Blame Mother: Mending the Mother-Daughter Relationship*, and winner of three national awards for nonfiction writing. She has taught at Harvard and been a Fellow in Harvard Kennedy School's Women and Public Policy Program.

Kathryn Clarke is a parent and part-time senior administrative officer at Edith Cowan University, Western Australia. Kathryn holds a BA (Hons) from the University of Melbourne. Kathryn draws on experience derived from her fortunate – if messy – life shared with dogs, cats, chickens, a delightful three-year-old daughter, and a superhuman partner of 28 years.

Rebecca Deen is Associate Professor of Political Science at the University of Texas at Arlington in the United States. Her work appears in *Women & Politics, Congress & the Presidency* and *Judicature*. Current research explores the politics of school-related volunteer organizations and their role in educational policy.

Dr. Keren Epstein-Gilboa is a nurse-psychotherapist, lactation consultant, childbirth educator, university lecturer, former stay-at-home mother, who has worked with families for three decades and resides in Canada. Her publications include peer reviewed articles, book chapters, and a book describing her original study on interaction and relationships in breastfeeding families.

Catherine Fournier is 54-year-old Canadian mother of six, she began her mothering career as a stay-at-home mom, then became a work-at-home mom and now works full-time outside the home. Catherine enjoys writing, creating gardens, clothing, and food, long distance canoeing, and anything to do with Roman history.

Dr. Janet Haynes is an international scholar at the University of Minnesota, Duluth, specializing in issues of social justice with an emphasis on marginalized youths and families. She holds a Masters of Social Work and a PhD in education from McGill University in Canada.

Valerie Heffernan is a Head of German at the National University of Ireland Maynooth. Her research interests encompass 20th and 21st century German-language literature, feminist literary theory and cultural studies. Recent research projects concentrate on contemporary literature, with a particular focus on women writers. She also has ongoing research interests in representations of motherhood in German literature and culture. Valerie Heffernan is a citizen of the Republic of Ireland.

Lisa Carley Hotaling is a mother and clinical psychology doctoral student at the Florida Institute of Technology. She completed her master's degree at the Saybrook Graduate School where she specialized in existential psychology. Her thesis work focused on the subjective experiences of mothers' shifting identities between internally felt and externally imposed liminal spaces.

Mary Jo Katras is an associate professor and Extension Educator at the University of Minnesota. She received her Ph.D. in Family Social Science from the University of Minnesota. Her current research and programs focus on access and opportunities concerning health and financial capabilities for limited income families. Citizenship: United States.

Ann-Claire Larsen is a legal sociologist whose research focuses on women's and children's concerns. She teaches international human rights, criminal law and professional ethics for the School of Law and Justice at Edith Cowan University in Western Australia where her research is associated with the Centre for Innovative Practice.

Jaerim Lee is an assistant professor at Sungkyunkwan University in Seoul, Republic of Korea. She received her Ph.D. from the Department of Family Social Science at the University of Minnesota. Her research interests include maternal employment, intergenerational support, family policy, and Korean families. Citizenship: Republic of Korea.

Professor Gayle Letherby is a Sociologist and the Director of the Institute of Health and Community at Plymouth University. She has written on a wide variety of topics within the area of reproductive and non/parental identity including perinatal loss, infertility and involuntary childlessness, teenage pregnancy and young parenthood, managing pregnancies complicated by long term conditions.

Darya Maoz is a senior lecturer in Hadassah College, in The College of Management, Academic Studies and in The Centre for Academic Studies, Israel. Her principal interests are in parenthood, romantic relations, gender, tourist behavior, host-guest contact and backpacking. She completed a Ph.D. in sociology and anthropology at The Hebrew University of Jerusalem (Israel) on Israeli backpackers in India. She contributes to a range of International peer-reviewed Journals and is the author of four books – three novels (*Vaya con Dios*, 2000; *India will Love Me*, 2002; *Maternity Home*, 2011) and a non- fiction *Romantic Relations* (2010).

Noelia Molina is a psychotherapist, lecturer and researcher. She lectures on the MA in Applied Christian Spirituality at All Hallows College (DCU). Her article: *'The Liminal Space in Motherhood: Spiritual Experiences of First-time Mothers'* was published by Ashgate, 2013. She is completing her doctorate on the transition to motherhood as a spiritual process.

Hallie Palladino is a Chicago based writer. Recent papers include, *Motherhood's Opening Chapter* (2012 MIRCI Conference in Toronto) and *Motherhood on the Message Boards* (2012 PCA/ACA Conference in Boston). She also a contributor to the forthcoming book *Intensive Mothering: The Cultural Contradictions of Modern Motherhood* (also from Demeter Press).

Pamela Redela holds a PhD in Spanish Language, Literature and

Culture and teaches in the Women's Studies Department of California State University, San Marcos. Her research focuses the Chicana/Latina female-authored short story with a focus on applied feminist theory and violence against women with an emphasis on Eco-Feminist thought.

Brianne Janacek Reeber holds an A.B. in Women, Gender, and Sexuality Studies from Harvard University, where she graduated with high honors. She currently works in digital marketing in New York City and resides in Stamford, CT, with her husband.

Dr. Elizabeth Reid Boyd is based in the School of Psychology and Social Science, Edith Cowan University, Western Australia. She is an Australian/British citizen. She completed her Ph.D. on mothers staying at home. Her publications on the topic have been included in *The Encyclopedia of Women in Today's World* and *The Encyclopedia of Motherhood* (Sage); *Motherhood: Power/Oppression* (The Women's Press) *Women's Studies International Forum and Mothers, Mothering and Motherhood across Cultural Differences: A Reader* (Demeter).

Dr. Stacey Rubin is a psychotherapist /psychoanalyst in private practice in San Antonio. She earned her Masters from Boston College and her Ph.D. from St. Mary's University in San Antonio, Texas. Dr. Rubin completed her certification in Contemporary Psychoanalysis from the National Institute for the Psychotherapies in New York in 2011. Her research and clinical interests center on the interplay between women's roles of mother and professional.

Yoshie Sano is an associate professor at Washington State University, Vancouver. She earned her Ph.D. in Human Development and Family Sciences from Oregon State University and her current research focuses on family well-being and functioning of low-income families. Citizenship: Japan.

Dianna Shandy is a professor of anthropology and *Karine Moe* is a professor of economics, both at Macalester College in St. Paul, Minnesota. They are co-authors of the 2009 book, *Glass Ceilings and 100-Hour Couples: What the Opt-out Phenomenon Can Teach Us About Work and Family.*

Beth Anne Shelton is Professor of Sociology at the University of Texas at Arlington in the United States. She has published extensively on women's time use, including time spent on household labor and volunteer activities. She is co-author (with Ben Agger) of *Fast Families, Virtual Children: A Critical Sociology of Families and Schooling* (2007).

Tara Ulbrich began motherhood with two Bachelor degrees in the Arts and in Social Administration followed by several years of social work practice in child protection and family therapy. Tara embraces parenting and radical homemaking as acts of social change. She currently home educates the youngest two of her four children, in the Meander Valley, Tasmania, Australia.

Dr Hester Vair is an Honorary Research Associate at the University of New Brunswick and a part-time instructor there, and at Saint Thomas University. Her primary interests are in mothering, women's paid and unpaid work, and feminist theory. Hester teaches a broad range of courses all with a liberatory social change focus.

Ana Villalobos, a U.S.-born Mexican-American scholar, completed her Ph.D. in sociology at U.C. Berkeley, working with Arlie Hochschild. She is now assistant professor of sociology at Brandeis University where the focus of her work is motherhood and gender. Her 2014 book, *Motherload: 'Making It All Better' in Insecure Times,* published by University of California Press, shows how a heavy expectation of mothers to provide security to children can actually undermine family security over time. Among her other publications is: "Mothering in Fear: How Living in an Insecure-Feeling World Affects Parenting" in Andrea O'Reilly's 2010 volume, *21st Century Motherhood.*

Pamela Weatherill is a digital social scientist, and research scholar at Edith Cowan Unversity. While a dual Australian/Canadian citizen, she currently resides in Queensland's Gold Coast hinterland and inhabits cyberspace as a freelance writer and computer-mediated communication blogger http://www.text-to-me.com - when not using the internet to keep in touch with her two grownup daughters overseas. She can be found on Twitter @PJ_Weatherill and contacted by email at pamelaweatherill@gmail.com